Fire and Water

D1559485

FAITH MEETS FAITH
An Orbis Series in Interreligious Dialogue
Paul F. Knitter, General Editor

Editorial Advisors
John Berthrong
Julia Ching
Diana Eck
Karl-Josef Kuschel
Lamin Sanneh
George E. Tinker
Felix Wilfred

In the contemporary world, the many religions and spiritualities stand in need of greater communication and cooperation. More than ever before, they must speak to, learn from, and work with each other in order both to maintain their vital identities and to contribute to fashioning a better world.

FAITH MEETS FAITH seeks to promote interreligious dialogue by providing an open forum for exchanges among followers of different religious paths. While the series wants to encourage creative and bold responses to questions arising from contemporary appreciations of religious plurality, it also recognizes the multiplicity of basic perspectives concerning the methods and content of interreligious dialogue.

Although rooted in a Christian and Maryknoll theological perspective, the series does not endorse any single school of thought or approach. By making available to both the scholarly community and the general public works that represent a variety of religious and methodological viewpoints, FAITH MEETS FAITH seeks to foster an encounter among followers of the religions of the world on matters of common concern.

FAITH MEETS FAITH SERIES

Fire and Water

Basic Issues in Asian Buddhism and Christianity

Aloysius Pieris

ORBIS BOOKS

Maryknoll, New York 10545

Library of Congress Cataloging-in-Publication Data

Pieris, Aloysius.
    Fire and water : basic issues in Asian Buddhism & Christianity / Aloysius Pieris.
        p. cm. — (Faith meets faith)
    Includes bibliographical references and index.
    ISBN 1-57075-055-6 (alk. paper)
    1. Catholic Church — Asia — Doctrines. 2. Theology, Doctrinal — Asia. 3. Christianity and other religions — Buddhism. 4. Feminism — Religious aspects — Christianity. 5. Feminism — Religious aspects — Buddhism. 6. Asia — Religion — 20th century. 7. Buddhism — Relations — Christianity. I. Title. II. Series.
BX1615.P54   1996
230′25 – dc20
                                    96–9441
                                      CIP

Dedicated affectionately to the memory of
my priest-brother and brother priest,
the late Father Theodore A. Pieris,
lover of God and friend of the poor.

Contents

Part III
SPIRITUALITY AND AUTHENTIC HUMAN LIBERATION

Foreword

PAUL F. KNITTER

In 1988, when I had the privilege of writing the Preface to Aloysius Pieris's first book to be published in the United States (Orbis Books, *An Asian Theology of Liberation*), I suggested that the book's significance and power lay in the dynamic dipolarity that animated it. Cautiously and creatively, Pieris connected the two dominant forms of pluralism facing Christianity and all religious communities — the question of the many poor and the question of the many religions. He boldly argued that neither question could be confronted, much less answered, without the other. The many religions of the world, in order to understand themselves individually and dialogically, must reach out to and listen to the many suffering victims of this world. And the pain and injustices afflicting the poor of the earth and the poor earth itself can be addressed and diminished only if the religious communities offer a coordinated contribution to the efforts of the politicians, economists, and social activists.

Pieris's message in that first book was that an Asian theology of liberation will be a dialogical theology — and that an Asian dialogue of religions will be liberative. Those who have been part of, or witness to, the proliferating life of the Asian churches and of Christian dialogue with Asian religions over the past ten years know how pervasively, profoundly, and often uncomfortably the voice and vision of Aloysius Pieris have been present to theological, pastoral, and ecumenical discussions in Asia. In addition, I can speak within and for a growing cluster of North American and European theologians who have been shaken and aided by his dipolar connecting of the plurality of religions and the plurality of victims.[1]

Much of what will engage and inspire the reader of this present volume creatively continues this conversation between the many religions and the many oppressed. But as the title of this book suggests, in the pages that fol-

---

1. Among the most significant in this cluster is Edward Schillebeeckx, *The Church: The Human Story of God*, Crossroad, New York, 1990, 167–68; Pieris's ideas guide the creative proposals in X. J. Alegre, J. Gonzalez Faus, et al., *Universalidad de Cristo, Universalidad del pobre: Aportación al diálogo interreligioso*, Sal Terrae, Santander, 1995.

low, Pieris describes and explores, from a variety of perspectives, a different (but much related) kind of dynamic dipolarity. In describing why the forces symbolized by "fire and water" call for each other, and how they can touch and vivify each other, he is responding to the broad challenge that David Tracy has recently put to practitioners and academicians of religion — that one of the most pressing and promising requirements for the understanding and practice of religion in our contemporary context is to explore how prophetic and mystical forces animate all religions and how these forces can be related among them.[2]

This book is a gripping example of what happens when this is done. It is precisely why and how two forces seemingly as divergent as fire and water are really two very different poles of the same religious energy — the mystical and the prophetic. Throughout these essays, Pieris contrasts and connects dyads which, like fire and water, are not synonymous with, but related to, the creative tension between mystical and prophetic experience: the unifying transcendent and the engaging particular, the metacosmic (transcending the finite) and the cosmic (informing the finite), the liberating freedom from need and the demanding freedom from want, and especially, the detachment of wisdom (*prajñā*) and the engagement of love (*agape*).

Not to maintain the dipolarity and connectedness between the mystical and the prophetic, to prefer one to the neglect of the other, is to distort the liberative nature of religion and to expose it to ideological abuse. In Part II of this book, the emphasis is on the destruction and corruption that can result when the mystical does not embrace the prophetic, or when the quest for transforming wisdom forgets the need to love the deformed world and the suffering neighbor. Some examples:

- The Christ who can find a place in Asia is not only the Christ of the ashrams discovered through dialogue with the mystics of traditional Hinduism but also, and today especially, the Christ of the Asian poor who calls for the transformation of society and of the Christian churches (chapter 7).

- To protect religions from the very real danger of factional exploitation (communalism), it is not enough to inculcate the wisdom of mystical practice; it is also essential that such mystics or religious persons of all traditions meet with, talk with, work with the poor and disenfranchised. The oppressed must be part of "interreligious dialogue" if such dialogue is to lead to the transformation of both personal and social consciousness (chapter 9).

- The mystic's search for "freedom from need" — i.e. detachment and freedom from greed — must be united to and shaken by the prophet's

---

2. David Tracy, *Dialogue with the Other: The Inter-Religious Dialogue* (Eerdmans, Grand Rapids, 1990).

search for "freedom from want" — i.e. freedom from the pain of imposed poverty and hunger. Christians in particular are called to embody these two freedoms, for they are called to follow Jesus not only in his total detachment and self-emptying obedience to the Father but also in his affirmation of Yahweh's "defense pact" with the oppressed (chapters 13 and 14).

But throughout this book, Pieris carefully keeps adjusting the balance; especially in Part III, he assumes the role of the spiritual director and guides his readers into the mystical spirituality of personal transformation in the Spirit, without which there can be no "authentic human liberation." Though his probing into the depths of religious life and the three vows will naturally speak directly to those in that life, his revelatory analysis of the mystical-liberative content of the practice of poverty and obedience and how such practice is expressed in chastity will enlighten and invigorate also the lay person's practice of these virtues. Only such a mystical living of voluntary poverty and obedient renunciation of Mammon will lead to what Pieris calls an "integral evangelism" — a service of the poor based on the church's mystical renunciation of power and self-aggrandizement.

The dynamic dipolarity and mutual nourishment that Pieris insists must be maintained between the mystical experience of *prajñā* and the prophetic demands of *agape* are grounded in his fundamental understanding of religious experience. The "saving" or "liberating" power of such experience bursts into a person's being as the realization of the "cosmic-human-metacosmic continuum" (52). To be "saved" or "enlightened," one might say, is to wake up to the given but still to be realized interplay between the metacosmic More and the finite Cosmos — a interplay that comes to particular expression and actualization in the human. In the human being the Transcendent and the Finite merge in an experience that is mystical insofar as it transforms the individual, and prophetic insofar as it transforms the world.

Such an understanding of religious experience as a marriage of the mystical and prophetic Pieris finds clearly contained and powerfully expressed in women's consciousness, especially as it is taking shape in Asia. Part I of this book contains Pieris's first public, written articulation of the challenge of women's religiosity and theology for all religions. In the religious experience of women and in the criticism they offer to traditional patriarchal religion, Pieris discovers a particularly powerful expression and nutrient for the dipolarity between the mystical and the prophetic. But not just "powerful" — for Pieris, the message he hears from so many of his Asian sisters appears to be "necessary for salvation" for the patriarchalized religions of the world. The gospel or good news lived and understood by women can be the saving grace that enables religious communities to regain the necessary balance between the prophetic and the mystical, between wisdom and love.

Pieris's own words show how seriously he wants to take this good though unsettling news: "Feminism...is a permanent feature in the struggle for full humanity in that it maintains the cosmic dimension [the mystical!] without which the experience of the metacosmic...is impossible." "...feminism is...the name for the endless struggle to retain the cosmic religiosity alive within these major religions" (62). "Feminism is the name of our perpetual struggle to maintain this salutary impact of love [prophetic involvement with the earth] on the power of knowledge [the mystical experience of wisdom]..." Therefore, we must allow "the woman in all of us to be born again" (55).

Notice that in these statements Pieris is not simply asserting that feminism represents the prophetic or agapic pole of religious life. Rather, he finds in the religious experience of women and in their criticism of given religious belief and practice a dynamic blending of both the cosmic and the metacosmic, or the prophetic and the mystical. In the wisdom resulting from the personal experience of mystical oneness, one is called to the prophetic engagement of love. And in the prophetic this-worldly struggle, one is touching and being touched by the Spirit. There is a mutual indwelling of love and wisdom, of mystical centeredness and prophetic struggle. As Pieris has experienced feminism, as he has opened himself to the mystical insights and prophetic criticisms of his female colleagues and friends, he has found a critique without which the established religions may not achieve the dynamic blending of the mystical and prophetic that they need: "...feminism...serves as a permanent critique of religion. Religion cannot survive in the future without appropriating the feminist critique, just as feminism cannot achieve its liberative goal without the aid of a religion so critiqued" (62).

If my introductory analysis of this third book of Aloysius Pieris in our Faith Meets Faith series is basically correct — that is, that the focus of this present work is the dynamic dipolarity between the mystical and the prophetic — then in a sense one can say that this third book expands the theme of Pieris's second book. In his *Love Meets Wisdom: A Christian Experience of Buddhism* (Orbis, 1988), Pieris showed that Christians can learn from Buddhists how to better integrate the prophetic reaching out of love with the mystical reaching in of wisdom. In this present book, starting with the insights of feminist experience, he broadens and deepens this meeting of prophetic love with mystical wisdom for both Christian spirituality and the wider ecumenical discussion. But in another sense, fire and water represent the extension and intensification of the focal concern of his first book, *An Asian Theology of Liberation*. As already stated, in that book Pieris called for a meeting of the many religions with the many poor; or, he called for the marriage of interreligious dialogue and liberation theology. In this book he shows, as it were, how such a marriage can work. If all the living religious traditions of the world would follow Pieris's advice and better integrate "love and wisdom" in their own communities, if, in David Tracy's words, there would be "in all the major religious traditions...a search for new ways to unite these mystical and prophetic trajectories,"[3] then the religious communities of our world would definitely be able to engage in a dialogue with each other in which the oppressed of the earth and the oppressed earth would be their starting point and ultimate concern.

There are those who are concerned that such an interreligious dialogue, which holds up the oppressed as its ultimate concern, leads to the exclusion of the Transcendent, or to a "reduction" of religious dialogue to "this-worldly liberation."[4] Such concerns would not be felt by religions and religious persons who have recognized and are trying to live out the dipolarity between love and wisdom, or the prophetic and the mystical. By maintaining this dipolarity and integrating it into the community's daily life, religious persons will affirm a difference, yes, but never a separation between the mystical and the prophetic. In loving and defending one's neighbor and one's earth, one is communing in that which is beyond all words. And in communing with the Beyond-all-names, one is linked with neighbor and earth. And so, a dialogue between religions that embraces suffering neighbors and suffering earth as its starting point and ultimate concern is not only possible but necessary. The dipolarity of the mystical and the prophetic calls for the dipolarity of the many poor and the many religions, which expresses the dipolarity of liberation and dialogue.

For some people, all this talk about dipolarities, about integrating the metacosmic and the cosmic, or the mystical and the prophetic, may tend to rise and evaporate in the upper spheres of abstraction. Not for those who know Aloysius Pieris personally. Since in this book he has made more personal revelations than in the past (especially in Part I and chapter 18), let me relate the abstractions of this Foreword to the concrete person — a man I have known for some ten years now and whom I had the exciting pleasure of visiting for one week in his Tulana Research Center, with my wife and two children. Aloysius Pieris is an amazing, exciting, surprising mix of, not "di," but multi-polarities.

He is constantly moving between different worlds with an alacrity and sensitivity that make his movements a bridge between these worlds. Most of these differing realms of experience or involvement fall, generally speaking, on either side of what we have been calling the mystical-wisdom and the prophetic-love distinction. His Tulana Research Center is both a center of academic rigor and pastoral-personal involvement; in his study, he has one desk for the meticulous examination of Buddhist texts and another for Christian theological-pastoral studies; "Aloy" can spend the morning discussing with Buddhist or Christian scholars and the afternoon conducting popular workshops among both Christians and Buddhists; he can connect his

---

3. David Tracy, "God Dialogue, and Solidarity: A Theologian's Refrain," *The Christian Century* (October 10, 1990): 100.

4. Pope John Paul II voices this concern in *Redemptoris Missio.*

interreligious conversations with his organizing experience in founding and directing the Christian Workers Fellowship (whose members are both Christian and Buddhist!); he can step from an engrossing study of Grillmeier's history of early Christology to fund-raising for the Interreligious Association for Hearing Impaired Children that he helped establish.

In very personal, real contexts, I have seen his "dipolarity" in action — when in the midst of a complex discussion on the Buddhist and Christian notion of the self he could turn, immediately, to console my daughter who was just frightened by a big spider in her room — when at a party for the Hindu-Buddhist-Muslim-Christian supporters of the school for hearing-impaired children, he moved from a complex religious discussion to add his voice to raucous merry-making — in his ability to reach out, be thoroughly present to, and offer sage, warm words of support to a woman-friend suffering the effects of sexual abuse. In such instances, and in the general content and tenor of his life, Aloysius Pieris embodies and struggles with the life-giving dipolarities that make his writings so rich and relevant.

Orbis Books and the Faith Meets Faith series are delighted and honored to offer the richness of Aloysius Pieris's writings to the English-reading world once again. We hope — better, we expect — that this book will nurture, in individuals as well as in ecclesial-religious communities, an ever-more fruitful union of mystics and prophets, of contemplation and action, of dialogue and liberation, of personal and social transformation — of wisdom and love.

Part I

Women and Religion

Buddhist and Christian Appropriation of Feminist Criticism

1

Autobiographical Reflections

A SYMPHONY IN THE FEMINIST KEY

Since the early seventies — that is, within the last two decades — I have hardly taught a course of theology in which I did not give a prominent place to feminism. The rubric under which I discussed this theme was *Woman in the Asian Religious Ethos*. The fact that this theme has not merited a focused treatment in my many writings of the last two decades has been lamented by a few Asian feminists.[1] On my part, I have frankly acknowledged this lacuna as far as my writings are concerned.[2]

The Oral Transmission as the Feminist Key

There was more than one reason why my lectures on this important theme have never passed into print. The one that carried most weight was that my rather idiosyncratic approach to the subject — that is, my appeal to symbolism and subliminality — defies the medium of writing, a medium that reduces one's message to a unilinear series of thought sequences. (Was not the art of writing created and cultivated by men?) So it was only after much hesitation that I decided to communicate, in this written form, a little of what I have been so far transmitting through the oral medium. The evocative language I employ in the first part of this essay, therefore, cannot be sustained without tiring the reader, unless I can bring in other modes of communication such as images and so on. I am constrained to fall back on the literary mode of unilinear analytical discourse in the other parts of this essay.

My tentative theological reflections on feminism — or *womanism,* as many

---

The first six chapters were first published in *Dialogue* 19 and 20, 1992, 119–203.

1. E.g., see V. Fabella, "Christology from an Asian Woman's Perspective," *We Dare to Dream: Doing Theology as Asian Women,* Orbis Books, Maryknoll, N.Y., 1989, 4.
2. See my *An Asian Theology of Liberation,* Orbis Books, Maryknoll, N.Y., 1988, xv. This source will be henceforward abbreviated as *ATL.*

non-Western women prefer to call it[3] — have reached many audiences in the lecture halls of universities and other institutes, always through the medium of oral transmission. In some courses, I have made lavish use of slides, diagrams, images, stories, poetry, parables, and paradoxes. The participants in my study sessions recall my warning, recurring like a refrain in the course of my lectures on feminism: "Listen attentively to what I am not saying!"

The reason was this: I had long realized that our education system, dominated as it is by the culture of literacy (writing and reading), has instilled in us a compulsion to "fill in the blanks." But in oral transmission — the womanist mode of communing from body to body — there is a way of connecting without eliminating the gaps. (To bridge the banks of a river, should I dam(n) its flow by filling the space in between?) The option is clear: feminists must either radically alter the art of writing, or employ (and even invent) adequate media to articulate this hitherto repressed dimension of our being.

Gut Reactions

In the mid-seventies, at the East Asian Pastoral Institute (EAPI) in Manila, when I first introduced women's issues as a central and all-pervasive aspect of Asian theology, a dear old friend on the EAPI staff chided me gently that I had forced into the Asian religious discourse a purely Western concern. "You are stepping out of your field, my friend," he complained. One year, a couple of students walked out of my class in protest; both of them happened to be white, male, clerical, and celibate. In another year, a highly confused Asian woman lost her nerve — perhaps because unpleasant and undigested memories of male oppression were let loose in her. I appreciate the intervention of the director, an American Jesuit, who "processed" the sad episode and helped bring about the much-needed healing. It revealed to me more than ever that when speaking of feminism within a patriarchal society, we are activating an atrophied part in the depth of our being; I realized, too, that my method of communicating the message was commensurate with the matter communicated.

Another male cleric, also an Asian, expressed his uneasiness at what he alleged to be "your indoctrination of our minds with your cunning use of images." That was his reaction to the persuasive power of the language of images, parables, and poetic utterances, and an admission that the subject touched him at his deepest.

On the other hand, these annual lectures in Manila had a positive impact on many others. The climax of the final lecture (a slide meditation on the image of woman) was always the figure of the living Asian Madonna; as I continue to hear in letters from former students, this image continues to haunt many people to this day.

---

3. Ann Moades (ed.), *Feminist Theology: A Reader*, SPCK, London, 1990, Introduction, 9.

I think back in wonder to the women at Union Theological Seminary, in New York, in Spring 1988, (among them some now prominent feminist voices such as Hyun Kyung Chung, Victoria Rue, and Catherine Poetig) who viewed my series of evocative slide images and listened to my out-loud meditations on these images. Why did they burst into sobs and sighs and plunge into torrents of tears, interlocked in sisterly embraces, even long after my lecture had technically ended? What really were they expressing? Was it the joy of being women that overwhelmed them? Or was it the excessive pain at recognizing how they were treated as unwelcome gifts, as pearls cast before swine? Or was it an in-depth awareness of having always been "an amazing grace" that men have consistently rejected as a menacing threat to their settled sexist system of managing practically all sectors of human existence, including religion?

THE DARK NIGHT OF GRACE

In their weeping I heard that other part of Christ lamenting religion's institutional resistance to Grace: "How often I have longed to gather your children together, as a hen gathers her chicks under her wings, *but you were not willing*" (Matt. 23:37; Luke 13:34)! This is God's and Woman's dark night of the soul:

> Grace, Amazing grace
> open your depths to my searching gaze
> that,
> washed in light and cleansed of doubt
> plunge I may
> into your abysmal bosom
> wherein to rest and fathom your ways.
>
> Why elude me then?
> For, your alternating icons
> — mother, sister and friend — confuse my vision
> one image drowned in the other.
>
> Grace, Amazing grace
> I hear your tottering steps
> toiling through the trajectory
> — from a supernal Source
> to a foreknown destiny — from all-loving Giver
> to an unreceptive addressee.
>
> Alas! Amazing Grace
> you cease being the gift
> if unwelcomed
> as redundant, unfit . . .

your pilgrimage aborted
by the barred gate of Man,
your mission frustrated
before his guarded tomb.

Or, has your icon changed?
Is it your features that stare at me
in the mirror that I face?
Am I you, O divine grace
destined to be a pilgrim of love?
on the way to being a gift
in the prospective receiver's shrine?
Will my pilgrimage end abruptly
before a covered niche?
Should I my steps retrace?

I dread the journey.
Unreceived,
I shall surely be
an ungraceful thing
sharing in that frightful fate
of all things that die: of being a weight
that none would carry save to the grave.

Grace, unfathomable grace
Has not thy icon changed again?
Thou art She from birth by name
she who fears the source
and doubts the grace
flees the pain of being the gift
shuns the torture of knowing
lest she too fall like Eve
from an ephemeral paradise
of innocence
to an insecure maturity.

'Tis her fear to be the gift
that makes her hurt
the Giver within
and hurt herself in turn.
Grace, Sweet Pain
have I earned your injury?

This poem, *The Dark Night of Grace,* was written in Spring 1982 as a
gentle appeal to a dear student-friend of mine, Grace, who feared to be a

woman and recoiled from answering the call of her baptismal name. It is not only men who are unreceptive to this amazing grace; women, too, there are, who fear the cost of being what men keep them from becoming. Fear, no doubt. That is the name of the demon to be exorcised.

2

The Fear of Woman's Power and the Power of Man's Fear

FEAR OF WATER AND THE POWER OF FIRE

This fear that my friend Grace and many women feel is not purely a psychological phenomenon or a sheer sociological datum. It is deeper. It is what I would call the cosmic tension between Fire and Water, the drama of a perennial struggle told and retold in so many ways by so many people — that familiar myth about Paradise, the Serpent, the Fall and the Redeemer. My version of this story comes from an Amerindian setting in Argentina.

A Story with a History

In the mid-seventies I read an interesting anthropological study on the culture change that the advent of Europeans had effected on the Toba tribe in Argentina.[1] What the social scientist Elmer Miller describes in this article is *history*, i.e., something "observed" to have happened in a particular place and time. But in an anthropological interpretation of events, I found a *story*, that is to say, something that happens in all places and at all times.

Concrete historical events can be interpreted by the observer to disclose a truth of cosmic proportions. Such an event is raised to the power of Myth. What I am about to narrate is the story or the myth that I recognized in the historical narration recorded in Miller's anthropological study.[2]

The story presupposes that Fire and Water are the natural sacraments of

---

1. Elmer S. Miller, "Shamans, Power Symbols and Change in Argentine Toba Culture," *American Ethnologist*, 2, 1975: 477–96.
2. Facts in themselves do not make history. It is the interpretation of facts that I regard as history. Elmer Miller's interpretation (history) is here taken as a basis for narrating a story which makes sense in the context of Asian feminism. I grant there could be other interpretations of this same event, e.g., Pablo G. Wright, "Toba Pentecostalism Revisited," *Social Compass,* 39, 1992/3, 355–75. It is the "story" that succeeds in communicating the great truths. It is the story that interests us here, not history.

our cosmic religiosity. Fire is always associated with the male and water with the female. This is a datum of our subliminal noesis, and it finds expression in the myths that anthropologists study and in the dreams that psychologists interpret, not to mention the sacraments that all believers celebrate.

The Toba Indians associated fire with their hunting, a male occupation, as they also used it for curing and tempering their weapons. It was their gender symbol. Did it occur to these men or to their shamans that it was this male element that their women-folk manipulated dexterously in their role as cooks? That is to say, these women were early technologists in whose hands fire transformed raw material derived from nature into something fit for human consumption. With their produce — cooked food — did they not mold and manage men, in the same way they also made and manipulated fire?

Thus it seemed good that the males, in their turn, also tried to calm their women through a deft use of fire, the fire of eros. It better be deft, for the women, according to the Toba credo, were endowed with "vaginal teeth" that could devour and devastate the menfolk! It is by kindling sexual passions out of the embers of female eros that men were able to tranquilize their ferocious partners.

Does this not indicate that the male fear of the woman was allayed with the power of fire? Or, let me put it in prosaic nonsymbolic language we unimaginative moderns use: Could sexual domination be men's response to their fear of woman?

Fire dreads an advancing column of water. Nor can water withstand the withering heat of fire. Yet people with a cosmic sense know that the wetness of water and the warmth of the fiery sun work together in nature's recurrent cycle of life and death.

> When Water and Fire
> meet, conspire
> does not the parched pebbled bed
> become, ere long, a floral spread? (AP 1976)

In the mythic Toba life, our imagination is made to stretch in quest of the ideal balance of sexes, the impossible dream of a Water-Fire merger.

> Can a drop of rain
> and a spark of fire
> which meet, retain
> their being entire?
>
> Can wetness send
> the flames still higher
> or, heat stop being
> a water-drier? (AP 1986)

A nonsexist cosmic spirituality has the perennial answer:

A paling *spark* of light in space
in passing through a *drop* of grace
is magnified to thousand *rays*
and showers down refreshing *sprays.* (AP 1986)

But *his* paradise was different. There, the fire reigned.

And now the Fall: Enter the serpent: the European colonizer. He desecrates the Garden of Eden — the sacred forest which is the Toba man's traditional seat of hunting, the sanctuary of his firepower. Agriculture introduced by the intruder results in the ascendancy of water over fire. Thus emerges the tree of good and evil. It is now *her* hour. The woman begins to be emancipated by the West as she lets this tempter creep into her bed. Intermarriage or just intercourse.... Step by step she "frees" herself from the grip of her traditional gender roles, flirts with the White Outsider and succumbs to an hitherto unknown cosmic catastrophe (that is, venereal disease) that challenges the competence of the medicine men. The omen "freedom" throws men out of balance; therefore, the whole Toba tribe falls.

And then Advent: Enter the time of waiting in hope, *aperiatur terra et germinet salvatorem* (Let the earth split open and bring forth a Savior)! *Nubes pluant justum* (Let the clouds rain down the Just one)! A cosmic power must rise and rescue the fallen. And what could this power be: water or fire?

The Hour of Redemption: It strikes when the white man's religion (the tempter's ideology) sweeps across the Toba land. Not in mystery and silence, not among the beasts of creation and the poor of the nation — as it was in Zero A.D. — but with fire and thunder, with din and dance, reminiscent of the fire ritual of hunting. It is the arrival of Protestant Pentecostalism, with its heavy accent on the baptism of fire over and above the baptism of water.

The inevitable happened. Conversion of the males to the new religion was quick and definitive, for it was the fulfillment of their secret longing. It was like a resurrection from the dead. Firepower returned with vengeance. Christianity restored the lost heritage of males. Men were the first to be saved by the colonial Christ; and women, too, thanks to their men; and with women, also their children.

We see here how the colonialism-woman-man sequence in the fall of the Toba Tribe was reversed to the Christianity-man-woman order of redemption. Looks familiar, does it not? The woman, by emancipating herself, helped mediate the destruction of the "good old order." But it was through man's mediation that the good old order was restored so that the woman could once more find her "proper place" in that order! That is what makes a story "true": it reveals history, namely, the interpretation that an ideology imparts to concrete events or even to a sequence of a narrative.[3]

---

3. My allusion here is to the patriarchalist and misogynic interpretation given by the theologians to the Fall narrative of the Book of Genesis, an interpretation that we have identified in the latter part of this essay as "the Eve-Mary polarity."

The Asian Version of the Story

This story has its many variants in many Asian cultures, not the least in countries that were once colonized by Christian powers. Kumari Jayawardene, a Marxist feminist from Sri Lanka, has furnished us with an array of facts which fall[4] into the general pattern of the Myth I have just narrated, though not without significant differences in many areas. The differences are important to note, or else the Asian womanists who are not aware of this story may fall into a blind alley in their search for the Asian brand of feminism, since many Asian feminists owe their emancipation to Western education! Let me give a skeletal version of that story as I read it in the above-mentioned author.

In most Asian countries, the ancient cultures are entrenched in a patriarchal social order supported by Asia's major religious traditions, mostly by those that I usually refer to as "metacosmic."[5] Now, the colonial presence, with its liberal democratic facade, did undoubtedly "emancipate" women from traditional social constraints by allowing them to come out of their homes to the office and factory, to the plantation and the mine...only to be exploited eventually as a cheap and cheated labor force in the hands of the postcolonial male capitalists.

Furthermore, most women from the upper strata freed themselves from cultural strictures in the process of anticolonial nationalist struggles when they joined hands with their male counterparts. But, often, the nationalism they struggled for was tinted and tainted by what is known as "orientalism," an occidental vision of the exotic East. Thus a return to certain traditional forms of women's subordination, legitimized by ancient religious traditions, was inevitable. What Christianity did to Toba culture, these religions, in their patriarchal form, continued to perpetrate on Asian women in general.

Thus in the Asian as in the Toban situation, the emancipation of women that came about under the influence of the Western (Christian) colonizers was short-lived and illusory. In both instances, traditional religions played a restringent role. Therefore, there is good reason to fear that a lack of proper analysis may drive Asian feminists to either of two extremes: to overestimate these metacosmic religions as a sure source of ideological inspiration in the women's struggle or to abandon religion altogether and resort to a *secularist* approach characteristic of some Western protagonists.

To avoid these two extremes, I suggest that we begin with the beginning of the problem, *gynephobia*, and note at once its subliminal linkage with the cosmic which — in opposition to the "secularist" model, as explained

---

4. K. Jayawardene, *Feminism and Nationalism in the Third World*, Zed Books, London, 1986.

5. As explained in my *ATL* (see chapter 1, n. 2 above), 71–74, 98–100. See also my *Love Meets Wisdom: A Christian Experience of Buddhism*, Orbis Books, Maryknoll, N.Y., 1989, 14–16.

below — is essentially religious or sacred. By holding three elements together we can find the starting point for an Asian feminism.

GYNEPHOBIA: THE SUBLIMINAL FEAR OF THE WOMAN

This is a fear that we (men and women) not only carry within us but also organize socially into gender-specific behavior which is ideologically justified as an immutable social order determined by Nature or ordained by God. The world's great metacosmic religions, especially Christianity, have served as a channel for handing down this ideology from generation to generation in the form of a sacrosanct tradition. Mariology (study of Mary's role in redemption) as traditionally taught in the Catholic stream of Christianity is not entirely free from such theo-ideology, as will be pointed out later.

Three Axioms in Asian Feminism

This brings us to three conclusions which must serve as axioms presupposed in the story of Woman which we are proposing and which can be learned only by narrating it. The first axiom is that feminism is not a temporary movement that lasts only until women's rights are restored; rather it is a permanent feature of our growth toward the *humanum*.

Secondly, feminism is indissolubly married to religion, for better or for worse. For, religion, as a "language of the spirit,"[6] is that which speaks *from* as well as *to* the subliminal region of our being where we are truly ourselves. This subliminal relationship between religion and feminism will make us question the secularist model of feminism, a model which even some Asian feminists have unwittingly adopted. But since religion can never operate in an ideological vacuum — that is, without a programmatic (action-oriented) worldview rationally justified as an ideal social order[7] — we must constantly keep in mind the ideology that transmits subliminal gynephobia.

I must declare, *pace* Malinowski,[8] that I am inclined to go by the hypothesis that in Asia (where pockets of matriarchal, and not just matrilineal, societies have survived to this day) there probably have been, in most parts, a patriarchal takeover from a previous gynecocentric social organization, and that all the major religions have arisen after the so-called patriarchal revolution, and consequently that it is within the ideological framework of gynephobic androcracy that all religions treat the role of women in society.

In this perspective, feminism is a permanent ideological critique of religion, something that religion cannot do without.

The third axiom is inseparable from the first two: Feminism is a subject that, by its very nature, can neither be fathomed nor articulated adequately

---

6. See Aloysius Pieris, "Faith Communities and Communalism," chapter 9 below, 100–102.
7. Ibid., 105–112; see also *ATL*, 24–31.
8. Cf. B. Malinowski, *Sex, Culture and Myth*, New York, 1962, 122–29.

except through an epistemic process that touches the most honest parts of our being — the subconscious and the body. Reason and intellect, by contrast, are the most cunning faculties of the human psyche. They often deceive us into believing the propriety or the impropriety of everything that we have subconsciously determined wrongly or rightly as profitable or unprofitable for our beings. But our subconscious is honest even where it makes wrong options, and our bodies neither deceive nor err because they record every message they receive and respond to it in an almost predictable manner. Feminism, therefore, attempts to reclaim and reaffirm the role of the subliminal and the bodily (or the cosmic) in our search for human authenticity.

In fact, ideology, which is often the rational justification of individual or class interests, is created by the faculty of reason that has not been exposed to the totality of the inner core of our being. This is eminently true of sexism, whether in its disappearing matriarchalism or in its present patriarchal form; it is an ideology that can be stripped of its deceptive rationalism only by exposing it to our subliminal selves.

One must, therefore, suspect that to use only the unilinear mode of knowing that generally characterizes written prose would be to place undue limits on the discussion of this theme. What we learn by the intuitive penetration of our own inner reality — something that religion is about — needs an evocative idiom, just as religion does. Here religion and feminism both must be allowed to use "oblique idioms" in an ideology-free manner — something that is well-nigh impossible in other forms of discourse.

The Religious, the Subliminal, and the Cosmic

In these three axioms taken together, the interpenetration of the religious, the subliminal, and the cosmic experience of reality is invoked as key to understanding the phenomenon of *gynephobia*, which itself is a religious, cosmic, and a subliminal experience. To appreciate the value of this thesis, one must learn to differentiate between (a) certain tendencies within the prehuman or purely *hominal* stages of the evolution, which can and must be transcended by human effort, and (b) the subliminal orientation of human consciousness toward the Cosmic — an orientation which determines the whole of human existence. The examples below are self-evident.

My conception in my mother's womb was heralded by an event which is hominal or prehuman, namely, the massive competition between several millions of my father's spermatozoa to meet and mate with just one single ovum released by my mother. Furthermore, the ejection of the semen was a conscious and deliberate choice on *his* part, whereas the release of the ovum was a cyclic event programmed into *her* physiology. This preconscious biological phenomenon of the male's conscious rivalry with other males and the female's often helpless reception does not and should not determine human behavior at the level of human culture.

A good analogy would be the so-called law of the jungle — what the

Buddhists and Hindus have aptly named *matsya-nyāya,* the law of big fish feeding on small ones. This prehuman tendency (the so-called "struggle for existence and the survival of the fittest") is not a binding law for humans. The humanization of cosmic evolution consists in transcending such sub-human tendencies. Similarly, the prehuman or hominal experience of male competition for nonresistant females, though culturally sanctified in some tribal and feudal societies, is not worthy of the humanum toward which we must relentlessly move.

But, this is not the case with the primordial experience of the human em-bryo, a postconception experience which is truly human and therefore not to be eliminated or transcended but to be handled consciously and cautiously. Our first human moments of incipient noesis consist of the awakening of our subliminal consciousness to the comfortable darkness of water in the womb of a woman. This fact once and for all establishes an unbreakable link be-tween the first awakening of our consciousness and our first experience of woman. Most accurately, our rudimentary awareness of the Cosmos (=water) coincides with our inchoative sentience of the Woman (=womb).

Thus we have all been irreversibly programmed by a gynecological, or more appropriately (to use Mary Daly's insightful pun), a gyne-Ecological orientation in our very mode of existence. The conclusion is obvious: Our human perception of reality is biopsychically determined to carry this sub-liminal connection (between the woman and the cosmos) as a permanent feature of the humanum, the humanum being the fullness of humanity, to-ward which we strive as the final goal of liberation (see chapter 6). It is precisely this massive gyne-ecological programming that justifies and calls for the creative intervention of males as an indispensable factor in the growth of a human person.

There is another facet to what we are urging, a facet that has to be included in any authentic feminist theology. The subliminal is also the un-known that eludes rational consciousness. Now, the fact is that the unknown or the subliminal, precisely in so far as it is unknown and subliminal, gen-erates fear. This fear of the unknown-subliminal explains the (ideological) defense mechanisms which operate not only in the mutual relationships be-tween sexes in human society, but also in our rapport with the cosmos — the cosmos being the ecological matrix in which we humans are evolving as a gigantic social embryo, awaiting our birth into a new humanity. Hence the interconnectedness between gynephobia and cosmophobia is fundamental to our perception of feminism. In other words, feminism is a way of handling the subliminal fear that makes males exercise power over women as well as over Nature.

3

The Cosmic in Feminism

THE COSMIC AS SACRAMENTAL

One implication of what we have said so far is that the "secularist" model, which some Asian feminists adopt unreflectively, seems both un-Asian and unfeminist in that it negates the gyne-ecological nexus. I want to emphasize that the *secularist* and the *cosmic* are as much opposed to each other as are the rationally explainable nonsacred world of liberal Western theology and the subliminally perceived religious worldview of the Asian Seers. Asian feminism cannot call itself Asian or feminist simply because it repeats the insights of pioneering Western feminists in the jargon of Asian statistics and data. A serious option must be made to use the cosmic worldview of Asia as the context for a truly Asian feminism. (See chapter 6.)

The Secularist versus the Cosmic

The secularism which we are talking about is not simply the emancipation of human institutions from the grip of organized religion — something I wholeheartedly welcome. Hence I accept and appreciate the stance of so many individuals who proclaim themselves to be secular in their life and thought. They justifiably refuse to be imprisoned in the ideological grooves that institutionalized religion tends to create. They have their own way of experiencing and expressing the transcendent as well as the sacred dimension of the cosmos. But they rightly dissociate themselves from the institutional and ideological grip that religion tries to exercise over their minds and hearts.

It is not the secularity of such people that I am contesting, but *secularism* or the *secularist* ideology that has its roots in the desacralization of the universe; such a secularism originated in the seventeenth century with the Cartesian reduction of the world to a lifeless machine,[1] and with the "masculinization of knowledge" by which Aristotle's *natura naturata*

---

1. F. Capra, *The Tao of Physics,* 1975/14th impression, 1988, Flamingo Paperbacks, 27ff.

(the passive mother-earth) is now "objectively" studied.[2] This is the origin of modern Western technocracy — the fruit of a heretical departure from biblical Christianity's teaching on Nature.

Although this mathematical and mechanistic model of the universe (which replaced Aristotle's teleological one) is said to be associated with Newtonian physics,[3] there was also another, older, concept of the world persisting in seventeenth-century Europe (which may also explain Newton's dabbling with alchemy). Nature was still considered the creation of an artist-magician who endowed it with beauty and mystery; thus the work of the scientist was seen as an ascetic task of unraveling Nature's hidden principles and secrets.[4]

Add to this the fact that sixteenth- and seventeenth-century authors, including Newton, were drawn to Tertullian's much-forgotten thesis that everything existing is corporeal,[5] including the spirit, whether human[6] or divine,[7] and that incarnation of God in matter would not be possible unless matter, in some subtle form, could be predicated of God.[8] Even though Tertullian's notion of the corporeality of spirit was very close to the biblical *ruah* and *neshma* and to the Greek *pneuma,* the idea did not strike deeper roots in Christianity.[9] The implication is that the metacosmic (God, Eschaton, Brahman-ātman, etc.) is not acosmic, as will be explained further below.

In fact, Teilhard de Chardin, in the middle of this century, struggled with this sense of the metacosmic within the cosmic in his theory of christogenesis. Sri Aurobindo, too, began to speculate on a parallel line but within a Hindu perspective. A Sri Lankan Buddhist philosopher, Martin Wickremasingha also made an effort to relate cosmic evolution to nirvanic emancipation in his controversial work *Bhavakarmavikashaya.*

The general perception of the universe among these scholars approximates what I call the "cosmic," in neat contrast to the "secularist" worldview associated with Western technocracy. The two paradigms are diametrically opposed. What is perceived as symbolic and sacramental in the one is often dismissed as magical or superstitious in the other. From the "cosmic" point of view, for instance, Water is not simply H_2O, as the secularist would see it; it is, rather, a gyne-ecological sacrament of life. So also is that other source of

---

2. Susan Bordo, "The Cartesian Masculinization of Thought," *Signs: Journal of Women in Culture and Society,* 11/3, 1986, 452.

3. Capra, 49, 63ff.

4. Walter Stangl, "Mutual Interaction: Newton's Science and Theology," *Perspectives on Science and Christian Faith: Journal of American Scientific Affiliation,* 43/2, June 1991, 82–83.

5. *De Anima, 7:* "Nihil enim si non corpus... nihil est incorporale nisi quod non est."

6. *De Anima,* 6.

7. *Adversum Praxean,* 7: "Quis enim negaverit, deum corpus esse, etsi deus spiritus est? Spiritus enim Corpus sui generis in sua effigie."

8. *Adversum Marcionem,* 2.27.1, 505.

9. Amos Funkenstein, *Theology and the Scientific Imagination from the Middle Ages to the Seventeenth Century,* Princeton University Press, Princeton, N.J., 1986, 42ff. I am indebted to this source for the quotations from Tertullian.

vital energy, *breath* (wind, *pneuma, ruah, neshma*, spirit, *marut, prāṇa, jīva*) which always appears in an andromorphic guise in mythology. It is more than the gaseous substance that the secularist speaks of. The same can be said of the other two elements: *earth* and *fire.*

The four elements, *āpo, tejo, vāyu,* and *paṭhavi* (Pali for water, fire, air, and earth), are not merely the cosmic stuff (*maha-bhutas*), but also the manifestations of the cosmic energy as female (water, earth) and male (fire, wind); the Buddhist monk-scholars in the scholastic era have interpreted these in terms of psychocosmic characteristics: water as cohesiveness, earth as resistance, fire as heat and light, and air as movement.

Gender in the Cosmic Language of the Bible

Gender differentiation in the four cosmic elements is not an arbitrary metaphor; it is a rich symbol, in that it truly shares in the reality experienced in the depth of human consciousness. But confusion arises when our cosmic experience — which determines and even constitutes our human language — is used to refer to the metacosmic that transcends such gender differentiation. The following examples clarify this observation.

First let us take St. Luke's description of Pentecost (Acts 2:1–4). The descent of the Spirit of God — despite the fact that *pneuma* (Greek for spirit) is neuter and *ruah* (the Hebrew equivalent) is feminine — is described in the mythical idiom of tongues of Fire and a great Wind, which are both symbols of maleness. Note that according to biblical anthropology, Mary and the church, upon both of whom God's Spirit descended, evoke a feminine image that resembles the deep and dark Water and the formless and void Earth on which the Spirit hovered to create the cosmos (Gen. 1:1–2).

Hence Pentecost (descent of God's Spirit on Mary and the church) is apparently expressed in terms of a male God recreating order (=cosmos) out of a female confusion (=chaos). The Creation story in the Book of Genesis is framed within the perspective of a rescue operation. Water assumes the guise of a source of evil and danger; other texts refer to Leviathan, the dragon living in the waters (Job 41:1; Ps. 104:26; Isa. 27:1); the exodus is a crossing of water (Exod. 14:21), recalling the Buddhist description of nirvana as crossing the sea of *samsara;* the last book of the Christian scriptures envisages the eschaton (final salvation in the end time) as a state wherein the Sea is entirely eliminated (Rev. 21:1)!

Fortunately, the same scriptures, elsewhere, counteract this tendency by using the two female symbols to express the salvific process. The Spirit is also the Water gushing out of Christ's side (John 7:38; also 4:10; Rev. 7:17; 21:6), while the image of the earth or rock or mountain are for the Psalmist a familiar symbol of Yahweh. Thus we can say that the bible alternates the male and female symbols in referring to Yahweh and Yahweh's saving activity.

We can conclude that, while cosmic elements are indispensable for expressing soteriological data, the alternation of the gender symbols prevents us from attributing to Ultimate Reality one specific sex at the expense of the other. There is one instance where the practice of alternation is done away with, namely, when the conjugal idiom is used in the First Testament of the bible. One never hears of God as the faithful wife and Israel as the adulterous husband! It is always the other way around! Such blatant patriarchalism is also evident in the marital image applied to the Christ-church relationship in the Second Testament (i.e., the Christian section) of the bible.

Even sacraments are administered within this same sexist model; the woman symbolizes the people to be redeemed, and male hierarchs represent the male redeemer. The Holy Eucharist and the Sacrament of Reconciliation — in the case of the latter, the confession of mortal sins to male mediators of God, which even in the revised tradition of the Roman church is a necessary condition for forgiveness except in special circumstances — are declared by the Roman Church to be all-male channels of communication with a male God!

Women's Mysticism against Men's Sacramentalism

Women have never failed to discover survival techniques within androcratic societies. They have learned to bypass the "sacramentalism" of a male clerical hierarchy by resorting to "mysticism," which provides as it were a hotline to God.[10] "This time, you listen to me, you male hierarchs!" the woman mystic seems to say, "God wants me to tell you something you men do not know. . . . " In sacraments men may claim to be the sole mediator; but in mysticism, allegedly a nonmediated experience of God, women could have equal claims; and yet even with mysticism, the prevailing "hiero-patriarchy" of the church requires that the ultimate authority to decide the authenticity of the mystical experiences of women happens to be a male prerogative! Here is an example: Margaret Mary Alacoque, the eighteenth-century mystic, had the Jesuit priest Claud de la Columbière as her spiritual director; through his mediation God's will was revealed to her. But she did finally reverse the gender roles by acting as God's mediatrix for her male confessor and his Jesuit confreres; the whole Jesuit Order believed it had received, through this woman-mystic, divine injunction to spread devotion to the Sacred Heart; and within a century (i.e., the nineteenth), the entire Jesuit Order would accept it as a revelation of God, and in the subsequent century (the twentieth), the Pope himself would issue an encyclical *Haurietis Aquas,* summoning the universal church to accept this message! It was a woman who became the medium of God's communication with man, thus reversing the androcentric order of the sacraments.

Mysticism offers women a way out of male sacramentalism, which relies

---

10. Ronald A. Knox, *Enthusiasm: A Chapter in the History of Religion,* Clarendon Press, Oxford, 1950.

too much on a male-female categorization of the Redeemer-redeemed relationship. The fault, in other words, is not with the sacramental nature of the cosmos, which we ardently uphold, but with the androcratic interpretation of the cosmos as woman and the metacosmic as man. Patriarchalism in religion, therefore, is an abuse of the sacramental nature of reality.

Hinduism and Tantric Buddhism

There is an instance in the Hindu tradition where this patriarchal bias in religious language is transcended not only by avoiding the Redeemer-redeemed categories couched in a technique of alternating the genders. Rather, an attempt is made to affirm one gender as an inseparable constituent of the other; hence the well-known adage: *Shavah shakti-vihīnah Shivah* (A corpse would Shiva be without Shakti). God's own energy or spirit is woman; God would not be God without her; suppression of the feminine is the death of God.[11]

In Tantric Buddhism, despite the absence of a belief in a personal and loving creator-redeemer God, we meet another manner of resorting to the sexual metaphor in speaking of nirvana as *parama-sukha* (supreme bliss). The conjugal idiom is employed in literature and iconography to express the belief that *karuṇā,* the compassionate involvement with beings caught up in samsara (rebirth cycle) and *prajñā,* the dispassionate withdrawal toward the state of nirvana, are inseparable facets of Buddhahood. Here the process of liberation (one's own and others') is conceived dynamically as a conjugal interaction between *karuṇā* and *prajñā.* Thus, statues showing the *prajñopayā* amplexus (the Buddha in conjugal intimacy with his consort), an image that hurts the sensibilities of Theravada Buddhists, are quite common in Nepal.[12]

Tantric Buddhism differs from the Shiva-Shakti theology of Hinduism in that what is feminine is not a constitutive dimension of the metacosmic, but the salvific process of one's disengagement from the cosmos (a movement toward the metacosmic), while the male principle is identified with the process of one's cosmic engagement.

Conclusion

Thus, whether or not one employs the conjugal idiom, we can conclude by formulating the following principle: Since liberation is a cosmic experience of the metacosmic, a soteriology is said to be conceptualized with a matriarchal ideology when the metacosmic is identified exclusively with the

---

11. However, the implicit belief seems to be that God is male though incomplete, and even useless without *the other* part of himself. The contemporary tendency of some Christian theologians such as Leonardo Boff to present the Spirit (the Third Person of the Divine Trinity) as a female energy coequal with the Father (the First Person) and eternally generating the Word (the Second Person) reflects this same androgynous model.

12. In public displays, however, it is the Diamond Rod and the Bell that are exhibited as the two sexual symbols. See Mahajra Bajracarya, "Kumari: The Virgin Goddess of Kathmandu," *Dialogue,* vols. 19–20, 1992–93, 88; 97.

female aspect of the cosmic; and conversely, a soteriology is said to be vitiated by a patriarchal conceptualization when the male aspect of the cosmic is exclusively used as a referent to the Metacosmic.

It is this observation that I am illustrating in the picture story given below (Figure 1).

THE STORY OF A GENDER CHANGE:
A PICTOGRAPHIC NARRATION

The stupa, a pre-Buddhist funeral mound (which the Buddhists inherited and transformed into a Buddhist symbol) tells this story to archaeologists and anthropologists even today. In composing this pictogram, I have been influenced by Lama Anagarika Govinda's profoundly insightful observations on this matter,[13] though the feminist critique which I associate with it, is not to be attributed to him.[14] I have chosen the (pre-Buddhist) stupa because it is one of the most well-known Asian religious symbols ever since the Buddhists had appropriated it as a sacred relic mound and because its pre-Buddhist history speaks of an Asian event relevant to our discussion of feminism. What follows is only a commentary on that pictogram.

The Cosmic Symbols in a Matriarchal System

In Nepal there are a couple of massive stupas, reportedly going back to Asokan times. The characteristic mark is their similarity with the Himalayan mountains that form their background. These massive stupas (wherein the dome is prominent, unlike in later stupas), as well as the mountains that form the background, give the impression that the Earth accentuates her femininity physiognomically in the form of rising rocks, protruding peaks, and massive mounds, as a woman does in her external form. But these signs hide the mystery of life within them, namely, Nature's power of nurture.

This power of hers is Water, that other feminine symbol which makes the earth awe inspiring and even frightening in its manifestations. For, water is a sign of life-giving love and death-bringing rage; of stillness and depth on the one hand, and of stirring motions on the other. When partnered by Earth, it makes a symbolic dyad that evokes in our hearts both the need and the fear of the feminine, the mystery of something beyond comprehension, which is at the same time our first uterine encounter with the cosmic.

The massive funeral mounds such as the pyramids in Egypt, or the stupas in pre-Buddhist India, or the megalithic tombs in pre-Christian Ireland

---

13. Lama Anagarika Govinda, *Psycho-cosmic Symbolism of the Buddhist Stupa,* Dharma Publishing, Berkeley, 1976, 71–98.

14. In his *Foundations of Tibetan Mysticism,* Rider and Company, London, 1960, 103, he insists that all the *mahābhūtas* (the four species of matter) constitute the feminine principle, in Tibetan Buddhism. I prefer to go by the general anthropological norm that Earth and Water are feminine while Fire and Wind are masculine.

are seen today in an androcentric perspective. But in a matriarchal context in which they had their remote origin, as Govinda suggests, they seem to have represented the incomprehensible horizon which the Cosmic Mystery of water and earth opened up — the horizon which we shall refer to as the "Metacosmic," something not to be confused with the "acosmic," a sort of a negation of the cosmic. As the prefix *meta* indicates, the metacosmic stands for a dimension which includes the cosmic and takes it beyond itself.

This metacosmic "Beyond" which we experience as the cosmic "Within" here and now had been perceived in the matriarchal period as a feminine expression of reality. This, of course, has been as sexist as the patriarchal model which we reject today. For, each of them is an inadequate response on the part of both males and females to the phenomenon of gynephobia.

This means that an investigation into that matriarchal paradigm is essential for our understanding of the patriarchal revolution which consisted of the other, equally one-sided response to the basic phenomenon of gynephobia. Thus the stereometric monuments which contained the remains of the departed seem to disclose — both in exterior form and location as well as in the belief-practice cycle surrounding them as religious symbols — the early matriarchal interpretations as well as the later patriarchal appropriation of that symbolism.

The Matriarchal Response to Gynephobia

Figure 1 on the left column illustrates the matriarchal response to gynephobia; and on the right, the patriarchal response and its consequences.

The (prepatriarchal) stupa, a gigantic dome (see left column, upper part) — evoking the image of Mother Earth's protruding breast? — was not a "functional structure" which served people's material needs as the local shrines did, but was an "aesthetic use of space," as Anagarika Govinda elucidates. It uplifts the human heart to the Universal Source of spiritual nourishment in the invisible spheres of ultimate release; it did not promise to satisfy one's legitimate cosmic needs such as food and shelter, health and wealth, as did the solar worship in the temples; nor did it ensure fertility and knowledge as did the Tree cult; rather, it elevated the mind to a realm beyond itself; to the mysterious springs of living Water. It symbolized the lunar (the menstrual?) cycle which alternated with the more regular and easily calculable solar rhythm of the males; this lunar cycle evoked the secrecy of the night and caused those stirrings of water — the tidal waves.

The ancient (pre-Buddhist) stupa, therefore, pointed to the unfathomable depths of the unconscious, to the indestructible life that hides beneath death, the eternal that succeeds the temporal, while the local shrine of (solar and astral) deities dished out the material requirements of day-to-day existence.

Thus the stupa — the lunar/aquatic/telluric symbol of the feminine — was understandably situated *outside* the human habitat, whereas the local shrine with its solar-astral deities together with the Sacred Tree (a symbol

FIGURE 1

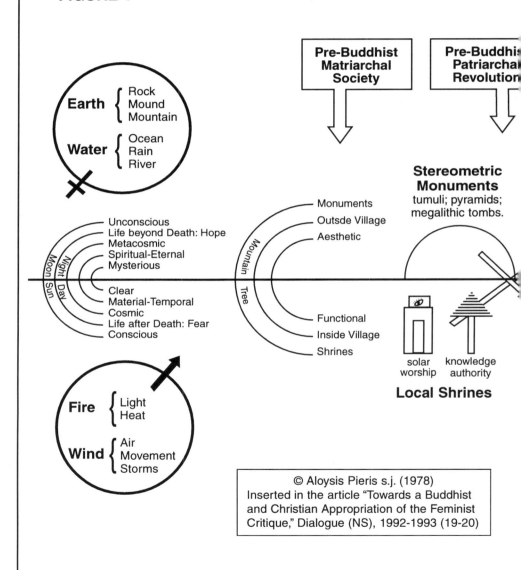

© Aloysis Pieris s.j. (1978)
Inserted in the article "Towards a Buddhist
and Christian Appropriation of the Feminist
Critique," Dialogue (NS), 1992-1993 (19-20)

Patriarchal Stereotypes
in Religions

♂ **Actus Purus**	♀ **Materia Prima**	
		Aristotle
Yahweh Spirit God Christ Spirit	Israel Chaos/Earth/Water People Church Mary	Judeo-Christain
Puruṣa Shiva	Prakrti Shakti	Hindu
saṃsāra Upāya	Paññā nirvāna	Buddhist

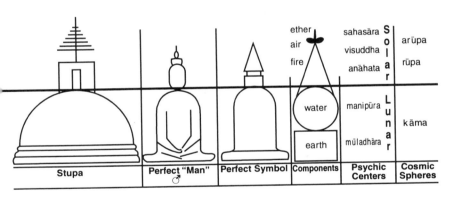

N.B. With psychic centers (cakra) one must also take the nāḍīs through which the masculine or solar forces and the feminine or lunar forces operate between the cakras (cf. Idā & Piṅgalā). Also to be noted in this regard: the union between wisdom (paññā = disengagement from saṃsāra = feminine and upāya (compassionate and loving engagement in Saṃsāra = masculine), cf. also the serpent symbol (Kundalini).

of practical wisdom and worldly authority) was always available *within* the village. These temples and sacred trees were tended by priests and mediators who knew the art of controlling the cosmic forces: not only regulating fire and wind in all their different forms (heat and droughts, storms and the human breath) but also appeasing, through rites and rituals, the exterior manifestations of Water and Earth.

In the right half of the diagram (Figure 1), I indicate the form of the stupa as the Buddhists inherited it (or as the Buddhists created it, according to Govinda) long after the patriarchal revolution. This form has combined the male and the female element into one harmonious whole — which makes the stupa one of the most powerful abstract symbols of Totality.[15]

The Patriarchal Takeover

There is, however, a problem, not so much with this abstract symbol as with the androcentric manner in which the male and female elements lend themselves to be interpreted. It is not the stupa or the statue that the Buddhists venerate, but the memory of the Buddha. The stupa and the Buddha figure are not just sacred symbols that mediate human veneration but also objects of contemplation (*mandala*). The universal symbolism of the cosmic elements combined therein should not be allowed to transmit a patriarchal message. What we said about sacraments holds true here. The danger does not lie in the symbol, but in the ideology of the beholder. Symbols (like sacraments) have to be redeemed from such ideological interpretations.

Thus we see that the dome has gradually assumed the role of the base on which the solar shrine and the Tree are mounted. The change is more than a mere spatial arrangement; there is here a reversal of gender symbols through an inversion of symbolic forms. What the nirvanic person integrates into a wholesome unity, the uninitiated reads separately. Hence many questions have to be asked: Does the new arrangement suggest that the cosmic is female and the metacosmic is male? Fire and Wind as well as the Tree are made to represent the higher, nobler pursuit of perfection. Does spiritual perfection amount to distancing oneself from the Cosmic? Do, therefore, water and the earth stand for the baser instincts of humankind and the lower strata of this world? Is it not precisely such patriarchalist differentiation that Buddhism tried to avoid, as Govinda seems to insinuate?

The geometric constituents which form the framework of the stupa are clearly discernible in some Chinese stupas to this day (compare Figure 2, a sketch of a stupa in the Chinatown of Manila). The cube (earth) and the globe (water), traditionally feminine forms, now seem to indicate the sensual and the enslaving elements within the human person, while the pyramid (fire) and the crescent (air) — topped by ether, often regarded as the finest element — refer to the spiritual realm which guarantees emancipation. The lunar and

---

15. Govinda, *Psycho-cosmic Symbolism*, 77.

the solar forces which operate in the human person as shown in Figure 1, coincide respectively with the lower and the higher psychic centers in Yoga discipline, too.

© Sketch drawn by D. Pieris from a photograph by A. Pieris

FIGURE 2
A Chinese Buddhist Temple in Manila

Are we here face to face with an ancient Indic cultural tradition which distinguished between "below the navel immortality" and "above the navel immortality"? In the earlier Brahmanic literature — presumably before the rebirth idea became clarified and widespread — one was believed to have attained immortality through one's offspring. In the later literature (especially in the Upanishads) one hears about the other, higher, spiritual mode of attaining immortality through renunciation of the lower, sensual activities of conjugal life.[16]

---

16. Cf. Patrick Olivelle, *Samnyasa Upanisads: Hindu Scriptures on Asceticism and Renunciation,* Oxford, New York, 1992, 3–100.

Buddhism arose at a time when the post-mortem survival of the individual through rebirth was a common belief and the samana ideal of renouncing
marital life was a widespread social phenomenon. Though *rebirth* and *immortality* are misleading terms when applied to the Buddhist approach to
life and death, its religious ideal falls under the rubric of "above the navel
immortality" of the Indic tradition.

What a mandalic contemplation tries (or ought) to avoid is the danger of
equating the lunar-feminine forces with the lower form of human experience
and the solar-masculine with the higher. Any suggestion that "the above the
navel immortality" is a solar movement and that the "below the navel" activity is symbolized by the woman, is tantamount to a patriarchal reading of the
symbol. No misogynic equation such as: *Evil = sensual = woman = cosmic,*
which evokes the parallel equation *Good = spiritual = man = metacosmic,*
should be allowed to be read in those symbols. For, this twofold equation
is the patriarchal response to gynephobia. It is parallel to the male-female
connotation attributed to the redeemer-redeemed relationship in Christian soteriology, with its subtle misogynic consequences which we have criticized
earlier.

The Feminist Critique

Feminism today aims at correcting this equation wherever it occurs, insisting that the metacosmic can be neither female nor male; that It/He/She is the
transcendence of both sexes. By referring to the Metacosmic as *dhatu*, Buddhists have avoided the sexist terms characteristic of a person, while the same
results are achieved in Vedantic Hinduism with its reference to *Brahman* in
the neuter.

The feminists too have more than one way of making this point. The first
is to alternate the gender in referring to God, as illustrated above. The recourse to androgynic language (Father-Mother God!) is the second way of
counteracting the sexist idiom in God talk. The Sri Lankan Buddhists do
this when they speak of the Buddha as both Father and (Immortal) Mother
(*budu-piyāṇo, amā-māniyo*).

The third, as indicated above, would be to eliminate both the genders in
one's religious discourse. In fact the early Buddhists understood too clearly
that Buddhahood defied all cosmic and human categories and was something
sui generis.[17] They had wisely refrained from making images of the Buddha
through fear of anthropomorphizing the Metacosmic. The early Buddhists
avoided "human figures" in illustrating the major events in the Buddha's
life, and had recourse to gender-free symbols such as the feet to indicate
the traveling preacher, the tree to symbolize the Buddha's enlightenment, the
wheel to express the Buddha's proclamation of the message of liberation,

---

17. Anguttara Nikaya, vol. II, 38–39.

and finally the androgynic symbol of stupa (ever to be guarded against any androcentric interpretation) to remind one of the Buddha's final release.

But once the human figure became an accepted medium of expression, the metacosmic had necessarily to be shown in the form of the historical male figure who later became the Buddha, and who remained male until parinirvana. The perfect symbols — stupa and samadhi statue (Figure 1, right column) — as appropriated by Buddhists of a later era need to be permanently guarded against any such interpretation.

One cannot help noting a parallel development in Christianity. The Risen Jesus began to be iconographically represented as a male figure, when in reality, Christ — whom Jesus became — is neither male nor female, but a transcendence of both. If "In Christ, there is neither male nor female" (Gal. 3:27), how can Christ be male (or female)?

TOWARD A FEMINIST CRITIQUE OF RELIGIOUS SYMBOLS

Symbols are more powerful than reality which they participate in, and which they "re-present," because it is as symbol that Reality or Truth invariably finds entry into the human heart. In all religions and cultures and philosophies, symbolism has indoctrinated humankind into an androcentric idiom not only in expressing but even in experiencing the Transcendent. Hence the feminist plea: that the liberative message of the great founders of religions must be continuously freed from the ideological captivity of a given symbolism in a given culture. Since all currently prevalent religions have been formulated in the patriarchal era, we must be conscious of the symbols (words in sacred scriptures, rites and rituals, objects of veneration or contemplation, and even lifestyles) which unconsciously trick us into misogyny.

Of all symbols, the human word is the most effectively evocative and the most frequently employed. The feminists have quite rightly battled against sexism that pervades the use of language. This, however, is not what I intend discussing here. I am more concerned with the patriarchal bias affecting the use of human words (i.e., the sacred scriptures) in expressing the Salvific Word — Dharma/Dabar. For we cannot deny that both the First and Second Testaments of the Christian bible, no less than the Buddhist Tripitaka contain misogynic texts that embarrass men and women sensitive to the feminine component of our human existence. Here the feminist critique has to be appropriated by scripture scholars and scripture readers of both religions.

There is, of course, many a way of handling these scriptural data. It would be wrong to gloss over the texts or treat them as sacred absolutes. The scriptures are not above their ultimate Source; human words struggling to express truth are not to be confused with Truth itself, which alone is the Ultimate Word. Feminists in the West, at least since the last century, have trained us to read the Hebrew and Christian scriptures in a nonsexist key. This method is yet to be employed with reference to Buddhist scriptures so that the feminist mode of religious experience hidden beneath an androcentric idiom could be reclaimed even within the scriptural text.

This is the next step we take in our search, as we try to understand and criticize the most obvious and all-pervasive androcratic bias — what I have called "the Eve-Mary Polarity"[18] — which pervades the Holy Writ of all religions.

---

18. A. Pieris, "Religious Vows and the Reign of God," see chapter 16 below, 180–181. See also "The Eve-Mary Polarity in Scripture and Tradition," chapter 4 below, 29–37.

4

The Eve-Mary Polarity in Scripture and Tradition

THE INDIC TRADITION

The Eve-Mary polarity is one of the most common expressions of gyne-phobia. It is the patriarchal way of categorizing women either as the temptress who is weak enough to succumb too easily to the seductive agent of evil (Mara in Buddhism; the Serpent/Satan in Christianity), or as the ideal woman who renounces all sexual (below the navel) activity. The Roman Catholic model of Mary (with a striking parallel in the Buddhist image of Maya, the virgin mother of the Buddha, a virgin before, during, and after the birth of the most pure Man) has been misused theologically to inculcate a patriarchal image of the ideal woman in Christian spirituality.

The Indo-European Roots?

The Hindu epic Ramayana does the same in presenting Sita as the ideal wife, but it does so with a twofold difference: the emphasis is on uxorial fidelity over and above virginity, and evil is personified in the Sri Lankan King Ravana. This Indic (or Indo-European?) vision of the woman corresponds to the view held also by the ancient Greeks for whom the faithful wife — an uneducated but glorified "slave" living happily at home with the other (real) domestic slaves — was a much revered person quite unlike that other kind of women, the *hetaerae* (courtesans) who were free, public, admired, talented, educated, and exerted influence on the lives of public men (e.g., Aspasia, the mistress who educated Pericles; Diotima, the courtesan who instructed Socrates; Leontium, also a prostitute and disciple of Epicurius); obviously, all these women, because of their beauty and knowledge (Greek ideals) were more admired than respected.[1] The Indic and Hellenic cultures seem to reflect a common Indo-European trend in creating this twofold image of the woman.

But already, a great Indian reformer of Tamil Nadu, Ramasawami Periyar, pioneered an antipatriarchal, and therefore, antisanskritic, anti-Brahmanic critique of this image of the women; he emphasized the crucial distinction between *nirpande karpu* or chastity imposed on women by a patriarchal society, and *suvecchai karpu,* or chastity voluntarily undertaken by women themselves, independent of that ideological pressure.[2] Our concern will be focused on how the image of the chaste woman has been forced upon our collective consciousness by centuries of androcentricism.

Goddess as Victim

By idolizing woman and placing her on a high altar — the altar being at once a place where an innocent victim suffers at the hands of the male priest and the place where the god(dess) is venerated — our society has tricked her into playing the role of a goddess-victim of hiero-patriarchy precisely because she is otherwise regarded as a demon, a temptress, the embodiment of sensuality and source of social deterioration. She cannot descend from that man-made niche and walk as a human among humans without losing the luster of the man-made halo that she is forced to wear; if she tries to leap down to her freedom from that exalted state, she is bound to crash-land and run the invariable risk of breaking into pieces, losing her allegedly "female identity," which, in reality, is the gender specificity determined by male hierarchs on the basis of an Eve-Mary polarity.

Thus the trend among some feminists to return to the idea of the goddess as a reaffirmation of the female in an "orientalist" manner — orientalism being a Western co-option of the eastern mystique — has to be carefully assessed.[3] The goddess idea, especially the mother-goddess cult, is not always and necessarily a liberative feminist concept in South Asia. The *devis* do often appear to be a faithful reflection of the state (or, more precisely, the fate) of women in Asia's androcentric society. Caring, nurturing, listening, healing, ever present and easily approachable — yes, but marginal and ubiquitously secondary and subservient to the powerful domineering devas of the Asian pantheon! Was it not this mythicization of the woman that nationalists in Bengal appropriated for political ends, turning it into a symbol of the patriarchal status quo?[4]

Note also that these same cultures — which raise the domestic(ated)

---

1. W. E. H. Lecky, *History of European Morals from Augustine to Charlemagne,* Longmans, Green and Co., (two volumes), 1911, vol. II, 287, 293, 297.

2. Gabriele Dietrich, *Women's Movement in India: Conceptual and Religious Reflections,* Breakthrough Publications, Bangalore, 1988, 29.

3. Kamala Ganesh, "Mother Who Is Not a Mother," *Economic and Political Weekly* (abbreviated *EPW*), XXV/42–43, October 20–27, 1990, 50ff.

4. Jasodhara Bagchi, "Representing Nationalism: Ideology of Motherhood in Colonial Bengal," ibid., 65ff.

woman to the level of a deity who is attired in the garb of chastity designed by males — invariably end up triggering a counterpoint movement of institutionalizing unchastity in women as in the case of "sacred prostitutes" (*devadasis*).[5] One is again reminded of Greek worship of Aphrodite and the courtesan-priestesses of so many temples in the Hellenic world.[6]

Later in this chapter, we shall see that prostitution and the cult of virginity are twin aspects of a patriarchal obsession. These two alternative destinies of womankind, which the anti-Brahmanic Periyar tried hard to eliminate, have reappeared in a modern version of *Illango Silappathikkam* of M. Karunanidhi — reversing the message of Periyar's version; for, here, to quote Dietrich,

> we are safely back to the compartmentalization of women into the chaste housewife Kannagi and the dancing girl Madhavi, the one plain and innocent, empowered by her chastity to let Madurai go up in flames to avenge the death of her innocent husband, and the other a dazzling damsel and skilled artiste whose moral disrepute finally gets redeemed by her becoming a Buddhist nun.[7]

Southern Buddhism and the Roman Catholic brand of Christianity, in the course of their early history, had begun to develop this same species of Eve-Mary polarity in their general attitude to women. The strong influence of a male-celibate hierarchy of "woman renouncers" may have contributed to this.

THE BUDDHIST EXPERIENCE

Buddhist Scriptures

A feminist Buddhist scholar, Karen Christina Lang, has made a very balanced comparative study of the contents of canonical texts, Theragatha and Therigatha, which are attributed not to the Buddha but to the early monks and nuns respectively.[8] Her feminist instinct has detected a radical difference between the two anthologies. The mystical poems of the monk-saints bear the stamp of gynephobia, i.e., the dread of the woman. She is said to be the hunter to flee from; and often, she or her body is referred to as *Mār'ūpāsa* or *Macc'ūpāsa*, i.e., the hunter's trap set up by Mara — Mara being the death-bringing seducer. On the one hand, the woman is the irresistible agent of (a male's) sexual enticement; on the other hand, she is also the disgusting source of polluting substances such as feces, urine, saliva,

---

5. See special issue on "The Devadasi Problem," by Asha Ramesh and H. P. Philomena, *Banhi: An Occasional Journal of the Joint Women's Programme,* 1981, especially 13–15 and *passim.*

6. Lecky, 291.

7. Dietrich, 30.

8. Karen C. Lang, "Lord Death's Snare: Gender Related Imagery in the Theragatha and the Therigatha," *Journal of Feminist Studies in Religion,* II/2, Fall 1986, 63–79.

and tears. These two characteristics of the female body appear — in the eyes of the male-celibate beholder — as a symbol and replica of this illusory world (samsara) with its seductive fascination, on the one hand, and its frustrating repulsiveness on the other! The misogynic equation "samsara=female=sensuality=body=evil" is complete. I presume that the woman, in this perspective, would be truly good (i.e., less dangerous for men) only when she renounces that natural state and becomes a renouncer herself.

Lang shows that in the Nuns' Poems, fortunately, there emerges another picture. These women mystics do not view man or the male body as a source of sexual enticement for them, as one might have expected, given the monks' attitude toward the opposite sex. Moreover, barring a few exceptions, the nuns generally do not share the monks' negative attitude toward their own female bodies as the tempter's snare for males or as a disgusting source of impure substances; the majority of these women arahans seem to relativize their bodies only in terms of the natural process of aging and death. In radical contrast to the misogyny of the monks, these women display a positive feeling about themselves and their own bodies.

Here I must recall an interesting conversation Fr. Herman Joseph Frisch and I had with the meditation guide at the Kanduboda Meditation Center in Sri Lanka. This monk, an ex-sailor who had renounced wealth, women, and the world, made it clear to us that he would not give the *asubha-bhāvanā* (meditation on the repulsiveness of the human body) to women, because they usually would not succeed doing it. "They love their bodies too much!" he explained.

This, precisely, is the contribution of women to religion: a positive understanding of matter, senses, body, and the world in general, and of the woman herself, in particular. They are that half of the human race that is capable of understanding the point where symbol and reality merge. I agree, therefore, with Lang's conclusion that a feminist critical hermeneutics of misogynic texts seeks to expose the androcentric social context which obscured the spiritual experience of these great women of the past, so that we may be able to "reclaim these long-dead women as part of our own human history."[9]

Though some of the misogynic texts found in the Buddhist scriptures sound coarse,[10] it would also seem that the Buddhist canon — together with the Vedic literature — remains unique among the sacred writings of any religion in including women among its canonical authors. The Therigatha are not just the work of males writing about women's experiences, as was thought by some Buddhologists,[11] but are authentically feminist in their sane and salutary approach to the cosmic reality, differing radically from the attitude adopted by the Theras. The implication is that the Buddhist canon already

9. Ibid., 79.
10. E.g., *The Book of Disciple*, Part I, 36; *Dialogues of the Buddha,* vol. II, 154.
11. Cf. C. A. F. Rhys Davids, *Psalms of the Earthly Buddhists,* London, 1909, enlarged reprint 1964, xxiii. See also Lang, 66.

contains a feminist critique of what I have called the Eve-Mary polarity, and this should be exploited to the full as an exegetical principle to eliminate sexism from all religious discourse and from all religious institutions.

A feminist reclaimer of this kind needs to be extended also to other parts of the Buddhist scriptures where the hand of women is conspicuously absent and where, therefore, the patriarchalism of the Indic society is accentuated by male-celibate compilers. Behind the androcentric screen of horrendous anti-woman prejudices *attributed* to the founder of Buddhism — some of which are so crude that they could never have come from the sacred lips of the Buddha[12] — we have to keep in focus who he really was: a Mahapurusa who had attained such heights of inner freedom as to be at home in the presence of women, unruffled by the gynephobia that harasses the beginners on that same path to freedom. The misogyny so blatantly attributed to the Buddha must reflect the mentality of the compilers. How could it be otherwise? The following considerations are valuable pointers toward a new way of interpreting these misogynic texts.

Reclaiming the Buddha's Feminism

There was, we know, a faction of rigid ascetics headed by Devadatta who criticized the Buddha for laxity. Ananda, the beloved disciple of the Buddha and a feminist, is presented as a nonsaint and a laxist, almost an immature person compared to, say, Kassapa the rigid ascetic.[13] Against this background one must critically assess the veiled protest made in the scriptures themselves against the Buddha's decision to found an order of nuns — which confirms that his decision was a rejection of the antiwoman bias of some of his own followers. This veiled protest can be noticed in the way Ananda, the beloved disciple, is severely criticized by the canonical authors for having misled the Buddha on this matter.[14]

Note here that the compilers are indirectly criticizing the Buddha himself; and quite contrary to the qualities of wisdom and discernment lavishly ascribed to him in the rest of the canon, he is made to appear as one who had been forced to make a grave mistake which he regrets later. Such a serious accusation against the Buddha boomerangs on the redactors of the texts. We have every right to indulge in what is known as the "hermeneutics of suspicion"; it makes us look for the ideology (here its name is androcracy) lying behind this contradiction in the texts. A sociological survey on the status of female renunciates in Thai and Burmese Buddhism has demonstrated that, just as in the scriptures, so also in contemporary traditions, women's equality with men is clearly maintained with regard to the practice of even the

---

12. Some of these texts have been gathered together in M. Spiro, *Buddhism and Society*, London, 1970, 297ff.

13. See for instance, S. II. 215ff.

14. Vin. II. 253ff. and especially 256ff.

highest form of religious pursuit; if there is any disequilibrium, it is noticed only in the organizational structure of religion.[15]

In other words, we are not wrong in concluding that patriarchy is to be found, not in the "core doctrine" of Buddhism (Truth and the Path) which is perennially valid, but only in the religious institution which necessarily reflects the cultural limitations of time and space. Hence it is a wise norm in exegesis to employ the perennially valid core doctrine — what is called the "canon within a canon" — to interpret misogynic texts which are culture-bound.

Let me insist in passing that the core doctrine which is intrinsically trace-able to the Buddha is the first of the four "Great Hermeneutical Criteria" (*mahapadesa*) which, according to the orthodox Buddhist manuals of exege-sis, are to be employed in discerning the authenticity of a given scriptural passage.[16] This exegetical principle would be greatly helpful in handling the misogynic texts in the Tripitaka.

Even without going into such intricacies, one can still conclude that pa-triarchy cannot be accommodated within the core doctrine of Buddhism; the core doctrine is that the absence of greed, hate and delusion (*alobha, adosa,* and *amoha*) constitutes nirvanic freedom. Now the oppressive ideology of patriarchy originates from male greed (*lobha*) for power and control over the body, labor, and sexuality of women; it manifests itself as species of *dosa,* a veiled hatred of women, which is what misogyny means. At the root of it all is *moha,* the great delusion arising from gynephobia and a tendency to con-fuse biological differences with socially imposed gender roles. This threefold evil, unless uprooted, will perpetuate the oppression of women in religious and in civil society.

A feminist hermeneutic, as I see it, will insist that all misogynic texts of the scriptures be interpreted in the light of the core doctrine preached by the Buddha, and in conformity with the litmus test given in his discourse to the Kalamas: what brings liberation is true. Both scripture and tradition must be submitted to this test.

THE CHRISTIAN EXPERIENCE

The Christian Scriptures

Also for Christians, the feminist critique does not intend to distort the message of the founder, but to redeem it from the androcratic strictures it has

---

15. Ingrid Jordt, "Bhikkhuni, Thilashin, Mae-chi: Women who renounce the world in Burma and Thailand, and the Classical Pali Buddhist Texts," *Crossroads: International Journal of South Asian Studies,* Special Burma Studies Issue, 4/1, Fall 1988, 31–39.

16. For an explanation of this exegetical principle (*yā hi catūhi mahāpadesehi aviruddhā pāli, sā pamāṇam*) as advocated by Dhammapala in his manual of exegesis (*Nettippakarana*), see Aloysius Pieris, *Some Salient Aspects of Consciousness and Reality in Pali Scholasticism as Reflected in the Commentaries of Acariya Dhammapala,* unpublished doctoral dissertation presented to and approved by the University of Sri Lanka, 1971, 19–21.

received from the patriarchy of the Judeo-Greco-Roman cultures in which it was formulated. In this way, women's experience, submerged so long by the dominant male worldview, can be reclaimed for the benefit of both male and female Christians.

Feminist critique has to begin with the observation that in the gospels which contain many Jesus-sayings, there is no sign of a "Mary versus Eve" or a "virgin-mother versus temptress" bipolarity in the understanding of women. Rather, what we detect is a very healthy but "hidden tradition" of two Marys: Mary, the mother of Jesus and Mary (Magdalene), the friend of Jesus; I say "hidden," because, as Elizabeth Moltmann-Wendel suggests, the mother tradition of the nascent church had already eclipsed the friend tradition.[17]

This, I think, is the twofold image of womanhood that has to be reclaimed through a feminist hermeneutic. For the same gospels as well as the other writings of the Second Testament clearly reveal the heavy hand of patriarchy distorting this feminism of Jesus.

From Jane Schaberg's illuminating detection of the male editorial hand hiding behind the gospel texts that speak of Mary Magdalene and other women,[18] I am entitled to conclude that there are at least three areas in which the feminism of Jesus is suppressed.

First, the witness value of women is doubted. Though Mary Magdalene is among the women who accompanied Jesus and gave financial support to his movement (Luke 8:1–3), and was the first to receive the Good News of the resurrection (Matt. 28:9–10; Mark 16:9; John 20:14–18), still, the contemporary patriarchal belief that women were unreliable witnesses seems scripturally confirmed when Peter and the others as well as the latecomer Paul are invested with an authority based on their experience of the Risen Lord. In the Lucan version (24:34) it is Peter who is the first to receive the resurrection appearance. Is it too rash to conclude that women, the first witnesses and the first believers, had at some moment in the nascent church ceased to enjoy credibility, and, therefore, also authority, in the Jesus movement?

Second, the various women figures are conflated into one. Contrary to the data in the Christian scriptures, the later generations have indulged in a conflation of the image of Mary the friend of Jesus with the figure of the woman who anointed Jesus' feet (John 12:1–8) or the repentant prostitute (Luke 7:36–50), and the woman about to be stoned for adultery (John 7:53–8:11) and the "loose" woman from Samaria (John 4:4–42), not to mention Mary, the sister of Martha who loved to listen to Jesus (Luke 10:38–42). Magdalene became her name!

---

17. Elizabeth Moltmann-Wendel, "Maria oder Magdalene — Mutterschaft oder Freundschaft?" in E. Moltmann-Wendel et al. [Herausg.], *Was geht uns Maria an?* Gutersloh, 1988, 51–59.

18. Jane Schaberg, "Thinking Back Through the Magdalene," *Continuum,* I/2, Winter–Spring 1991, 71–90.

Third, the prophetic status of women is diluted. In Mark and Matthew the (unnamed) woman is not a prostitute; and her act was one of anointing Jesus for burial, i.e., a prophetic act. This is a case of Jesus being prophetically *anointed*, i.e., "made Christ" by a woman — and not just declared Christ as was done by Peter (Matt. 16:16) or Martha (John 11:27). In the Lucan theology which highlights heavenly joy when sinners repent, this significant event vanishes into the drama of a prostitute's conversion.

Thus we have inherited, in the course of time, the now familiar tradition of the two Marys — not Mary the mother of Jesus and Mary the friend of Jesus — but the sexually *innocuous* Mary (the virgin-mother of Jesus) and the sexually *seductive* Mary (the sinner whom Jesus transformed into a contemplative saint). This tradition of the Eve-Mary polarity continues to determine the attitude of official Christianity toward the moral and institutional status of women.

The Church's Laws

Nowhere is this more notoriously evident than in the way prostitution (which, as we know, is a patriarchal institution) is viewed in medieval ecclesiastical law. Brundage's study on this question warrants the following observations.[19]

The legal tradition of the Roman church, bearing the stamp of its male celibate authors, seems to assume that it is natural for women to become sexual enticers of men and therefore recommends practical toleration of prostitutes while indulging in a theoretical condemnation of prostitution as such. Nicholas of Lyra even holds that prostitution is necessary for public good! The paradox accepted by canonists seems to be that, despite its moral turpitude, prostitution keeps the social order (of males?) from collapsing; says Augustine: *Aufer meretrices de rebus humanis, turbaveris omnia libidinibus; constituite matronarum loco, labe ac dedecore dehonestaveris.*[20] The male celibate priests (who alone have the power to absolve the sins of men and women) are advised to be merciful and understanding toward these naturally frail creatures who are inclined to sexual lapses (with males) while the pimps who employ them are to be treated severely for exploiting the females' innate sexual weakness. What we see here is the embodiment of a belief that is clearly aired about in the early Christian ascetical writings (third and fourth centuries) wherein women seem to be safe only as consecrated virgins (and widows) or as homebound spouses. No third way could be presumed to have existed for them, save, perhaps, that which led them to Eve's fate.

In all this, the lasting impact of Greco-Roman beliefs on the church is evident. It continues to this day. This explains, as I have conjectured else-

---

19. James A. Brundage, "Prostitution in the Medieval Canon Law," *Signs: Journal of Women in Culture and Society,* University of Chicago 1/4, Summer 1976, 830, 835–37.

20. *De Ordine*, 24 [PL 32/1000], quoted by Brundage.

where,[21] why during the Romantic period of European history there appeared so many works of art (poetry and paintings in particular) which extolled Mary Magdalene — the prostitute and mystic lover of Christ. We might say that this was a desperate humanist search for a via media between Eve and Mary, a synthesis of chastity and charity, or even of agape and eros. Or was it an unconscious attempt, successful or not, at reclaiming the "mother/friend" tradition of the gospels?

But centuries before the Romantic period, already in the Middle Ages, the Christian humanism of Dante and Petrarch [*pace* Deviataikina[22]] and of the great romantic saint Francis of Assisi had started this project of recovery. Indeed, feminism has had many beginnings in the history of Christianity, and many setbacks.

---

21. Aloysius Pieris, "Religious Vows and the Reign of God," chapter 16 below, 180.
22. N. T. Deviataikina ("The Problem of the Meaning of Human Existence in Petrarch's 'Confessions,'" *Soviet Studies in History,* New York, XIX/2, Fall 1980) questions the widespread acclamation of Petrarch as a humanist.

5

Religious Abuse of Woman

The consequences of the gynephobia contained in the Eve-Mary polarity are many and varied. In this chapter, I will deal with three of them: (a) the abuse of the mother-ideal; (b) the desexualization of women through the cult of virginity; and (c) the instrumental role imposed on and accepted by women.

THE RELIGIOUS ABUSE OF THE MOTHER-IDEAL

Buddhist and Christian hierarchs are quite justified in proclaiming the sanctity of marriage and the importance of the family as a unit of society. But there is something they tend to forget about their founder's view of marriage and family and consequently about the authentic role of woman in and outside the family.

Feminists complain that religion uses the mother-ideal to keep women under control in a male-dominated home. Motherhood is extolled as a service that takes in all the burdens of the home, allowing the men to occupy the seat of power. The context within which such ideological manipulation is made possible, in Asia in particular, is the traditional notion of the family and civil society.

We cannot insist enough, however, that neither the Buddha nor the Christ accepted uncritically the model of the family and society taken for granted by their contemporaries. The woman's role in Buddhism and in Christianity, therefore, has to be defined within this new horizon which Gotama and Jesus opened up for humankind.

Relativization of Family and Civil Order

The Reign of Yahweh was the goal that Jesus held up as the *summum bonum*. It does not restrict itself to an individualistic type of internal liberation, but embraces a new set of social relationships governed solely by love, a new society in which natural limitations of biological and emotional ties

38

must fade away into a new order of human freedom and fellowship. Marriage is meaningful only as a sacrament of God's Reign; family is a worthy pursuit only when it reflects this new society which Jesus preached at the risk of death. Unlike his contemporaries, he did not absolutize the family, nor take for granted the social structures of his times. This explains the revolutionary change of heart and mind — *metanoia* — which he demanded from his followers before they could become cocreators and coheirs of the new human family.

A parallel teaching can be noted in Buddhism. Total human liberation requires that marriage and family lose their cramping effect on the irresistible human quest for nonpossessive love (*alobha*), forgiving love (*adosa*), and the pleroma of wisdom (*amoha*). At the time of the Buddha, "priesthood and marriage" were inseparably joined together and symbolized in the perpetual maintenance of Fire (*agni*). Fire served as the sacrificial element for the male head of family who was equally the priest, while it was also the focus of the culinary chores of the home-and-hearth-bound wife. This notion of the household neatly fitted into the religiously sanctioned caste order which constituted the civil society of his day.

The Buddha, as a renouncer of both family and priesthood, followed the *anagni* ("fireless") path of celibacy and mendicancy, a path that created a dent in the civil order of the day. In his preaching, he did not reject the family but relativized it before the ideal of the *ariya-savaka-sangha*, a communion of those in pursuit of nirvanic freedom. He did not subvert the order of the family, as charged by his enemies, but made it subserve this new order.

For, besides the wife-mother role with a heavy burden attached to it, women in ancient Indian society (according to the evidence found in Buddhist literature), had the chance of choosing from two vocations of a much freer nature: that of a prostitute and that of a *bhikkhuni;* of these, the latter enjoyed not only the esteem of the society but also far greater independence and social mobility than the former.[1] The Buddha gave women the opportunity to enjoy freedom from all burdens of the biological family in order to join the noble community of disciples where they could pursue the highest freedom — nirvana — on a par with male renunciates. It was a respectful alternative to the traditional image of women as wives and mothers.

Thus, with the relativization of the family, the conventional role of women was also challenged in the new dispensation inaugurated by the founders of Buddhism and Christianity.

Freedom of Woman in the New Order

Many Jewish women flouted the accepted canons of family and society, when they dared to become travel companions of Jesus, the new rabbi, a

---

1. Uma Chakravarty, "The Rise of Buddhism as Experienced by Women," *Manushi: Journal about Women and Society,* no. 8, 1981, especially 8–10.

man who had no time for marriage and family; he was fully involved with the work of initiating a new order of values. He invited men and women to leave father and mother, spouses and children, for the sake of the Kingdom. The majority of his male and female disciples were married, but when they joined the ministry, their families, too, joined them, so that henceforth marital and family life — which were never renounced as such — found their proper function only in relation to the task of advancing the Reign of Yahweh.

An analogical species of emancipation is acknowledged also in Buddhist scriptures. The mystical utterances in the Psalms of the Sisters (Therigatha), while referring to the nirvanic freedom enjoyed by their female authors, make also many unambiguous allusions to the freedom they gained from troublesome husbands, family bonds, and household labor.[2] In other words, the holy writ advocates the legitimacy of such freedom for wives and mothers.

If, as we have seen, the Buddha and Jesus gave women the chance of freeing themselves from a male appropriation of their bodies, labor, and sexuality, then we are wise in maintaining that fatherhood is also a word for household responsibility, just as motherhood also evokes a societal responsibility. Where labor is shared by man and woman in both family and society, one sees a form of sex differentiation which does not know gender discrimination. This is what feminists aim for in their critique of religion; it is also what Asian cultures desperately need.

THE CULT OF THE VIRGIN AND THE DESEXUALIZED WOMAN

Female Renunciates

From a feminist perspective, it is intriguing to notice that the investiture ceremony of female renunciates in most religions consists of a symbolic hiding of their feminine identity. In spite of liberalization after Vatican II, a few congregations of Catholic nuns, particularly in Asia, continue the custom of cutting the hair or even shaving the head completely. The female form of the body is hidden beyond recognition. Males are not subjected to this custom. Does it imply that a woman cannot attain total human freedom without ceasing to be a woman?

This question is multifaceted. One aspect of it is whether celibacy is a renunciation of genitality only or of sexuality as well. Sexuality is a physiological, physiognomic, and psychological orientation of an individual in terms of the dominance of maleness or femaleness in him or her. This includes the variety of heterosexual and homosexual orientations. Sexuality is a natural and inalienable quality of a person's cosmic existence. Since liberation is the cosmic experience of the Metacosmic, sexuality can and should

---

2. Ibid., 10.

never be renounced.[3] Hence two clarifications are in order: (1) what feminists call into question is not sexual differentiation but gender stereotypes imposed by a patriarchal society; (2) what celibates renounce is not sexuality — which is part and parcel of the human mode of relating to things and persons — but of genital activity as the medium of expression in relationships. The desexualization of women through suppression of their femininity in any form, even in the name of consecrated virginity, originates from the second of the two types of confusion mentioned above.

Christian Appropriation of Parthenolatry

One form in which such desexualization is fostered by religious patriarchs is "parthenolatry," the cult of virginity (and/or veneration of virgins) which appears in various guises in various epochs. Nowhere is this so evident as in Roman Catholicism. It is, in fact, a Greco-Roman heritage that mitigates against biblico-Christian foundations of religious life.

The vestal virgins were a symbol of pre-Christian Rome's veneration of virginity. Their purity ensured the state's prosperity. The Roman poet Virgil saw something divine in the bees because they were virgin-mothers (just as Plutarch believed that virgins were never attacked by bees!). Virgins were so sacred that they could not be executed in ancient Rome. When Sejanus fell, the Senate wished to execute his daughter, but being a virgin she was deflowered by the executor before he put her to death, as if it were sacrilegious for a virgin to die in captivity.[4]

Greek culture, that other component of traditional Western Christianity, brought a contribution of its own. The Parthenon (Virgin's Temple) was the noblest religious temple in Athens. Athene and Artemis were venerated for their chastity. "Virgin, defend the virgins," prayed the suppliant in Aeschylus — an understandable prayer in the midst of unbridled sensuality that wrecked ancient Greece.[5]

But Christianity, in its founder's version, would hear of no cult other than the worship of Yahweh, which, in its turn, consisted of service to fellow-beings. But in its Greco-Roman version, Christianity had succumbed to many cults. The cult of virginity is just one of them! In Christ's perspective, virginity (like marriage) could have no value except in relation to the Reign of God, which alone is absolute — "eunuchs for the sake of God's Kingdom." Yet in the Romanized and Hellenized churches of the empire, virgins began to acquire a high social status, as did the male clerics. They were offered special seats of honor in the Sunday liturgy. After their death, they were liturgically commemorated immediately after the martyrs and confessors of faith. Virginity was the only way for Christian women to be respectable among

---

3. See A. Pieris, "The Vows as Ingredients of Authentic Humanism: An Autobiographical Essay on the Religious Vows," chapter 18 below, 212–214.

4. Cf. Lecky, I, 106–7.

5. Ibid., 105.

men and intellectually acceptable among male hierarchs.[6] It was a status symbol.

Alas, God's Reign ceased to be the standard for valuing human institutions; in fact, the new criterion for evaluating marriage seemed to be virginity! "I praise marriage," declared St. Jerome, a notorious misogynist of the early church, "because it produces virgins for me."[7] He was "the most outstanding spiritual guide of Roman virgins, first in Rome and then in Palestine."[8] He surrounded himself with unmarried female devotees, complaining at the same time of being afflicted with wild sexual fantasies about women even during prayer, as did so many other monastics who were obsessed with the cult of virginity![9]

Note, in passing, how the male celibates and clerics who were already controlling women through the administration of nearly five sacraments — those "all-male" mediations between God and women — would now assume the role of spiritual counselors and take over the only domain where women could establish a nonmediated contact with God, the domain of mystical life (see chapter 3). Thus began an unhealthy tradition — in vogue even today — of certain male celibate clerics specializing in being exclusively spiritual directors of consecrated virgins!

On these "spiritual gynecologists" — I have no better word to describe them — consecrated virgins are made to depend for their spiritual health, in violation of the very purpose of virginal consecration, namely, total reliance on God alone. This tradition keeps women in perpetual infancy as "spiritual daughters" of underdeveloped Fathers, lest by maturing as adults they would question their gender role in a male-dominated church. Are such male celibates emotionally dependent on this profession of directing women, as indeed was their prototype, Jerome? Should not there be a more egalitarian approach to mutual spiritual direction among religious and consecrated women?

Indeed the cult of virginity — not virginity as such — indicates a male compulsion to desexualize women. This is a compulsion that is a veiled obsession with woman as an object of genital satisfaction. The cult of virginity and the cult of sex are two sides of the same coin. This is what happens when anything other than God begins to reign as supreme value in Christianity: idolatry and, in this case, parthenolatry. This is how Mariology, as the study of Mary's role in Christ's Redemption, often turns into a veritable "Mariolatry," a cult of a desexualized Mary.[10]

---

6. Anne Yarbrough, "Christianization in the Fourth Century: The Example of Roman Women," *Church History*, 45/2, June 1976, 159–60, where reference is made to the case of Paula, who studied Hebrew under Jerome, and Melania, her sister, who got involved in getting Origenism condemned.

7. Jerome, Epist., 22.20 quoted in Yarbrough, 161.

8. J. A. Mohler, *The Heresy of Monasticism,* New York, 1971, 92.

9. Lecky, II, 117.

10. Space does not permit me to discuss here the current Mariological disputes resulting from a greater feminist awareness in theology. The greatness of Mary and even her uniqueness

Asian Forms of Parthenolatry

Asian cultures are saturated with parthenolatry. The custom of showing the stained cloth after the wedding night is a social norm that indicates the double standard employed in patriarchal ethics. The Indian form, in which conjugal and virginal chastity are made a cult, has already been mentioned. In the popular religiosity of South India and Sri Lanka, we have the desexualized Pattini, the virgin-mother, contrasted with the hypersexual Madevi, the harlot-mother.[11]

Perhaps the cult of the Royal Kumari in Katmandu, one of Nepal's many virgin-goddesses, could be cited as a very instructive example of parthenolatry.[12] This vestal virgin is usually a beautiful girl selected according to astrological criteria. The candidate is confirmed if she can remain unruffled during "kalatripuja," a gory animal sacrifice performed in the dead of night during a blood-curdlingly terrifying ritual of mask dances portraying the battle of demons.

Venerated by Buddhists and Hindus alike as "Vajradevi," she is annually taken in procession with state honors. She is decked in red (the tantric color for lust), with a red eye marked on the forehead. However, at the very first menses (or also in the case of serious mental or physical illness) she ceases to be the goddess, gets demoted to the level of common humans, and is replaced by another virgin.

Two observations need to be made here. First, the belief that the virgin cult validates lust as a means of experiencing the nirvanic pleasure — *parama-sukha*[13] — reveals again the fact that a cult of virginity is inseparably bound up with the cult of genitality. Both cults are a male obsession that treats women as a mere tool of sexual gratification — a persuasion that has seeped into the female's own religiosity.

Secondly, the belief that the Kumari loses her divine state of virginity on becoming a menstruating woman reflects a widespread patriarchal dogma that woman is an immaculate goddess as long as she is in a genitally inactive or impotent state and that she can be harmful to (male?) social order unless maintained in that state by what Periyar (quoted above) has aptly called "imposed chastity" (*nirpande karpu*) as opposed to chastity defined and determined freely by women (*suvecchai karpu*).

A deity, in most Indic cultures, is a symbol of an ambivalent power that can harm unless tamed through rite and ritual and locked up in a shrine. Most cults and customs surrounding women in South Asia (puberty, marriage, and

---

are never questioned; on the contrary, traditional Mariology fails to do justice to Mary both as a woman and as a special creature destined to collaborate with Jesus in the work of redemption. I intend taking up this question in a separate study in the near future.

11. Gananath Obeysekere, *The Cult of the Goddess Pattini,* Motilal Banarsidass, Delhi, 1987, 455ff.

12. Cf. Bajracarya, 91.

13. See Philip Rawson, *The Art of Tantra,* Thames and Hudson, London, 1973/1978, 83ff.

renunciation rites, rules on clothing and work, etc.) have been designed on the basis of this principle.[14]

This is why we cautioned Asian feminists against the return-to-the-goddess trend of their Western counterparts! The same warning must be extended to Asian women who look for a straightforward feminist thesis in the cult of Kuan Yin (Kanon) in Chinese (and Japanese) Buddhism.

THE INSTRUMENTALIZATION OF WOMEN

Patriarchy has been rightly defined as the male appropriation of (and man's control over) the bodies, labor, and sexuality of women both in the family and in public life.[15] This ideology was operative in the East and the West long before Descartes reduced Nature to a desacralized and mechanized material object to be controlled through knowledge and through the power that knowledge gives *man.* Women and the cosmos have always suffered as covictims in any androcratic society. Given the gyne-ecological nexus, the violent use of nature can be seen as a male reaction to cosmophobia, just as men's violent use of women is their response to gynephobia.

This violence is registered in the traditional religious perception of both marriage and celibacy. Hence Buddhist and Christian traditions, which have each deviated from their founder's vision in this regard, can find their way back if they are exposed to the feminist critique.

As for Christianity, it has to revise its theology of marriage by carefully sifting certain sociological and ideological underpinnings that continually make women the "means of man's fulfillment." We have already criticized the religious propensity to absolutize marriage and idolize the mother-ideal as a way of locking women in the prison-shrine of the home. Now, I wish to discuss the other, even more pernicious, dogma hiding beneath the so-called "two ends of marriage."

The Two-Ends Theory

For centuries Christians have been taught that the primary goal of marriage is the procreation of children. Being primary, it determines the morality of the secondary or the subordinate goal of marriage, namely, the consolidation of conjugal intimacy. The latter, negatively and pejoratively defined in certain moral theology manuals as a *remedium concupiscentiae* ("a remedy for concupiscence"), is judged sinful to the degree that the primary end is de-

---

14. See Kalpana Ram, *Mukkuvar Women: Gender Hegemony and Capitalist Transformation in a South Indian Fishing Community,* Kali for Women, 1992, 59. I have not read this book, but gained access to it only through the insightful review made of it by Gabriele Dietrich, "Caste, Class and Patriarchy," *Economic and Political Weekly,* XXVII/10, March 6, 1993, 389–91.

15. Cf. Dietrich, *Women's Movement,* 15ff.

nied its priority. This is one of the arguments lurking behind the theological repudiation of birth control.[16]

There is a sociological origin to this theory. Ancient agricultural societies needed to produce many children as labor hands at a period of time when the infant mortality rate was very high. In other words, children had to be produced in sufficient quantity for economic reasons, just as in today's industrial societies, the need to limit children is equally dictated by economic reasons. To justify either practice theologically is an ideological abuse of theology. This is why we reject not only the classical theological argument against birth control but also liberal attacks on *Humanae Vitae*. Both fail to question the instrumental role of women.[17]

Our concern has to do with this androcratic theo-ideology which is clearly operative in the classical (Augustinian) argument that a wife who avoids bearing children while mating becomes a virtual prostitute in that she refuses to be a mother and that sexual intimacy is a disorder permitted in view of (and in compensation for) the painful but necessary process of begetting children.[18] The brunt of this argument is on the woman and her motherhood. Presupposed here is the persuasion that the wife is the instrument by which children are produced for men (primary end) and also the instrument of men's genital and emotional satisfaction (secondary end). The nobility of conjugal companionship, the salvific beauty of marital intimacy, as well as women's equality in that partnership have no weight in that argument.

The separation of the two ends — with one given priority over the other, but both so formulated that women's companionship is eliminated in favor of her instrumental role — is more evident in the metacosmic side of the religious spectrum than in the cosmic. For instance, in the Vedic religiosity, with its strong cosmic emphasis, the two ends (i.e., fertility and companionship) are given equal emphasis with regard to the woman's sexuality,[19] but as we proceed toward highly elaborate jurisprudential theology of the Dharmasastras, one notes the dominance of the instrumental approach based on gynephobia.[20] The German Jesuit, Joseph Fuchs of the Gregorian University, who was stopped from teaching by the Vatican in the sixties (but later reinstated by Pope Paul VI), became famous for his definition of marriage as "a fruitful interpersonal union" (*unio interpersonalis fecunda*). His

---

16. A third-world theology has its own critical approach to the question of birth control, which differs both from the Western liberal approach (Cf. A. Pieris, *ATL,* 6), and from the official position which we are questioning in this article.

17. In fact, Paul VI, the author of *Humanae Vitae*, is sensitive to the fact that the use of artificial birth-control methods could risk turning women into playthings or easily available instruments of pleasure for man.

18. Cf. Augustine's "Soliloquies" in *Fathers of the Church*, Ima Publishing, New York, 1948, vol. I, 10.

19. Srabhi D. Sheth, "Woman's Sexuality: A Portrayal from Ancient Indian Literature," *Manushi: A Journal about Women and Society*, no. 71, July–August 1992, 15.

20. Ibid., 17ff.

definition avoided the dichotomy between the two ends of marriage. When
a student asked him why the classical division between the two goals was
eliminated, Fuchs — according to legend — answered in the words of Jesus,
"What God has put together, let no person put asunder." Fact or fiction, the
story makes the point that a unitary definition is closer to the true nature of
marriage. Whether Fuchs thought of it or not, his view of marriage avoids
the androcratic overtones of the classical definition.

In fact, the theory of the two ends of marriage, if really believed in, can
be so taken to its logical extreme as to justify the practice of Christendom's
many past rulers who had an official queen for begetting the heir to the throne
and a mistress for the secondary end of marriage. Macho husbands who exemplify this belief abound in many third-world cultures. I can never forget
Ignace Lepp's humorous remark about someone envying his friend for "loving his wife as if she were his mistress" — a remark that seems to convey the
absurdity of the two-end theory. It is an absurdity compounded into a tragedy
because of the instrumental role of the woman implied by it.

Instrumentalization of the Female Renunciates

Tantra, a sort of esoteric trend in Buddhism and Hinduism, has developed a kind of "mystical marriage" in which a female ascetic (*yogini*) plays
the role of the Great Sign (*Mahāmudrā*), that is to say as a medium for the
male's acquisition of ultimate liberation.[21] Buddhism initiated the Tantric approach, in a noble way,[22] and this healthy approach is still maintained in
mainstream Buddhism in Tibet.[23] But it did give birth to certain degenerate
sects advocating sexo-yogic cults. What intrigues us is the application of the
patriarchal theory of marriage to its mystical form: woman as the instrument
which males use for a soteriological end, which is primarily defined as a
male achievement.[24]

One of the greatest Asian spiritual leaders of our time has shocked us with
what is sometimes referred to as "self-temptation," namely, an experiment by
which he tested his chastity, believing that his absolute purity was a *conditio sine qua non* for the efficacy of his prayers. Sleeping seminude in close
proximity to a young woman, he tried to see whether he had perfect control over his body! Probably, he had the required degree of control. Probably
he was pleased about it. But what was the woman other than an instrument
for testing his virtue? Can the underlying assumption be any other than that

21. B. Bhattacharya, *An Introduction to Buddhist Esoterism*, Varanasi, 1964, 27, 33–34, 39,
66–67.
22. Govinda, *Foundations,* 100.
23. See Tsong-ka-pa, *Tantra in Tibet: The Great Explanation of Secret Mantra,* with a
commentary by the Dalai Lama, George Allen and Unwin, London, 1977.
24. See S. B. Dasgupta, *Introduction to Tantric Buddhism*, University of Calcutta, 1958,
102ff. and 179ff.

the woman is a sex object, a sex tool which makes her a potential source of temptation? Eve again!

There is mention in the Buddhist scriptures (*Vinaya,* III. 37–38) of a woman sleeping with a monk who, being an Arahan (one who has reached the acme of perfection), is declared by the Buddha to have incurred no guilt.[25] This is a text that needs to be understood in its proper context. Fortunately, this statement has not been misused by self-proclaimed Arahans to justify their experimentation with female ascetics, except perhaps among the *vāmācārins* (left-handed mystics) in Tantric Buddhism, already referred to above. But such an abuse of scriptures did take place in mainstream Christianity very early and in a very big way. I am referring to the species of androcratic asceticism recorded in the early church in regard to virgins and widows who formed a group of "consecrated women." Despite their massive numbers, they did not have convents of their own and were therefore constrained to live with monks and ecclesiastics; invariably, they became the men's domestic servants.[26] Not surprisingly, they also became instruments for males to test their capacity for "angelic life." Writing in another context, I referred to this experiment as "eschatological illusion."[27]

I coined this name because at the root of it all was a misapprehension of Jesus' reference to the end time (*eschaton*), or final resurrection, as an entry into an angelic dimension of life wherein marriage would be made redundant (Matt. 22:30). Some celibates presumed they were living already in the fullness of God's Reign, thanks to their life of renunciation. What better proof could they offer than to vindicate their ability to live in heterosexual intimacy, as if their need for marriage had been transcended? Evagrius, in the fourth century, expressed admiration for men who had so controlled their passions that "neither sight nor touch nor woman's embrace would make them relapse into their natural condition."[28]

One of the earliest compilers of church history records[29] that the Synod of Antioch accused and condemned Paul of Samoasta for the scandal of living with young women (coining a special name for them: *Gynaikes syneisaktoi,* in Greek[30]). The scriptural basis for this practice of "syneisaktism" was 1 Cor. 7:36–38, where St. Paul declares that it is not sinful for a man either to marry a virgin (with whom he presumably has a friendship) or not to marry her after *he* has settled the matter in *his* own mind and has suf-

---

25. For the English translation of this text, see *The Book of Discipline* (I. B. Horner, tr.), Pali Text Society, London, 1938/1982, Part I, 58.

26. Elizabeth A. Clark, "John Chrysostom and the Sub-introductae," *Church History*, 46/2, June 1977, 182. There had been allegedly 3,000 such women in the Anthocyan church alone, according to Chrysostom, Hom. 66, Matt. 3.

27. Aloysius Pieris, "Religious Vows and the Reign of God," chapter 16 below, 181–182.

28. Lecky, II, 150.

29. Eusebius of Caesarea, *Historia Ecclesiastica,* 7/29.

30. Clark, 173.

ficient self-control. In fact, St. Paul declares the second opinion to be of higher value.

Many a male celibate who had a virgin friend (*mulier subintroducta,* in Latin) took refuge in a laxist misinterpretation of the Pauline counsel and tried to live with a virgin in a spiritual marriage, which invariably turned out to be concubinage! They lived like brothers and sisters until some sisters became mothers! That was literally St. Irenaeus's comment on the Valentinian scandal![31] Save for St. Euphraim, the Syrian, who accepted this interpretation, all the Fathers of the church condemned the practice as well as the scriptural interpretation behind it; furthermore, about six councils in the fourth century banned the custom — such condemnation being carried up until the Middle Ages.[32]

Thanks to a more highly developed feminist consciousness, when such practices are detected today, they are called by their proper name: *sexual abuse,* or a reduction of woman to a mere tool. Regrettably, however, the concern of the church in condemning the practice revolved around monastic chastity. Was there any recognition, let alone condemnation, of the injustice of treating women as tools of a male experiment? Even in marriage, was not woman's instrumental role simply taken for granted? Did religious life, after all, differ from marital life with regard to the instrumental role of the woman?

No wonder, the very idea of women-priests sounds horrendous. How could domestic servants be allowed to usurp the role of their masters? How could instruments function as agents or tools as their own users?

From the Instrumental to the Sacramental

To conclude, let me repeat here what I have said elsewhere:[33] our attitude toward the cosmos (or creation in general) can be either instrumental or sacramental; "using" creatures as a means of arriving at God, as advocated in some brands of liberal Christianity, is just as sacrilegious as the capitalist economics that puts all persons and things at the service of Mammon (increase of capital for profit). In the sacramental approach, by contrast, one sees the Other — both things and people — as one's own personal extension, and reveres the world as one's own body, thus reflecting the one body from which man and woman differentiated and the one body they are meant to become. In this sense, then, feminism is the summons from the universal human conscience to all humankind to restore the sacramental praxis in a world desecrated by instrumentalism.

---

31. Irenaeus, *Adversus Haereseos,* 1.6.3., quoted in Clark, 172.
32. Clark, 173–74.
33. Aloysius Pieris, *Love Meets Wisdom,* 14–16.

Hence no discourse on feminism is complete without projecting to the future an authentically religious view of a social order wherein these feminist summons remain a permanent feature. This is the final task we wish to undertake in this section.

6

The Feminist Critique and the New Religious Vision

SEARCH FOR A THEORETICAL PERSPECTIVE

Five False Starts in Feminist Theories

In September 1992, I was invited by Virginia Fabella to a Filipino women's group in Manila for an exchange of ideas and concerns. I was challenged there by a question that was said to have been raised by an Indian feminist (whose name was not revealed) at another forum. It concerned my writings on the Asian theology of liberation. "Why," it was asked, "should greed or self-centeredness be named as the root of all evil, since only males are self-centered and exploit the selflessness which is natural to women?"

Mary Grenough, the American Maryknoll nun who has given her life for the poor and lived among women of all classes, accompanying me after the session, confessed to me that she wondered whether the Indian feminist ever knew either the poor or women! As for women, the question can be asked: Is possessiveness — that species of greed or selfishness which invariably generates jealousy and suspicion — never known among them? Are women so immaculately conceived that there is no trace of any exploitative instinct in them? Here then is a false start in feminism, false from the point of view of feminist psychology.

The idea that the oppressed are selfless saints, whereas the oppressors alone are selfish hogs, is the basis for a pathological messianism. It is more than just bad theology. The bible is clear: the poor are not saints nor are the poor covenanted with Yahweh because of their holiness. The basis of a liberation theology is that Yahweh enters a pact with the victims of oppression because they are victims of oppression, not because they are holy. They become holy only when they take up their covenantal responsibility seriously (for which they need to be conscientized) and join Yahweh's struggle against the principalities and powers of oppression.

This applies also to the feminist struggle. To be oppressed on the basis of sex is not necessarily a certificate of holiness. Or else women's salvation would depend on their victimhood — which is precisely the presupposition of patriarchal theology that Christian feminists are indignant about. Women are as much a part of the human predicament as are men. Grassroots groups know only too well the selfishness of women that even keeps other women in subjugation. They know now that even among the oppressed, selfishness or greed is not a vice confined to the male psyche. The mere fact that the men use women as instruments in an androcratic society is no guarantee that women are free of the tendency to exploit others on racial, religious, or class basis. To think otherwise is to make a false start in the theology of feminism.

Saraswati Raju has exposed the fallacy of fragmented approaches to the study of women's issues (labor, health, literacy, etc.) in India; she shows why to set up gender specificity as the first-order theoretical framework is to place gender studies in a theoretical vacuum. Gender issues, she therefore argues, have to be perceived in the wider context of class formation; this makes clear that women are just as much influenced by their social class as anyone else.[1] To think otherwise is a false start in the sociology of feminism.

In fact the question raised above, based as it is on the assumption that greed is not a woman's vice, is the result of approaching gender issues in a theoretical vacuum, rather than placing them in wider social, especially class, structures. One fails to see that both the active victims of greed (the greedy) and the passive victims of greed (those exploited by the greedy) extend across gender and class lines. The failure to see this, I believe, constitutes a false start in the theology, psychology, and sociology of feminism.

A fourth false start has occurred in the politics of feminism. It consists of reducing feminism to a "rights movement," a struggle for equality of women with men. Some of the Asian feminist literature emanating from Christian women reflects this rather narrow concern. In fact the whole of the "rights language," couched as it is within the framework of liberal democracy, may make feminism just another name for an uncritical acquisition of self-centered individualism characteristic of today's dominant model of social theory.[2] But feminism, as we had pointed out earlier, has to be a permanent feature of the human condition, not something that terminates with the winning of rights.

This last observation imposes on us the task of providing a lengthy refutation of the fifth and final deviation: the tendency among certain theologians, including a few feminists, to set the cosmic in opposition to the human. They declare that it is a cosmocentric worldview, and not an anthropocentric

1. Saraswati Raju, "Gender and Deprivation: A Theme Revisited with a Geographical Perspective," *Economic and Political Weekly,* XXVI/49, December 7, 1991, 2827–39.
2. I presuppose here the thesis I have begun to develop in two articles: "Human Rights Language and Liberation Theology," chapter 10 below, 113–126; "Three Inadequacies in the Social Encyclicals," chapter 8 below, 79–96.

worldview, that constitutes the ideal framework for feminism. Are they confusing anthropocentricity with androcentricity (male-centeredness)? To see a cleavage between the cosmic and the human is a false start in the philosophy of feminism.

Since the primary concern in this last part of this section is to construct the proper framework which can retain feminism as a permanent feature, I am constrained to take up immediately the last mentioned misapprehension and deal with the mutuality of the cosmic and the human dimension of liberation.

The Cosmic-Human-Metacosmic Continuum

Our definition of liberation as the cosmic experience of the metacosmic makes sense only if we understand "experience" as a self-reflectively noetic act supereminently proper to the human component of the cosmos which alone can dream of the metacosmic. For, wherever imagination and reason work in alliance to form the creative and innovative current in the cosmos, we have the human.

Therefore, as we shall soon indicate, techno*logy* and religion are direct expressions of hominization; they witness to the gradual manifestation of the human center of the cosmos and ensures the continuity of that evolution toward the metacosmic (the humanum). Conversely, for the same reason, techno*cracy* and irreligion constitute a regression to the inhuman and reflect an instrumental approach that spells gyne-ecological disaster.

The metacosmic is the human heart's infinite potentiality that must be dreamed by our imagination, grasped by our intuition, strategized by our reason, actualized by our personal and collective effort, but always under the perennial impulse of love. Thus the human is the experiential link between the cosmos and the metacosmic. Hence soteriology can also be defined as the "cosmic-*human*-metacosmic continuum."

We need to recognize that the metacosmic is the hidden future of the present moment, the "beyond" which acts as the "within" of the cosmos. This self-transcendent capacity immanent in the cosmos, this power to unfold within itself *the Other,* which is ever present from the first moment of cosmic evolution, is the human. Thus the "human" — that is, whatever pertains to men and women as self-conscious, other-oriented, and dreaming components of the cosmos — has the capacity to carry the cosmos to its ultimate perfection; and for want of a better word, let this point of perfection be called "the humanum." The act of "carrying the cosmos to its perfection" (*technē* or *ars movendi*), as we shall indicate soon, is the coordinated task of both technology and religion. The humanum is also that which is anticipated in any "Easter Person" (a Christian who lives the life of the Risen One) or in a "Nirvanic Person" (a Buddhist who has followed the path of the Awakened One) and their equivalents in other religions. The metacosmic and the humanum, therefore, coincide as the self-consciously active and self-transcendently immanent nucleus of the cosmos. Thus the human is the conscious link between the cosmic and the metacosmic. That is why we have already spoken of liberation in terms of a *cosmic-human-metacosmic continuum.*

If, therefore, the human is none other than the openness of the cosmos to the metacosmic, it follows that the so-called cosmocentric view (which results from the expulsion of the human from the center of the cosmos) is only a euphemism for downright secularism; it is the belief in a closed world with no transcendental horizon. It is the world of technocracy and irreligion. This is precisely the worldview we repudiate as unfeminist and un-Asian.

Here I must explain why I identify the humanum with the metacosmic. Words such as *divine, divinity,* or *deity* could be misleading in an Asian context since they seem to designate "cosmic powers," whereas in Christianity the "divine" is synonymous with the metacosmic and is, therefore, the Christian homologue (not the equivalent) of Buddhist nirvana. The word *God* when I use it here, designates this Christian meaning. On the whole, I try to use the common expression: metacosmic (*lokottara*) or *humanum* to designate the salvific horizon of both religions: for Buddhism: nirvana/ Buddhahood/arahatship, for Christianity: Yahweh/God's Reign/eschaton); and I insist that the cosmos (*loka*) is not the negation of the metacosmic, but the only context in which it can be realized.

This is quite evident in the case of Christianity: the cosmos ("heaven and earth") has not only a metacosmic origin (creation by God) but also a metacosmic destiny (a re-creation of a "new heaven and a new earth," that is to say, a cosmos permeated by the fullness of the humanum).

Buddhism gives a similar message within a nontheistic paradigm. Govinda clarifies that Buddhism, especially in its Theravada form, advocates the primacy of (cosmic) experience over metaphysical speculation and has laid an earth-drawn (not earthbound) and empirical foundation for its project of liberation.[3] In other words, both religions, each in its own way, affirm the cosmic-human-metacosmic continuum.

MALE-FEMALE DIALECTICS OF THE CONTINUUM

A Possible Christian Model

This continuum is not a straight line, but a zigzag path as proper to any goal-oriented movement. The human (spirit), which establishes the continuum, does so through the dialectical interplay of its two subliminal impulses or interior movements. Of these, the female impulse is *agape*, the male is *gnosis*. By calling them dialectical tendencies, I am affirming that they are never found in their pure form; love is always lit up with knowledge; and

3. Lama Anangarika Govinda, *Psycho-cosmic Symbolism*, 11. Govinda, however, is quite mistaken in thinking that other religions are busy with heaven and not the earth.

knowledge is warmed up with love. The spark that illumines the mind with wisdom is the same that inflames the heart with the glow of love. The light of gnosis that dispels the darkness of ignorance and the warmth of agape that thaws every estrangement are manifestations of the same Fire which is at the heart(h) of the earth: the humanum.

Thus, Descartes's "masculinization of knowledge," deplored by feminists such as Susan Bordo, consists of removing knowledge from the agapeic (feminist) sphere of influence. Science or knowledge, thus divorced from love, has become brutal by mating with power and thus giving birth to that hideous monster called technocracy. Women and the earth, obviously, have been the first casualties.[4] Both women and nature were reduced to the level of things to be known, tools to be used, machines to be managed and of course, prospective victims of rape.

If love without knowledge is blind, knowledge without love is beastly. The lover who is armed with knowledge empowers the loved one; the knower who is starved of love steals power from the object known. Love enlightened by knowledge invariably turns even things into persons; but knowledge untouched by love treats even persons as things. Technocratic scientism is gnosis minus agape, which has turned humans into means of production, slaves of *man*-made tools. By contrast, technology plus religion, which implies a dialectical interplay of knowledge and love, would remake companions of labor even out of inanimate tools.[5]

Lest one receive a simplistic image of the gnosis-agape dialectics, I need to make an important qualification here. The reason for the agapeic thrust to disappear in Christianity is the rejection of true gnosis; for as I have demonstrated elsewhere,[6] the instrumental theory of creation ("all are things to be used in so far as they help one to go to God") was the direct result of diminishing and consequently distorting the love-idiom of Christianity by depriving it of its gnostic component so that a deviant form of gnosis (scientism and technocracy) — i.e., "a nonagapeic gnosis — affirmed itself in the Christian cultures: all persons are instruments at the service of Mammon/ Capital."

This axiom (namely, agape minus gnosis results in a gnosis minus agape) is vital for understanding the feminist critique. For such simplistic gender stereotypes such as "male aggressiveness and feminine passivity" result from treating the two instincts as separate entities, as if each could retain its respective identity independent of the other. It is not that the male principle (gnosis) is in itself aggressive, but that without the other it is no more the male principle but its monstrous aberration. Similarly, the female principle, if it is passive, has already ceased to be female, because the other which

---

4. See Capra, as cited in n.1, chapter 3 above.
5. See A. Pieris, *Love Meets Wisdom,* 14ff.
6. See ibid., 9–10, 26–28.

elicits its femininity is absent. Thus the neognosis of scientism and technocracy, which is "knowledge without love," has its remote roots in "love deprived of knowledge." This is the doing of a Christianity that has ceased to be Christian.

Feminism is the name for our perpetual struggle to maintain this salutary impact of love on the power of knowledge. No amount of creation theology and feminist theology can restore the ruptured gyne-ecological nexus unless the neognosticism of technocracy (the irreligious urge to control or instrumentalize persons and nature through scientific knowledge) is tempered and transformed by a worldwide rediscovery of our agapeic potentialities, by a massive reactivation of this atrophied part of our being, that is to say, by allowing the woman in all of us to be born again.

The Buddhist Paradigm

Obviously, the observations made above spring from the experience of Christianity which is an agapeic religion. In Asia, where gnostic religions such as Buddhism exert a dominant influence over our cultures, the aberration, if any, is not the degeneration of technology into technocracy and irreligion, as in the West, but the relegation of technology to the nonreligious sector of human experience, as has happened in many Asian cultures.

In the Buddhist scheme, we have to infer that any gnosis (*prajñā*) that is divorced from cosmic engagement (i.e., *karuṇā* or compassion) ceases to be wisdom and tends to be an "other-worldly knowledge" (acosmic gnosis). The great technological achievements of Asia, for instance, in hydrologic engineering, did not enter the ola leaf manuscripts, which were written mostly by a spiritual elite dedicated to pure spiritual knowledge. Hence, science and technology failed to develop into a body of knowledge placed at the beck and call of laypersons; most of this Asian science/technology (save medicine) has disappeared together with the oral tradition that was its only vehicle.

The fault lay in the dichotomy that occurred between gnostic detachment (*prajñā*) and agapeic engagement (*karuṇā*) — a dichotomy that is totally contrary to the Buddhist view of the cosmic-human-metacosmic continuum. Thus, the fading away of the early technological initiatives in Buddhist cultures is not due to an inherent weakness of Buddhism, as some have proposed (see below); rather, it tells the story of a Buddhism that has failed to be Buddhist.

Hence we cannot concur with Peter H. Lee's insinuation that the voluntary poverty or gnostic detachment of Buddhists is a hindrance to development. This diagnosis is based on the observation that countries with a Confucianist cultural base (rather than a predominantly Buddhist one) have advanced quickly in technological development. He refers, of course, to the four dragons, namely, Korea, Hong Kong, Taiwan, and Singapore.[7] Those who advocate this thesis perhaps do not ask themselves whether these four supposed "success stories" tell us about technological development or about a technocratic incursion of the West into Asia. Buddhist gnosis, as I argued at another forum, is a necessary condition for authentic technological progress — a lesson we learn from the Christian West's neglect of that dimension.[8]

Buddhism is a zealous advocate of the reciprocity between *karuṇā* (which approximates agape) and *prajñā* (salvific gnosis). It is in Mahayana, and particularly in Vajrayana, that the sexual metaphor is used in a very effective manner to express the fact that each is incomplete and unproductive without the other and that total liberation is the fruit of their union.

In such schools of Buddhism, however, gnosis represents the female aspect, and compassion the male aspect of soteriology. This is the opposite, or more accurately, the mirror image of the (Christian?) paradigm we presented above. This Buddhist paradigm, nevertheless, has been detected also in the wisdom literature of the bible — that part of the bible where the influence of the gnostic religions is clearly evident. For wisdom is treated in the bible as a feminine principle, just as in Buddhism. The current Christian feminist theory that promotes self-love and self-acceptance as the women's need of the hour (see below) has recourse to this sapiential paradigm of the bible.

Feminism and the Sapiential Paradigm

The ages-long "instrumentalization" of women by men and the resultant image of women as self-sacrificing partners whose only mission was the well-being of men, as well as the guilt feeling that accompanies a woman's legitimate effort to assert her self-worth or simply enjoy loving her own self — all these undeniable injuries require redress. The feminists have, therefore, come out with the remedial measure: self-love and self-acceptance as the essential precondition for a woman's offer of love to others. "Love your neighbor as yourself!" Elizabeth Moltmann-Wendel has quite convincingly appealed to the much neglected wisdom theology of the bible as the feminist basis of this thesis.[9]

Two implications of this proposal merit our attention. First, there is the question of winning lost rights. It is argued that women, systematically deprived of their personal dignity and self-esteem, must now affirm their personal rights — more precisely their "biblical rights"[10] to such dignity and

7. Peter Lee, "The Four Little Dragons, the Great Dragon and the Phoenixes," *Inter-Religio,* no. 15, Summer 1989, 21–25.

8. In my address to Asian Theological Conference of the EATWOT in 1979, reprinted in *ATL,* 79–81.

9. Elizabeth Moltmann-Wendel, "Self-Love and Self-Acceptance," *Pacifica: Australian Theological Studies,* 5/3, October 1992, 288–300.

10. Based on "love thy neighbor as thyself," Ibid., 299.

esteem. Here, I presume that the basic axiom almost taken for granted is the sovereignty of the individual and the supremacy of the self, an axiom that manifests its cutting edge in the human-rights theory couched in the Western framework of liberal democracy. This is a theme I will take up more carefully below. Second, there is the question of repairing damages. The emphasis in the second issue is quite rightly on self-acceptance as a condition for self-fulfillment, not on self-fulfillment dictated by the conventional expectations of an androcratic society. Moltmann-Wendel equates this species of self-love with eros, which, she says, is not a love that controls or patronizes others.[11] By erotic love she seems to mean nonexploitative self-love. At any rate I am delighted that by restoring the indispensable role of sapiential language, or the idiom of gnosis in theology and spirituality, Moltmann-Wendel has rediscovered the complementary role of nonselfish self-love (agapeic eros?).

I endorse Moltmann-Wendel's thesis as a kind of remedial feminism which is not without its own value. But I am more concerned with the total liberation (cosmic experience of the metacosmic), as well as with the permanent role of a feminism that aims at more than winning lost rights or repairing past damages. Therefore, individualist liberalism based on personal dignity and worth (very much a part of the West's rights language but not exactly the language of the bible or of Asian religions[12]) does not seem to me to be the ideal framework for feminism here in Asia. The theory of self-love and self-affirmation could be salvaged from the pitfall of liberal individualism only if the larger perspective of self-transcendence is allowed to dominate our ethics.

Self-Abnegation and Self-Transcendence

I am painfully aware that words such as *self-denial* irritate many theologians, a fortiori feminists. Centuries of abuse have made these expressions loathsome. Slaves had to deny themselves for the sake of their masters, and wives for the well-being of their husbands. This fact is undeniable and, of course, deplorable. But we must ask: wherein lies the fault? Is it in the idea itself or in those who abused it? Is there anything noble in this world that has not been abused in such a manner? Yet as the ancients said, *abusus non tollit usum,* "the misuse of a thing does not preclude its (proper) use."

The paradox about the seed that must die in order to bring life, or the need to lose one's life to find it, as well as the hard saying about self-denial and the taking up of one's cross as a prerequisite for becoming a Christian, or about the exaltation of those who humble themselves and vice versa, not to mention the definition of love as friendship proved by the laying down of one's life — all these teachings of Jesus sound bitter, unrealistic, and ex-

11. Ibid., 299.
12. See A. Pieris, "Three Inadequacies in the Social Encyclicals," chapter 8 below, especially 93–96.

aggerated in the current social context of liberalism and individualism. The Buddha's equally paradoxical doctrine which welds together "self-effort" and "self-negation" meets with a similar fate in a world of competition and consumerism. What can feminism offer in such a context if it refuses to preach to all the masters and husbands the liberating message of self-transcendence through self-denial that Gotama and Jesus have preached?

It is a curious fact that in modern liberal societies, where the doctrine of self-denial is increasingly questioned, there is also much self-discipline that goes into their work ethics and wealth acquisition! And what about the rigorous program of self-abnegation (in diet and exercise) that the modern woman willingly accepts as a necessary condition for maintaining her health and beauty? Who would ever repudiate it as masochism? Does not the interior freedom of persons as well as the collective growth into healthily related communities of males and females merit a similar kind of self-sacrifice?

Furthermore, are we to dismiss the basic intuition of the author of Genesis that there is within each one of us a serpent, i.e., a pre-Fall tendency to crave for knowledge that begets power (rather than love that begets knowledge), an ambition to enthrone one's own self as a god, a greed that is satisfied when one succeeds in manipulating others as tools in one's own service? The spiritual crisis of our times results from ignoring, or perhaps encouraging, the serpent dimension of sin, that prehuman or hominal urge which needs to be contested, controlled, and conquered by every individual human being, male or female, rich or poor, Christian or Buddhist. The incessant struggle against this destructive instinct is what all religions mean by self-abnegation, self-denial, or self-discipline; it is a guarantee of interior freedom and healthy relationships, a sure path to eliminate a weak self-identity of individuals and groups.

Thus, a philosophy of self-indulgence which allowed male oppression of females cannot be held up as an ideal. An authentic love of self cannot tolerate a self-indulgence that destroys one's own as well as the other's personality. Patriarchy is the story of males diminishing their own humanity by refusing to foster it as their own in the other. They tried to master nature and women instead of mastering themselves, that is to say, instead of resisting the serpent within. In this lay their oppression of women and nature as well as their self-destruction. Does one remove the oppressiveness of the oppressor by appropriating it as a virtue? Males must be compelled to practice what they so selfishly demand only of women: self-abnegation leading to self-transcendence. Unless both parties adhere to this basic principle of spirituality, both succumb to slavery. That is the lesson we learn from patriarchy.

The Common Spirituality of Buddhists and Christians

Is it not significant that Buddhism and Christianity, which are so divergent in their emphasis — as a sapiential spirituality differs from an affective one — do nevertheless converge on the doctrine of self-transcendence through self-denial? This is precisely how gnosis and agape — like the male and female principles *prajñā* and *karuṇā* in Tibetan Buddhism — meet and mate to form one soteriology. The merging point is self-transcendence through self-abnegation: the message common to Buddhist gnosis and Christian agape.

As a gnostic religion, Buddhism focuses on the individual as the locus of the nirvanic experience; but it also gently sows the seed of social transformation through the compassionate love that it incorporates into its gnostic soteriology. The converse is true of Christianity. Its agapeic emphasis on our peoplehood as the focus of our God encounter succeeds in also eliciting our personal transformation through the discerning knowledge that love generates. The transition from self to the other in Buddhism, and from people to the person in Christianity, is through the common spirituality of self-transcendence, which implies self-denial.

Christianity, which sees salvation as the worship of God through loving service to people, identifies sin as self-worship, which is anti-God, and as self-isolation, which is antipeople. Buddhism sees nirvana as the total freedom of the mind and singles out self-belief (i.e., belief in the existence of a permanent unchanging immortal personality) and self-centeredness (acquisitiveness, accumulativeness, or greed) as fetters that keep humans in bondage. The wisdom of the cross (gnosis born of agape) that Jesus offers as the path of freedom runs side by side with the Buddha's eightfold path that culminates in knowledge (*amoha*) accompanied by a love that is at once unselfish (*alobha*) and forgiving (*adosa*). They are each a path of self-discipline leading to the freedom of self-transcendence.

TOWARD A GYNE-ECOLOGICAL FRAMEWORK

The Secularist and the Cosmic Perspectives

The crucial question raised at this juncture is once again the old one: Is the secularist perspective — a cultural ethos vitiated by an acquisitiveness-consumerism cycle, engulfed in technocracy and saturated with the self-indulgent individualism of liberal democracy — the most suitable context to spell out Asian feminism? Or, does the cosmic-worldview wherein the affirmation of the earthly, the bodily, and the womanly blossoms in an atmosphere of religious socialism based on self-transcendence provide the *gyne-ecological* framework for Asian feminism?

More specifically, secularism is the product of a desacralization of the cosmos, a loss of the sense of the transcendent. It is a world without an absolute future or a metacosmic horizon. On the other hand, the cosmic is the world unfolding within itself its own metacosmic destiny. The latter accounts for technology and religion; the former for technocracy and irreligion.

Technology and Religion in the Feminist Discourse

I have had other occasions to spell out the interface between technology and religion along this perspective.[13] Technology is the continuity between the cosmic and the human. Religion is the continuity between the human and the metacosmic. Thus there is a continuity between technology and religion. Such is the cosmic worldview within which Asian feminism has a chance of preserving the gyne-ecological nexus.

Technology is not a matter of creating instruments for various human achievements. That would be technocracy. Technology results from the cosmos reaching a self-reflective stage known as the human. The human awareness of the whole cosmos as one body makes a dramatic change in biological evolution. Instead of developing human limbs and senses as means of movement and cognition, the hominized beast begins to develop and sensitize cosmic matter as its own limbs and senses: the wheel and the propeller would be the extension of the human leg; the telephone, the extension of the human ear; the telescope, the extension of the human eye; the computer, the extension of the human brain; and so on.

This way of being continuous with the cosmos helps men and women to acquire a deeper cosmic awareness, and this manifests their incipient religiousness. The hominized beast becomes aware of the humanum as its own destiny. The upward thrust of evolution passes through hominization characterized by the rise of technology and continues as humanization with the deepening of religiosity. Thus technology and religion in their continuity portend a sacramental rather than an instrumental approach to the cosmos. What *homo faber* achieves is not the invention of an instrument to achieve a particular end, but an extension of one's own self. This precisely is the womanist mode of relating the self to the other.

Religion and technology in their inseparable unity reflect the typically human "art" or "style" (*technē* in Greek) of moving the cosmos to its acme of perfection: the humanum. The Latin phrase by which medieval Europe recognized early forms of technology (the mechanical clock, the windmill, etc.) was *ars mechanica,* "the art of moving"; and I like to think that technology is continuous with religion in constituting the *ars movendi,* the typically human *technē* or art of moving the cosmos to its metacosmic destiny. This is a religious vision of technology, and a feminist vision too.

The sacramental approach that accompanies technology and religion, if I may repeat, consists of regarding all that is outside of me as my own body, rather than as a tool to be used for my self-growth. But the enthronement of the instrumental theory with self-centered individualism as its philosophical basis began to be more and more evident in modern times precisely because the self was isolated as an independent knowing subject and the cosmos was reduced to a mechanical knowable object, and all beings were diminished to

---

13. A. Pieris, *ATL,* 108.

the state of things at the service of the human self either in a bid to gain access to Mammon (i.e., accumulation of money and power, as in capitalist technocracy) or in its desire to gain access to God (as in liberal Christianity with its individualistic pietism). This is the secularist model within which many brands of feminism (and mainstream Christianity) have evolved. In Asia, today, this model is readily available with all the other accessories: self-fulfillment theories and rights language, religious fundamentalism and economic liberalism.

The philosophy of self-transcendence which embraces the Other as one's own extended self in a context of a religious socialism based on an ethics of mutual obligations (*dharma*) is the contribution that Asian feminists can offer as an antidote to secularism and instrumentalism that has generated a self-destructive hedonism. It alone ensures the dignity of both woman and nature.

The Cosmic and Feminist Component of Liberation

From all that we have been saying so far, it should now be easier to understand why we have repeatedly alluded to human liberation as a cosmic experience of the metacosmic. The experience of the metacosmic is not a liberation from the cosmic, but a liberation from secularism. The cosmic dimension is never lost in human liberation. Hence, to conclude, I can list the following implications of the thesis I have been trying to develop in this chapter:

1. The cosmic approach is sacramental; it sees and says more than the secularist perspective, which, being reductionist, stops at what the senses perceive. If the instrumental approach to the world is a product of secularism, the feminist approach is cosmic by nature.

2. Self-love and self-affirmation point to a mere remedial measure to cure the effects of instrumentalization of women; but it is not a preventive measure unless we abandon the secularist model with its liberal philosophy of self-indulgence and individualism which has accelerated the current gyne-ecological crisis.

3. The cosmic is dialectical, with male and female forces (gnosis and agape) interacting in its journey toward self-transcendence. This is not an undue "genderization," but a description of the subliminal instincts of the human psyche which continue their dialectics with the predominance of one or the other of them whatever be the sexual orientation of a person, be it homo- or hetero-. Hence the next observation:

4. The secularist view being what it is — a perception of a desacralized, mechanized and masculinized world — does not maintain the tension between male gnosis and female agape, which is an indispensable el-

ement of the movement for liberation; but the cosmic, by maintaining this bipolarity, prevents masculinization.

5. Consequently, a cosmic spirituality preserves the womanly, the earthly, and the bodily contribution to the salvific experience.

6. The cosmic implies religiousness which is associated with openness to the metacosmic or the humanum; the secularist approach is a sealing of the world against its own transcendent destiny. Thus a cosmic worldview is also human centered.

7. Feminism, therefore, is a permanent feature in the struggle for full humanity in that it maintains the cosmic dimension without which the experience of the metacosmic (i.e., absolute liberation) is impossible.

8. Hence all religious systems that overemphasize the metacosmic pursuits at the risk of ignoring the cosmic roots of religious experience tend to be patriarchal; feminism is, therefore, the name for the endless struggle to retain the cosmic religiosity alive within these major religions.

9. All this means that feminism also serves as a permanent critique of religion. Religion cannot survive in the future without appropriating the feminist critique, just as feminism cannot achieve its liberative goal without the aid of a religion so critiqued.

Part II

Theology, Religion, and Society

7

Does Christ Have a Place
in Asia?

A PANORAMIC VIEW

In this chapter, I attempt to spell out how a committed and reflective minority of Asian Christians might answer the question: "Does Christ have a place in Asia?"

Obviously, the question has to be divided further: *Which* Christ? and *Why?* Here, one has to sort out the various "Christs" claiming Asia's allegiance: the *Euro-ecclesiastical Christ* of the official church; the *non-Western Christ* of scholars and intellectuals; and the *Asian Christ.* History's response to our initial question, however, is harsh and clear: they are all out of place in Asia, but each for a different reason. History being a reliable teacher, I have allowed its verdict to set the agenda for my investigation.

Asia has always been impenetrable to Christianity (a mere 3 percent converted after two millennia). This was not necessarily or primarily due to Christ's colonial appearance; nor, conversely, would an indigenized Christ have tricked the Asians to accept Christianity. In Parts I and II, I cast a doubt on these assumptions, in order to isolate the real issue for our discussion in Parts III and IV.

THE EURO-ECCLESIASTICAL CHRIST
OF THE OFFICIAL CHURCH

Riding on the waves of colonialism, the Euro-ecclesiastical Christ swept to power in Latin America as he did a little later among the non-Islamicized tribes of Africa and continues to do so in Oceania. Why, then, did he fail

First published in *Concilium,* 1993/2, 33–47.

to capture Asia, except in a few well-defined areas? I offer what I think is a plausible interpretation of this strange phenomenon.[1]

My explanation presupposes two types of religiosity: the cosmic and the metacosmic, which we have discussed above in other contexts. The cosmic embraces all tribal and clanic cultures whose religiosity consists of revering nature and its forces, either in the form of a numinal being or a numinal complex of beings who is/are, nevertheless, so much part of the world as to be encountered in the context of an ecological spirituality. *Animism* is a pejorative misnomer for it. The cult of the spirits and cosmic forces, such as the Bons (Tibet), Devas (S. Asia), Nats (Burma), Phis (Thailand, Laos, and Cambodia), spirits of ancestors (Confucianist cultures in Korea, China, and Vietnam), Kamis (Shintoist Japan), and so forth, are constitutive elements of this religiosity.

The metacosmic refers to the so-called great religions which posit the "existence" of an immanently transcendental horizon (Brahman-Atman, Nirvana, Dao, etc., in the "gnostic" religions; YHWH of Moses, Abba of Jesus, and Allah of Muhammad in the three "agapeic" religions), Which/Who is salvifically encountered by humans, through liberating knowledge (gnosis) and redemptive love (agape) respectively.

The mechanism involved in the rejection of Christ in Asia can be explained by what we might facetiously call "the helicopter theory of religious expansion." The theory is based on four historical observations.

The first is that the metacosmic religions are like helicopters, while the cosmic religions serve them as natural landing pads. Their encounter is one of mutual fulfillment, as they are complementary. Hence there is no radical conversion from one to the other. Thus, "inculturation" means none other than a metacosmic religion finding its natural point of insertion in a cosmic religion. This is how all non-Christian religions spread in various parts of Asia. The spread of Christianity in the Philippines, as also in Africa and Latin America, seems to have followed the same pattern.

The second trend seems to be "First come, first served." Buddhism came to Thailand before Christianity. Christianity came to the Philippines in those areas where no other metacosmic religion had preceded it. That is why Thailand is Buddhist and the Philippines are Christian, today. Tantric Hinduism in Java was of a cosmic type, and Islam did not find it too difficult to penetrate its culture.

Thirdly, it is usually the case that once a helicopter has landed, another cannot land on the same pad. This means, for example, that the Philippines will not become a Buddhist country, just as Thailand will not be Christian. In other words, mass conversions from one metacosmic religion to the other are improbable. Only where a cosmic religiosity still prevails (e.g., Oceania and certain pockets of Laos and Cambodia and the tribal regions of

---

1. I have also done so in A. Pieris, *ATL*, 71–74, 98–100.

India, as well as certain parts of Korea where Buddhism is more Confucianist than metacosmic) is there evidence of a Christian breakthrough. In certain parts of Indonesia (North Sumatra, Ambonia, Moluccas) Christianity had won (a few millions of) converts, probably because a cosmic religiosity had a stronger sway over the masses than did Islam. The rest of Asia would not let Christianity sweep across its religious cultures.

Fourthly, the possibility of a helicopter being forced off of its landing pad is not to be ruled out. A metacosmic religion could replace another by exerting prolonged and persistent political or military pressure or even through demographic changes (i.e., through migratory colonization). The history of religions in central and western Asia abounds in examples of this.

These four trends, by no means absolute but indicating a historically observed pattern of religious expansion, explain why colonial Christianity did not strike roots in most parts of Asia. It is not necessarily the colonialness of Christ that is rejected, for we see his Euro-ecclesiastical figure being successfully enthroned in cosmic cultures that are being Christianized today. In fact, the Encyclical of John Paul II, *Redemptoris Missio,* singles out Asia as a field for a quantitative expansion of Christianity (See par. 37). "Open the doors to Christ!," the Pope proclaims (See par. 3). But our prognosis, based on the observations made above, is that the cultures that have absorbed the great religions — that is over 90 percent of Asia — have no room for Christ, except perhaps as one cosmic power among many, i.e., as one more deity in the pantheon of cosmic forces, rather than as the one Lord and Savior.

THE NON-WESTERN CHRIST OF INTELLECTUALS

Our focus, here, is mainly on attempts made by some Christians or groups of Christians to break out of the existing theological molds in order to communicate the Christ-event in the context of the other Asian religions and cultures. Let us reflect on four such attempts, two in China and two in India.

The first on our list is, so to say, the "Buddhist Christ" of the Nestorian community, which flourished in China from 635 to 845 C.E. Judging from extant records,[2] we could call their experiment "inreligionization" as distinct from inculturation.[3] The latter, as I explained above, is the unchallenged entry of a metacosmic religion into the ethos of a cosmic religion. But in the Nestorian experiment, we see a metacosmic religion (Christianity) developing a new Asian identity within the idiom and the ethos of another metacosmic religion (Buddhism) — something that falls outside the general pattern observed above.

---

2. E.g., the catechetical writings of Alopen, a Nestorian missionary who arrived from Mesopotamia in 635 C.E., and also of Ching Ching (or Adam, to use his Christian name), as well as in the well-known stele erected in 781 C.E. by Yazedbouzid (Ching Ching's father), whose family came from Balkh, a Buddhist stronghold.

3. Pieris, *ATL,* (n. 1), 52.

Thus, for the first time Christian soteriology was reformulated within the Buddhist worldview, with the Avalokitesvara/Kuan-Yin model serving to form a "Buddhist christology."[4] To appreciate the bold originality of this experiment, one must contrast it with the syncretism of the third-century Manichaeans, who concealed the person of Jesus in a forest of Buddhist terms and concepts.[5]

Obviously, in other parts of Asia the Nestorians had different experiences, and the documents of their headquarters in Mesopotamia witness to both dialogical and hostile attitudes toward Buddhism.[6] At any rate, if the "Buddhist Christ" of the Chinese Nestorian communities did not last more than about two centuries, it was not because of any ecclesiastical intervention, but because of Emperor Wozong's ruthless suppression in 845 C.E. of all so-called "foreign religions" — which included both Buddhism and Christianity.

Hence we have no way of ascertaining how far the "Buddhist Christ" of the Nestorian scholars appealed to the Chinese masses. We can only conjecture that Nestorian christology and the monastic witness of that community might have contributed much to the emergence of this "Buddhist Christ" who, nevertheless, remains dead and buried in the writings and inscriptions of the past.

The second breakthrough came a millennium later when Matteo Ricci arrived in China. Rejecting Buddhism as incompatible with Christianity, he built on the cosmic religiosity of Confucianism, thus opting for inculturation rather than inreligionization, as we now see retrospectively.

His becoming a Mandarin scholar in China is paralleled by Roberto de Nobili's becoming a Brahmin Sanyasi in South India. Both these men made many converts and established Christian communities. Misunderstanding within the church caused the end of their efforts. Had they not been suppressed, what would be the fate of such communities today in China with its anti-Confucianist socialism or in modern India with its growingly anti-Brahmanic self-assertion of Dalits (about whom, see below)?

As for the People's Republic of China, where Ricci is still not without honor, we know that the Patriotic Church did look for a Christ with a Sino-ecclesial expression within the framework of anti-Confucianist socialism,[7] whereas the Underground Church repudiated such attempts as a treacherous compromise with an atheistic ideology and confessed their adherence to Christ in conformity with their inherited ecclesiastical mode of relating to the Western churches. The universal church waits anxiously to see how Chinese

---

4. For a neat summary with reference, see David Scott, "Christian References to Buddhism in Pre-Medieval Times," *Numen* 32/1, July 1985, 88–100.

5. See Hans-J. Limkeit, "Jesus' Entry into Parinirvana: Manichean Identity in Buddhist Central Asia," *Numen* 32/2, January 1986, 224ff.

6. Scott, "Christian References," 91.

7. For a very concise analysis of this attempt, see Frank K. Flinn, "Prophetic Christianity and the Future of China," in J. K. Hadden and A. Shupe (eds.), *Prophetic Religion and Politics*, New York, 1984, 307–28.

Christians will resolve this conflict. What kind of Christ will emerge from their reconciliation, and what place will such a Christ occupy in this gigantic segment of Asia? Since such questions are not yet answered, this case is left out of our critical evaluation.

In India, too, there were new developments. As de Nobili's work faded into history, there emerged another figure of Christ, the "Gnostic Christ" of the nineteenth-century Hindu Renaissance: a God-man, in whom the divine and the human enjoyed moral (rather than an ontological) unity, perhaps a Christ severed from his ecclesial body, but familiar with the idiom of metacosmic Hinduism.

Significantly, however, this Christ emerged mostly from the pens of well-meaning Hindu and Christian scholars of the so-called high castes. Obviously the Hindu masses would not have been aware of these attempts, nor did all of the Hindu elite welcome this new incarnation,[8] while the church as a whole was reluctant to absorb this trend. One wonders whether this Indian Christ of the nineteenth and early twentieth centuries really survives today anywhere else but in the historical studies of this period.

To sum up: none of these four Christs has found a place in the hearts of the masses or in the minds of the majority of today's elite. The reason in each case differs, as explained above.

As for the authenticity of these Christs, however, we have two ways of making an assessment: One would be to embark on a long and laborious analysis of the christological worth of these creations; the other — this is what I propose to do — will be to place them side by side with the Asian Christ.

THE ASIAN CHRIST

The Asian Christ is my shorthand for the "Christ of Asia" whom the Asian bishops addressed in their liturgy at their pan-Asian conference of 1974. But my focus here is not so much on the "Asianness" of this Christ as on the *Christness* of those categories of Asians who alone can reveal his Asian features. This emphasis has guided me in selecting four such categories for discussion.

The Broken Body of the Indian Christ

The humiliations of India's broken Christ have been woven, since the 1970s, into what is known as Dalit theology.[9] *Dalit* means "broken, trampled upon, destroyed" by the nefarious system of discrimination between the

---

8. See Richard F. Young, *Resistant Hinduism: Sanskrit Sources on Anti-Christian Apologetics in Early Nineteenth-Century India,* Vienna, 1981, 137–38.

9. My two main sources are: M. E. Prabhakar (ed.), *Towards a Dalit Theology,* Delhi, 1989, and Arvind P. Nirmal (ed.), *A Reader in Dalit Theology,* Madras, 1991.

so-called high, low and scheduled castes in India.[10] Their weak self-identity as untouchables and outcasts is derived from centuries of cruel segregation in matters of habitation, education, marriage, meals, burial, access to water and even to temples, and from a deep-seated socioreligious stigma of being a polluted and a pollutant species of nonpersons. Since the 1970s all backward castes, tribals, and landless laborers, who maintain the primary sector of service in contemporary India, seem to have gradually earned the name *Dalit.*

Mahatma Gandhi's condescending term *Harijan* (God's people) appeared offensive to the enlightened sections among them; they refused to be coopted by the oppressive caste-system prescribed by Hindu Canon Law (Dharma Sastras), which Gandhi adamantly defended as a sacrosanct and inviolable part of Hindu religion. Dalits prefer to be called what they have always been: Dalits, a broken people. (This brokenness presumably also includes numerous caste divisions and conflicts among the Dalits themselves![11]) Their stance is clear: their brokenness rather than their Christianness remains their identity and, consequently, also the basis of their christopraxis.

In the Dalit perspective, the Gnostic Christ was only a phantom which the Hinduizing Christians created while treading on the body of this authentic Indian Christ. Those great pioneering indigenizers[12] are now standing trial before the Dalits. Even Christian ashrams that dialogue with Hinduism's metacosmic religiosity, without ever allowing the broken Christ to utter a word of challenge, are a party to this sin against the Body of the Lord! The third-world theologians, too, have been severely criticized for speaking of the Indian poor in general without singling out the scandalous plight of the Dalits even within the church.[13] For the great majority of Christians are claimed to be Dalits (in some areas 60 percent, in others almost 90 percent), but 90 percent of church leadership and of the theological community is alleged to be in the hands of a minority of "upper-caste" Christians! The broken Christ has no place even in the church, which, therefore, could not be the body of *that* Christ.

Many Dalit theologians reject *in toto* the Marxist tools of social analysis so dear to some "third-world theologians" of India. For not only did the Indian Marxists fail to grasp caste structure — most of them were from

---

10. The words *high castes* and *low castes* have now been replaced with the less odious *forward castes* and *backward castes* in contemporary Indian literature.

11. See Ghanshyam Sha, "Dalit Movement and the Search for Identity," *Social Action,* 40/4, December 1990, 217–35.

12. E.g., Upadhyay, Sundar Singh, Nehemia Gore, Krishna Pillai, Appasamy, Norman Vaman Tilak, Chencia, Chakkarai, to name the major figures, were all from forward castes!

13. However, it must be recorded here that at the Delhi Meeting of the Ecumenical Association of the Third World Theologians (EATWOT) in 1981, a hearing of the Dalit case was a major item in the exposure program. In my input at that meeting (now Chapter 8 of *ATL*), I made a case for the Dalit and tribal struggle for liberation as a more important element for an Asian theology than the overemphasized Hindu Renaissance.

the "upper" castes and had no firsthand experience of the Dalit reality — but Marx's own theories about Indian society and its prospective liberation relied too blindly on indologists like Max Müller and on the administrative reports of British colonizers who did not have an inside knowledge of caste-infested rural India.

Thus, in Dalit theology, the Exodus text dear to the liberation theologians yields place to the confessional formula of Israel's historical roots: Deut. 26:5–12. Since Dalitness is the constitutive dimension of their theology, the broken Christ whom they identify themselves with, follow behind, and minister to, is for the most part non-Christian! Hence, their participation in the Dalit movement in general is an essential part of their christopraxis.

Since it is not only in civil society but also in Christian communities that the Dalit Christ is refused a place, the struggle is both against the Euro-ecclesiastical Christ of the official church and against the Hindu Christ of ashramites, both of whom fear the consequences of abdicating their place in favor of the Broken Christ. An official option on the part of certain groups (religious congregations) to "go Dalit" in ministry and even in their recruitment is rumored. If it is true, the Indian church will soon climb the cross, where it will be fragmented before being gathered into a Christ that India aspires to.

The Han-Ridden Body of the Korean Christ

In the Minjung theology of Korea,[14] the same Asian Christ appears with a *"han*-ridden body." *Han* is a mixture of many things: a sense of resignation to inevitable oppression, indignation at the oppressor's inhumanity, anger with oneself for being caught up in that hopeless situation, and a host of other emotions which are all accumulated to form a powerful source of psychological energy possessing a revolutionary potential if released in a socially organized fashion. In day-to-day life, this revolutionary energy is released in small doses through rite and ritual with the aid of shamans. But the most dramatic release of *han* is the mask dance in which prophetic humor is exercised by the Minjung (the oppressed people) against the Confucianist elite and the monastics (of metacosmic religion which, in Korea, is Buddhism) who side with the oppressive system. It is a symbolic enactment of the Minjung's unconcealed aspiration for freedom.

A distinction is made between *daejung,* the (confused) masses, and *minjung,* the (conscientized) people.[15] Does it not imply two moments in the life of the Korean Christ: the *han*-ridden moment and the *han*-releasing moment of the messianic people? Does not the passage from one to the other constitute the Korean christopraxis?

---

14. The main source on which I base my reflections is *Minjung Theology: People as Subjects of History,* Orbis Books, Maryknoll, N.Y., 1981, revised edition, 1983.

15. Kwon Jin-Kwan, "Minjung Theology and Its Future Task for People's Movement," *CTC Bulletin* (CCA Hong Kong), 2 and 3, May–December 1991, 16–22.

This brand of Asian theology emerged in its present form only in the 1970s, in the words and deeds of imprisoned and/or tortured farmers, workers, students, professors and journalists, who discovered their prophetic role by a *reditus ad fontes,* a return to the ancient (non-Christian) Korean sources of liberation: the *minjung* tradition. *Minjung* theology was a theological appropriation of a *minjung* Christianity which, in its turn, was a Christian appropriation of the (non-Christian) *minjung* tradition.

The Christianization of the *minjung* tradition occurred in the nineteenth century in a way that marks Korea as the first Asian country to sow the seeds of a theology of liberation. For the first time, an Asian nation received the bible, not as the aggressive foreigners' holy book — for Korea's colonizer was Shinto-Buddhist Japan, and not the Christian West — but as a sacred history of the *minjung.* Japanese and Chinese being the languages of the Korean literati, the appearance of the bible in Korean language (and in the Hangul script) had an explosive effect on the *minjung.* Here was a God in solidarity with the *minjung,* announcing the word of liberation in their own despised language and through their own folk idiom of narrative, drama, and poem, so different from the abstract jargon used by the God of missionary catechesis!

From its inception, therefore, Korean Christianity was a politicized faith and played a significant role in the national liberation struggle, unlike other Asian countries, where it was the non-Christian religions that stirred nationalist sentiments against Western colonizers. No wonder that the books of Exodus and Daniel were banned in Korea as potentially subversive! So we can draw this conclusion: the bible, when made accessible to the oppressed in Asia, easily becomes the seed of an authentically Asian Christianity, as it allows the best of Asia's (non-Christian) liberative traditions to be absorbed into the church's conscience. No wonder that there was a concerted effort by pastors to depoliticize and privatize the faith of Korean Christians, and not without success.

Even today, collusion between the neocolonialist Christianity and developmentalist ideology conspires to keep the unshepherded masses (*daejung*) from leaving their chains and exercising their role as a messianic people (*minjung*). The Passover from the *han*-ridden state of the Suffering Servant to the *han*-releasing hour of exaltation is the only way for the Asian Christ to manifest himself in Korea as the covenant between God and the oppressed. What hinders this Korean christophany is the perverse order of Mammon, which reserves a place only for a Christ without a cross, a Christianity which is comfortable with that disorder.

The Breast-Feeding Christa of Asian Womanhood

Asian women have no place, even where they wear themselves out at the service of males: in homes and offices; fields, forests and factories; tourist resorts and nightclubs; and, of course, temples and churches. Their Christhood has been powerfully captured by Chung Hyun Kyung in her wood-cut painting of the "Korean Christa," an open-armed Shaman-woman stretched on a cross and mounted on a lotus, with a sword in one hand and a bowl of rice in the other; the pierced side of the Crucified One issuing the waters of the Spirit is depicted in the form of an exposed (female) breast ever available for suck.

This image emphasizes the fact that a woman-shaman does not occupy a reputable place in society but remains the most accessible source of consolation and comfort for the *han*-ridden masses of women. She is the "priest of *han*."[16] Extending this observation to all cosmic religions of Asia, Chung notes:

> The existence of women-defined popular religiosity in Asia, such as Korean Shamanism, folk Chinese Buddhism which venerates Kwan In (female goddess), Filipino worship of Ina (mother-god), is powerful evidence of women's resistance to patriarchal religions.[17]

Here one might add South Asia's Kali, Pattini, and other female manifestations of divine justice, to whom the poor and helpless appeal against their oppressors.[18]

Note that all these cults belong to the cosmic level of the great Asian religions. For all metacosmic religions condone or even commend patriarchalism in the sacred scriptures of their traditions. Like casteism, sexism, too, is a religious and not merely a socioeconomic oppression. Often, not always, it is at the cosmic end of the Asian religious spectrum (popular religiosity) that women discover religious symbols to protest directly or indirectly against their servile state or create some space for themselves even within religion.

The cosmic approach to feminism differs from the secularist one. The latter reflects the antireligion of feminists reacting against the antifeminism of religion. But the "cosmic" is a blend of the earthly, the womanly, and the religiousness of the poor. The involvement of women from the oppressed classes in ecological movements,[19] therefore, is a distinctive feature in Asian feminism. Hence in Asia there is a tendency to appropriate theologically what was condemned as "popular" (and in my vocabulary, "cosmic") religiosity. For it is the religiosity of all the four categories of the Asian poor mentioned here. It is the spirituality of the Asian Christ among whose members discrimination in terms of "male and female, high-caste and low-caste, or Christian and non-Christian" (Gal. 3:28) is less accentuated than among those who refuse him a place.

---

16. Chung Hyun Kyung, *Struggle to Be the Sun Again: Introducing Asian Women's Theology,* New York and London, 1990, 66.
17. Ibid., 112.
18. At the time of writing, the mothers of children who have disappeared in torture chambers in Sri Lanka are reported to be gathering frequently in shrines dedicated to these goddesses, demanding justice and seeking liberation from their pain.
19. See Gabriele Dietrich, *Women's Movement in India: Conceptual and Religious Reflections,* Bangalore, 1988, 129–201.

The Third-World Christ of Asia

The continuous use of the phrase "Third World" irritates people who think it has lost its meaning since the collapse of the Second World. This is because they take the term *third* to mean "number 3" in a numerical series, whereas in its original (French) usage it designated "something different" from both the First and the Second World, a "third way" of organizing society, an "alternative" to the two existing models — a meaning that inspired the nonaligned movement.[20] Secondly, it also means the "Two-thirds World," the teeming masses of the destitute who form the vast majority on our planet. Further, it includes the idea that this world of the poor is in reality the waste product of a plutocracy led by the First World.

To these three meanings, the Afro-Asian and Latin American theologians add a fourth "biblico-christological" significance: "Third World" stands for the humble of the earth whom God has elected as the covenant partner in God's project of human liberation. It is also the Christ in whom Jesus continues as in his own members: through, with and in him alone the church is called to relive its mission and *thereby* recreate its ecclesial identity.

The starving children of Jacob, who turned westward to wealthy Egypt in quest of economic aid, only to become the donor country's political and cultural slaves, were chosen by Yahweh to create a "third way" of being a community in a land that significantly stood between Egypt and Babylon, the two superpowers of that time. Understandably, therefore, the Third World, summoned to partner Yahweh in building the new dream world of justice and love, has now become a theological and even a christological challenge, in that the majority members of the body of the third-world Christ are both Asian and non-Christian.

THE ASIAN CHRIST: A SIGN OF CONTRADICTION

Asian theologies evolve in a dialectical process of resolving several conflicts, four of which are singled out below. Asian Christians need both time and freedom to resolve these conflicts in their own way.

The Three Christs in Conflict

In traditional christology (through which I can make the Asian quest intelligible to the rest of the church) *Christ* is a compendious title which has absorbed all that we believers have attributed to Jesus ever since the Easter experience. The elements crucial for our purposes are three: the name of Christ overlapping with the name of the Trinity (God's salvific presence in history) as in the earliest Asian (Syriac) anaphoras; Christ the Risen Jesus bound to his earthly body, the church, as in the Pauline catechesis; Christ as the continuity of Jesus' history on earth in the lives and struggles of the

---

20. See "Three Inadequacies in the Social Encyclicals," chapter 8 below.

poor and the dispossessed who, as victims of human neglect, are also the eschatological judge of nations (Matt. 25:36ff.).

Thus the preponderantly "non-Christian" character of Christ has become a determinative factor in the four brands of Asian theologies explained in pp. 69–74 above. This poses no problem if we abide by the traditional belief that though all of Jesus is Christ, not all of Christ is Jesus (*Jesus est totus Christus, non totum Christi*). Jesus cannot grow to the full stature of Christ unless all his members (most of whom are non-Christians), together with the cosmos, struggle like him, even unto death, in ushering in God's Reign on earth.

The Christian members of basic human communities operate on this christology in the light of which the three images of Christ discussed above are subject to the following verdict: The Christ of the official church is not only European but also ecclesiastical, i.e., a clumsy body that hides its head, which is Jesus. But the non-European Christ of the Asian elite suffers from the other extreme of not being *ecclesial;* it is a head minus the body, a Jesus truncated from the total Christ. In contrast to both these, the Asian Christ (as recognized, announced, and served in the basic human communities) — at times called the non-Christian Christ — is the true body, even if it has not yet named its head.

Two Missiologies in Conflict

Understandably, therefore, the Asian theological quest involves two conflicting missiologies, reflecting the three images of Christ. The one defines mission as somehow or other procuring a place for Christ in Asia; the other spells out the missiological consequences of recognizing and proclaiming Christ as the one who has no place in Asia.

The Euro-ecclesiastical Christ began to grow weaker in Asia thanks to the postconciliar development of the theology of the local church; thanks to this theology, the mission to Christianize Asia was somewhat deemphasized in favor of the mission to Asianize Christianity. Some Asian churches, refusing to be a mere extension of the Western Patriarchate, strove to be for all Asians a readable sign and an accessible means of God's Reign experienced in Asia from time immemorial.

Now, christology is the first casualty of this new ecclesiology, while proselytism is the second! For the "Christ of Asia" that the Asian bishops addressed in their liturgy at their pan-Asian conference of 1947 seemed to have been in Asia long before the church arrived there and is at work even today far beyond the church. Were they all aware of their tacit acknowledgment of the "non-Christian Christ" and his claims over the Asian church? The christological reflections accompanying the new ecclesiology were breeding missiological confusion and much apprehension in the church.[21]

---

21. See Felipe Gomez, "Uniqueness and Universality of Christ," *East Asian Pastoral Re-*

Pope John Paul II's encyclical, *Redemptoris Missio,* is an attempt to confirm these fears rather than to allay them. Despite reiterating many a conciliar teaching, it reveals its hidden agenda in the introductory paragraphs. One gets the impression that the church, which has lost its grip on the secularized West, would like to gain control of the religious South; the South is fast becoming the new center of Christianity in both numerical and qualitative terms, besides being the traditional arena of global conflicts. Alluding presumably to the sixteenth-century missions to Asia and the Americas, which helped to renew church life in Europe, the redactors of the encyclical want missionary zeal to be whipped up again in terms of the "planting the church" (*plantatio ecclesiae*) model of mission, which, I suspect, guarantees a quantitative expansion of the Western Patriarchate's ecclesiastical control in the Third World.

The encyclical warns against placing the emphasis on the "Reign of God" alone as the goal of mission. The purpose of mission is to expand the church — to get Asia to "open the doors to [the Euro-ecclesiastical] Christ"! This is a missiology that seeks to create a place for Christ everywhere in Asia.

Some Asian theologians, as indicated above, have been as irrelevant as the encyclical. They have endeavored to invent a non-Western Christ that would have a "respectable place" in the minds of the religious elite, rather than discover the Christhood of the Asian poor who, like Jesus, have no decent place to be born in (Luke 2:7), no reputable place to live and work (John 1:46), no safe place in their own country to hide from oppressive rulers (Matt. 2:13–14), or no honorable place to die (Luke 23:23), and no place of their own to be buried (Matt. 27:59).

Two Ministries in Conflict

Hence it is the discovery of the Christhood of Asia's placeless and religious (mostly non-Christian) poor that has inspired a new theological quest along the second line of missiology mentioned above. Its goal is not to provide place for the displaced Christ, but to be ministerially involved with him.

Now, in this ministerial praxis, too, we note two trends. One group exercises the church's healing ministry toward the Asian Christ. The other group seeks to participate in the prophetic ministry that the Asian Christ exercises toward the church and society. The former trend is represented not only by Mother Teresa and her sisters, but by countless men and especially women, whose heroic charity is all the more Christian for being done without the public media advertising it at the expense of the poor. They work within church structures.

---

view 1983/1, 4–30, and Aloysius Pieris, "Christology in Asia: A Reply to Felipe Gomez," *Voices from the Third World,* XI/2, December 1989, 155–72.

But the other species of ministry can succeed only in the basic human communities operating on the periphery of the official church. It is a mission which promises no consolation of the type that the first group enjoys. It is a massive plunge of faith into the project of human liberation and social transformation, based on the belief that the Asian Christ's placelessness in Asia is constitutive of the sin that infects both the civil and the religious society (including the church).

That is why the Asian Christ does not plead for a place in this sinful system; for he is its victim-judge, not an accomplice. The Christian mission, as articulated in the basic human communities, demands a conversion of Asian societies to Christ's order. Baptism is not a convenient mechanism to expand the church at the expense of the Asian Christ. It consists of "making disciples of nations" (Matt. 28:19) along the *via crucis* of greedless sharing so that the life of each nation will be radically reordered in terms of the demands made by the Asian Christ.

The separation of these two ministries is an obstacle to the coming of God's Reign. The healing ministry can only serve to perpetuate the sinful order if the Asian Christ is not prophetically announced in word and deed as God's judgment over nations (Mother Teresa, pay attention!). But the prophetic activity of basic human communities can lead to ideological grooves through despair, unless healing miracles illuminate their word of liberation with a spark of hope, i.e., with glimpses into eschatological wholeness. The reconciliation of these two groups is crucial for another purpose which the Asian Christ demands: the reevangelization of the official church by the basic human communities, something that requires the mediation of ministers of healing who operate within the church structures. Hence my final observation.

The Center-Periphery Conflict

The official church, because of its minority complex, has often compromised its evangelical mission by its alliance with the ruling class, running institutions that produce the elite. Alienated from the Asian Christ, it may indirectly contribute to his placelessness. The official church's apostolic authority depends on its continuity with Jesus of Nazareth; but this continuity is strained if the church is not one continuous body with the Asian Christ. The basic human communities provide the channel through which it can reestablish this link and regain its lost authority, thus also loosening the chains of Euro-ecclesiastical feudalism.

For in basic human communities the story of Jesus is appropriated as an Asian drama of liberation. The Christian members (though a minority in the basic human communities) retell this story as the story of the Asian Christ, declaring in word and deed, in liturgy and life, that "Jesus of Nazareth whom they follow is the living Christ whom they serve here in Asia." The hierarchical center of the church is the first addressee of this "new evangelization" taking place on the periphery!

But such conversion at the center, as I observed, is difficult unless the two ministries (the healing ministry *to* the Asian Christ and the prophetic ministry *of* the Asian Christ) merge into one christopraxis.

If that happens, the Asian Christ, a rock that God has placed for the church to stumble and fall on, may begin to serve as the rock of its salvation (see Rom. 9:32–33). Then the church will not waste its energy "trying to procure a place for Christ in Asian societies"; it will rather wear itself out in "transforming societies that have no place for the Asian Christ."

8

Three Inadequacies in the Social Encyclicals

Lest I be misunderstood, I wish to begin with a declaration of support for the century-old papal tradition of issuing periodic encyclicals on social questions and of creating an awareness in and outside the Christian community that a response to such questions falls within the church's mission (EN 29–38, SRS 41, CA 54, etc.).[1] It would have been a tragedy if the See of Rome had never spoken on this matter! During the last hundred years, "the Magisterium of Peter" (EN 64) has set a precious example to the heads of other local churches by its conscientious effort to develop what has come to be termed "Christian/Catholic social teaching."

Regrettably, the majority of bishops, priests, religious, and the laity in Asia — especially those who are vociferous in their protests of loyalty to Rome in matters of church discipline — have not shown the same enthusiasm for these papal teachings. Some of them have even scrapped the Peace and Justice Commissions that were set up partly to translate the Roman Catholic social teaching into practice. Their "selective obedience to Rome" inhibits my critique of the Roman Catholic social teaching, through fear I might in-

First published in *Vidyajyoti Journal of Theological Reflection,* 57/2, February 1993, 75–94. I am grateful to Gabriele Dietrich, Michael Amaladoss, David Hollenbach, Cecilia Tan, and Beda Liu for their critical remarks on the original version of this chapter, which was presented at the Asian Seminar on the Future of Catholic Social Thought in Hong Kong in March 1992. Their comments have been taken into consideration in preparing this revised version.

1. A note on abbreviations: In referring to papal documents in this paper, the following abbreviations are used: CA for *Centesimus Annus* (by Pope John Paul II, 1991); EN for *Evangelii Nuntiandi* (by Pope Paul VI, 1975); LE for *Laborem Exercens* (by Pope John Paul II (1981); MM for *Mater et Magistra* (by Pope John XXIII, 1961); OA for *Octogesima Adveniens* (by Pope Paul VI, 1971); PP for *Populorum Progressio* (by Pope Paul VI, 1967); PT for *Pacem in Terris* (by Pope John XXIII, 1963); and SRS for *Solicitudo Rei Socialis* (by Pope John Paul II, 1987). I also use the abbreviation DV for *Dei Verbum* (The Vatican Council II decree on revelation).

directly contribute to their callous disregard for the papal teachings on social justice.

On the other hand, I am aware of Joseph Ratzinger's elucidation that "criticism of papal documents is possible and necessary to the extent that these pronouncements are not covered in Scripture and Creed."[2] However, in my criticism of the Catholic social teaching, I shall try my best to emulate such pioneers in the field as Dorr and Hollenbach, who have edified us with their constructively critical loyalty to the magisterium.[3]

This critique, undertaken in that same spirit, has two aims in view: the first is to persuade the Primatial See of the Western Patriarchate to listen to and learn from concerned individuals and groups of other local churches when preparing such documents so that their contents will be truly "catholic," that is to say, universally credible and credibly universal; the other aim is to persuade the local church leaders in Asia that they are duty bound to evolve a Catholic social teaching (i.e., a programmatic vision of their social responsibility) by consulting the experiments of those individuals and groups, who, in word and deed, in liturgy and life, are witnessing to the Social Gospel within Asia's own economic and cultural context.

It is with this twofold motive that I have chosen to indicate below three perspectives that I miss when I read the social encyclicals, first as a person from the Third World, then as an Asian, and finally as a Christian summoned to anchor myself in God's Word, spoken through Holy Writ and contemporary history.

THE THIRD-WORLD PERSPECTIVE

The authentic concept of a Third World has not been adequately appreciated in the papal writings. Pope John Paul II, in one instance, refers to "the so-called third world" (LE chap. 4) and, in another, to "the nonaligned movement" (SRS 21), but does not elaborate on the nexus between the two. The Third World he so frequently mentions is just a geographical area on the globe where the poor are manufactured by a heartless First World. This is only a fraction of what "Third World" means for us. Neither he nor any of his predecessors has taken serious notice of the crucial meaning it has for those who have begun to see it as a theological category.

With the collapse of the Second World and following the trend in the First World, John Paul II seems to employ the phrase and the concept of the Third World as a convenient synonym for the other two frequently used phrases, "the South" and "the developing countries." This vocabulary indicates an oversight on the part of the redactors of papal encyclicals with

---

2. Quoted in Richard McCormick, S.J., *Critical Calling*, Washington, 1989, 160.
3. Donald Dorr, *Option for the Poor: A Hundred Years of Vatican Social Teachings,* Gill and Macmillan, Dublin, 1983, reprint 1985; David Hollenbach, *Claims in Conflict: Retrieving and Renewing the Catholic Human Rights Tradition,* Paulist, New York, 1979.

regard to a significant historical movement that has penetrated the Christian consciousness in the Third World.

The primary sense in which the phrase "Third World" became part of our vocabulary needs to be restated here. When the French demographer Alfred Sauvy introduced it as a newcomer to the political parlance of the 1950s, he was thinking of colonized nations that were just beginning to acquire independence from the colonial masters in the First World. Given the then prevalent polarization between the First and the Second Worlds, we can surmise that the term *third* had the more nuanced (French) connotation of a new or an alternative world rather than the popular idea of something occurring as "number 3" in a numerical sequence. This numerical idea has led some to invent a superfluous "fourth" world, a misnomer for third-world pockets within the First World itself. The Pope seems to appropriate the rationale behind this enumerative approach when he sees the world as divided into four worlds (SRS 14).

Even the contemporary attempt (not by the Popes) to rename it the "Two-thirds World" misdirects our attention to the mere fact that the Third World constitutes a numerical majority on the planet today. Though I fully endorse the significance of this all-important fact, I regret that the neologism "Two-thirds World" eclipses the idea of a third way or a new way which imposes itself on the political consciousness of the world's secular and religious leaders. At any rate, it was in this latter sense that the word was appropriated by the leading figures of the Third World itself, in the sixties and seventies.

The architects of the now moribund or defunct nonaligned movement, which is associated with the authentic meaning of the Third World (this connection is vaguely insinuated in SRS 21), desired their countries to group into a third force in response to the Cold War between the other two worlds. Though not all the countries in the Third World joined this movement and not all the member nations of the movement were from the Third World (as, for instance, Tito's Yugoslavia, which resisted the Second World's claims over it), the basic idea of an alternative force was strongly stated in the world forum.

No doubt, one may have reservations about some of the leaders who advocated the movement. (Are the leaders of the other blocs paragons of integrity?) But their appeal to the Western and the Eastern bloc was for a new political spirituality. They demanded especially from the Christian powers of the West a new order of values. The following words of Nehru, directed against two Catholic nations that were tactically delaying to grant independence to their respective colonies, are too clear to need any comment:

> Something we in the Third World consider a great sin is looked upon (by the Western [Christian] powers) as a minor misdemeanor which can be passed by, and something we consider a minor misdemeanor is

perhaps considered a great sin [by those powers]. So our *values* differ. Apparently our *standards* differ.[4]

The notion of the Third World as a third force demanding a new morality in the world order could not fail to attract a few theologians of these countries. But a widespread Christian appropriation of this clamor for a new order of social ethics was not possible in the sixties because the First World's developmentalist ideology neutralized the profound idea of a truly third way by reducing the notion of the Third World to a merely economic category.

The West was not ignorant of what it was doing; nor were the leaders of the Third World economically independent enough and morally courageous enough to resist the tide. No one could raise the consciousness of the Western powers to the pernicious results of their ideological posture, just as no one could awaken a person who is pretending to sleep. Was the church, especially the Western Patriarchate together with its Primatial See, too much a part of the First World to perceive this move? At any rate it failed to raise its voice in solidarity with the aspirations of the third-world leaders, most of whom, significantly, were non-Christians. This makes it even more regrettable that all the encyclicals of this period (MM, PT, PP) took the developmental ideology as a given thing and tried to humanize and Christianize it in the way that the "Daniels" of our own decade wish to tame capitalism into whose den they have been thrown (cf. CA).

Referred to as "developing countries," the third-world nations came to be defined in terms of and in subordination to the economically developed First World. It is, therefore, not difficult to understand why the neocolonialist dependence of these nations on the two superpower blocs made the Popes only moralize over its unjust nature, whereas the economists and ideologues of the Third World (e.g., Furtado, Frank, Cardoso, etc.) resorted to the more radical stance of a liberation from rather than a development toward the other two worlds. Though their "dependency theory" may not have adequately explained the whole phenomenon of underdevelopment in the Third World and particularly in Latin America,[5] its liberationist perspective did succeed in highlighting the inherent weaknesses of developmentalism.

The desperate search for a new path on the part of Julius Nyerere, in Tanzania, and Ho Chi Minh, in North Vietnam, in the very next decade (the seventies) has amply demonstrated how well-nigh impossible it is for a third-world country to survive the bear-hugs of both Western and Eastern benefactors!

Thus it was in the seventies that the concept of the Third World began to

---

4. Chanakya Sen, *Against the Cold War,* Asia Publishing House, 1962, quoted in Guy Arnold, *The Third World Handbook,* Cassel Educational, London, 1989, 44. The words in the square brackets as well as the emphases are added.

5. See Arthur F. McGovern, S.J., "Dependency Theory, Marxist Analysis and Liberation Theology," in Marc H. Ellis and Otto Maduro (eds.), *The Future of Liberation Theology: Essays in Honor of Gustavo Gutiérrez,* Orbis Books, Maryknoll, N.Y., 1989, 272–86.

sharpen itself into a "theological category" as well as a point of reference in what emerged as liberation theology. This is how the EATWOT (Ecumenical Association of Third World Theologians), formed in that decade, began to work out an alternative to the First World's developmentalist paradigm which had left its stamp on the papal encyclicals. The liberation perspective, which had already entered the Medellín Statement, in 1968, made a timid appearance in the Document of the Synod of 1971, thanks, in both cases, to the fact that third-world bishops had a say in them.

The encyclicals, on the contrary, have not generously entertained the influence of Third World's spokespersons within the church. Even *Octogesima Adveniens* of 1971 is not a radical departure. In granting the right and the duty of local churches to develop their own social praxis and their social doctrine, what the Pope seems to expect is simply that they adapt the papal Catholic social teaching to their social situations. This means that this teaching is universal and what is required is its application to the local needs. An autonomous approach to the social question is not envisaged for the local churches of the Third World.

Understandably, the seventies were also the decade in which the Third World theologies surfaced under the rubric of "liberation theology" in stark opposition to the developmentalist theology of the Western Patriarchate.[6] Their anti-Western slant, therefore, was not surprising and was perhaps further accentuated by many significant events of that decade, e.g., Red China's becoming a world power through self-reliance, independently of the two superpowers; the Viet Cong's definitive victory over the greatest military power of the West; the Sandinista Revolution in Nicaragua.

In fact, EATWOT, formed in that decade, was increasingly becoming the forum of this emergent theology. The starving children of Jacob going in search of economic aid to the rich country of Egypt in the West and becoming the political slaves of their benefactors seemed an apt biblical paradigm of "Third-Worldness."[7] Yahweh joins them in forming a society in contrast to dominant societies and places them between the two superpowers: Babylon and Egypt. It is a third way.

However the anti-Western bias of this theology, or rather, of some of these theologians, was, as explained above, an understandably negative reaction to the developmentalist accent in the Western Patriarchate's social doctrine. But this anti-Western slant was, unfortunately, accompanied by an attitude of uncritical silence or naive adulation toward the Eastern Bloc, where unprecedented social gains were marred by a tendency toward state capitalism. The caution I voiced on this matter in 1979 at the EATWOT's Asian Con-

---

6. E.g., see Gustavo Gutiérrez, *A Theology of Liberation*, Orbis Books, Maryknoll, N.Y., 1989, 272–86.

7. A. Pieris, *ATL*, 87.

sultation[8] gave rise to a polarization which was resolved only after several years of debate.[9]

The recent collapse of the Second World may bring in a more realistic understanding of the Russian experiment, but that cannot justify any attempt at doing away with the idea of a "Third World" and its historical implications for a new order. Our fear of being swept off the ground by the First World (which since the Gulf War has usurped the Third World's rhetoric of a "New Order" — a euphemism for the Bush Administration's *Pax Americana*) is even more justified now than when there was a Second World to check such a tendency. The church is not faithful to her mission to the nations if the liberation theology of the third-world theologians who have been developing a Catholic social teaching authenticated by a Christian social praxis is not given a positive hearing. The Vatican on the whole has not been part of this Christian effort; on the contrary, it has been issuing threats and warnings instead of dialoguing with bishops, theologians, and the basic communities who are the authors of this Catholic social teaching.

Besides, the option for a "socialist" model of society, which not only counters the capitalist-developmentalist model proposed by the West but also differs from the Second World's version of socialism, is greeted with suspicion by the Roman church, which had other experiences associated with the word *socialism* (CA 4).

One sees a calculated reluctance on Rome's part to appreciate these "liberational" and the "socialist" aspirations of various third-world movements both within the theological community and outside it. Though a clear avowal is made to the effect that the Roman Catholic social teaching does not present a concrete social model as a third way between capitalism and socialism, being a "category of its own" (SRS 41), it does seem that what it pines after is no more than a desecularized West, that is, a re-Christianized version of the First World as the safest social model. A careful reading of all the encyclicals (especially *Redemptoris Missio*) drives one to this painful conclusion. If the magisterium of Peter renounces its obligation to be imaginative and creative in directing the nations into a new path, will there be another prophetic voice in the world to guide us if and when capitalism collapses because of its inbuilt suicidal mechanism and perhaps because of demographic changes that will take place with population depletion in the North and inevitable South-to-North emigrations?[10] Is there no person or community to resuscitate humankind's desperate longing for a truly *Third* World? It is possible that the Basic Human Communities in Asia could perhaps be one such voice that cries in the wilderness.

---

8. This intervention appears as chapter 7 in *ATL*, especially, 76–78.

9. See *Voices from the Third World*, June 1979, for a sample of this debate.

10. See Immanuel Wallerstein, "The Cold War and the Third World: Good Old Days?" *Economic and Political Quarterly*, XXVI/17, April 27, 1991, 1103ff.

THE ASIAN PERSPECTIVE

The Third World is not monolithic geographically, culturally, or even economically. Asia, Africa, and Latin America differ from each other in almost everything except in their common fate of being culturally and economically colonized by the powerful nations. They meet under the rubric of the Third World. Yet Third-Worldness expresses itself in an unrepeatable way in each of the three continents, as well as in small enclaves of the marginalized in the First World.

What, then, are the Asian features of the Third World? The main characteristic of the Third World in Asia is that it is almost totally (97 percent) non-Christian; to be more specific, Asia is shared between regimes governed by atheistic Marxism and those dominated by antitheistic capitalism, whereas the masses believe in religions that are predominantly nontheistic or polytheistic, while only Islam, as well as one or two brands of Hinduism, together with a small minority of Christians, profess their theistic faith in a personal creator-redeemer God. But these masses, even while adhering to the aforementioned (metacosmic) religions, are still profoundly rooted in a cosmic religiosity — a species of ecological and creation-conscious spirituality that would rather die than coexist with technocracy, which is part of the package of modern agro-industrial technology.

The social doctrine of the Popes is not only framed within a perspective that does not comfortably accommodate Asia's Third-Worldness, as indicated in Part I, but it is also couched in the theological language and idiom of Western Christianity.

I grant, however, that there are three principles that can be extracted from this Western Christian formula and translated into a non-Christian idiom acceptable to Asians. First, the theological basis of the social doctrine of the encyclicals is the dignity of the human person and this is common to practically all Asian religions, even those that are nontheistic. The idea of the *imago Dei* may be absent, but there are other ways of formulating the primacy and the superiority of man and woman.[11] But superiority, as a Buddhist monk-scholar warns, should not imply supremacy of humans over the rest of existence[12] — this being a major difference between the cosmic (ecologically integrated) approach of Asian religiosity and the Western Christian habits of thought that are currently being corrected by the emergent emphasis on creation theology.

Secondly, a parallel can be noticed between the principle of Natural Law or Right Reason invoked in the Catholic social teaching, and the *dharma/Tao*

---

11. See *Human Rights and Religions in Sri Lanka: A Commentary on the Universal Declaration of Human Rights*, Sri Lanka Foundation, Colombo, 1988, 3 (Hindu Commentary on Article 1), 6 (Buddhist Commentary), and 8 (Islamic Commentary).

12. Ven. K. Anuruddha, "Religion and Peace," *Dialogue*, Colombo, XI/1–3, January–December 1984, 3.

which forms the eternal principle of righteousness in the cultures permeated by some of Asia's gnostic religions. Here again there is a proviso: whereas in the papal social doctrine duties are derived from rights rooted in the dignity of each person — a characteristic of the West's "human rights language" absorbed into Christianity and "confirmed" biblically[13] — the religions of Asia reverse the process: it is *dharma,* duty or obligation, that justifies rights. That means that the dignity of the human person is not the source of rights; rather, as we shall explain later, it is responsibility toward the others that seems to define the status and dignity of humans.

Thirdly, there is a convergence between the ancient Christian belief in the sovereignty of the common good over individual rights to private property (a doctrine reiterated in several social encyclicals) and Asia's traditional sense of reverential obligation toward the common natural resources which are considered too sacred to be manipulated or appropriated by any single person or a privileged group of persons. The most criminal violation of this basic principle is the practice of segregation by some caste Hindus, one of the great scandals in Asia, the only parallel being apartheid in South Africa. The Dalit movement in India as well as the liberation theology that accompanies it, reaffirm the sacrality of cosmic resources and the commonly shared stewardship over them (see footnote 25 below).

The three aspects just mentioned (the centrality of the human person, the human rights language, and the primacy of the common good) are woven into a Christian theory of justice in which commutative, distributive, and social justice are interconnected, with the last mentioned form of justice serving as the all-embracing and determinant component. In fact this constitutes the core of the so-called social doctrine of the church, or rather, the "lasting paradigm" for such a doctrine — to borrow a phrase which the present Pontiff applies, perhaps too narrowly, to the message of *Rerum Novarum* (CA 5).

Now our question is this: Can and should Christian Asia (which is statistically a mere drop in the ocean) develop a social doctrine within this paradigm, accommodating the nuances and modifications I referred to above? This, I presume, is the expectation of the See of Rome (cf. OA). Besides, it would be the height of chauvinism to reject a doctrine simply because it is Western or advocate an alternative paradigm on the grounds of its alleged Asian inspiration. Nor do we believe that the papal Catholic social teaching (which, in our opinion, is only the Western Patriarchate's response to the social question) should be forced to include Asian (African and Latin American) options and become a kind of doctrinal fruit salad!

But my doubts about the applicability of the Catholic social teaching in Asia arise from another set of considerations based on the total historical context of the papal teachings. Let me situate the discussion in that perspective.

---

13. See chapter 10.

The papal Catholic social teaching grew out of a critical Christian stance adopted by the Popes vis-à-vis the socioeconomic and political developments in the West. I do not deny that it reveals a Christian concern for the victims of both capitalist and communist domination in the Third World; but with the recent disappearance of the Eastern Bloc in Europe, Catholic social teaching is moving in the direction of warning capitalism of its inherent dangers, on the one hand, and encouraging a humane version of it, on the other.

Now, in Asia this might sound fine in some Christian enclaves which welcome the socioeconomic and political incursions of capitalism into Asia; I'm thinking of contemporary Japan and the four dragons (Korea, Taiwan, Hong Kong, and Singapore) which some theologians see as "success stories"[14] — though, from a different perspective, they can also be seen as questionable experiments. For it is one's standpoint which influences one's viewpoint. Hence the question: How do enlightened Asian Christians and their non-Christian co-pilgrims who take a stand against this encroachment of the First World's technocratic culture into Asia (not technology as such) receive the Catholic social teaching of the encyclicals? They, I am able to report,[15] see the Roman Catholic social teaching against a background of an Asia dominated by the First World, with its developmental model linked to capitalistic technocracy and with so many virtual dictatorships maintained by the very same powers that manipulate the First World. In other words, the Catholic social teaching comes out as a prescription given but never taken seriously in the First World for a disease created in the First World and now exported to our continent. Does one expect a numerically insignificant Christian minority to apply such a prescription to the Asian reality? Should not we Asian Christians (a minority in dialogue with the non-Christian majority) perceive the social question in the perspectives of our own standpoint?

The next observation is this: The papal doctrine, in the eyes of the actively engaged non-Christian Asians, seems tied to the West, on whose colonial waves Christianity was carried to the shores of Asia. The Catholic social teaching nowhere makes a sincere confession of sinfulness in this matter, and even in *Populorum Progressio,* where some acknowledgment is made of the ill-effects of colonialism, not without patting it on the back for the good side-effects, the Patriarch of the West does not own the Christian sinfulness so clearly stamped in Asian history.[16]

Thus, it is understandably difficult for non-Christian Asians, who know this fact, to dissociate the Western Patriarch's Christian concern for Asia's

---

14. Peter H. Lee, "The Four Little Dragons, the Great Dragon and the Phoenixes," *Inter-Religio,* no. 15, Summer 1989, 21–25.

15. This is the impression I gather from the participants of seminars I have been conducting for various groups of Christians and non-Christians on the CST during the *Rerum Novarum* Centenary (1991).

16. For a neat summary of this sinful history, cf. J. Dunn, *Missionary Theology: Education in Development,* Catholic University of America Press, Washington, D.C., 1986, 9–36. This author, however, appeals for a theology of development.

social evils from the contemporary West's blatantly colonialist expansion of its technocratic power in Asia today. What is at stake is the credibility of Catholic social teaching.

The third observation is that this doctrine is what it is: a mere doctrine, a theoretical statement, which the Popes would have us translate into practice (MM 226–30). There is here the old Greek concept of the "universal" which is abstracted from concrete reality and then "applied" to individual instances. The Christian experience, like all other religious experiences, has another perception of the universal. Just as the universal church is not an abstract body but a communion of particular churches, an *ecclesia ecclesiarum*, so also a doctrine is universal when the social gospel lived in concrete situations is gathered together into a coherent teaching.

Put more bluntly, Roman Catholic social teaching has no roots in a Christian social praxis, unlike liberation theology which includes a Catholic social teaching drawn from a grassroots third-world experience. No social doctrine can be pastorally effective if it does not spring from a praxis. The church can boast of a eucharistic doctrine because it has had an unbroken tradition of a eucharistic praxis. Can the same be said of Roman Catholic social teaching?

When slaves and the marginalized sections accepted Christ in the first years of Christianity in the Roman Empire, they were gathered into a true Jesus-Community. But despite the timely warning given in the Apocalypse against the seductive power of the Roman Beast, the church gradually abandoned the ways of the Lamb who was slain and evolved an imperialistic and feudal structure of government. Since then a permanent tradition of a radical Christian social praxis was not seen in the official church. There were sporadic liberation movements in the fringes of the churches, from which even now one can draw much inspiration.[17] Such movements, however, did not always reflect the praxis of the official church, which formulates the Catholic social teaching. Quotations from the bible, and a few from the Fathers and recent Popes — a sort of potted history summing up twenty centuries, as done in LE for instance[18] — do not warrant the conclusion that there was an unbroken tradition of social praxis in the official church.

These considerations explain the sense of diffidence we feel toward the magisterium's Catholic social teaching, as we with our non-Christian friends yearn for a new political spirituality rooted in firm humanistic values, living as we are in an ethos of a religious humanism and a religious socialism still available in their monastic and tribal versions,[19] now systematically destroyed by the "economic miracles" brought in from the First World. Whereas communist regimes, in Asia, have purified religion and strengthened its roots

---

17. See Clodovis Boff and George V. Pixley, *The Bible, the Church and the Poor,* Orbis Books, Maryknoll, N.Y., 1989, 159–84.

18. As pointed out by Peter Hebblethwaite, "Popes and Politics: Shifting Patterns in 'Catholic Social Doctrine,'" a LADOC reprint from *Daedalus,* 1982, 22.

19. Cf. Pieris, *ATL,* 40–45.

by persecution, capitalism and its technocracy wither it away right before our eyes, fostering a right-wing fundamentalist version of it to the detriment of its liberative thrusts. We need a Catholic social teaching that meets this challenge.

Here, the Roman See has very little to offer. But the Basic Human Communities are evolving their own Asian Catholic social teaching by valiantly moving against this current as well as opposing sinful structures indigenous to Asia (caste, bonded labor, etc.). There, the scriptures and social praxis combine in eliciting a liberative Word, a Word that truly comes from the One who has built her tent among the poor. And this brings us, finally, to

THE BIBLICAL PERSPECTIVE

During the Reformation there seemed to have been a polarization between those who advocated "scholastic theology" as a Roman defense against the Reformers, and others who rejected it in favor of a "positive theology," which was said to be of biblico-patristic inspiration and associated with a spiritual praxis.[20] The counterreform mentality of the Roman church had nurtured the apologetical and rational trend of scholastic theology to the extent that in the subsequent centuries even positive theology gradually ceased to be a distinct theological method and became a mere function of scholastic theology.[21] This function was to provide a biblico-patristic support, plus other proofs from the *praxis ecclesiae,* to confirm what the scholastics have been traditionally saying. Roman theology retains this scholastic tradition in that it uses the bible for proof texts but does not submit itself to the Word of God. The challenge of rationalism in the nineteenth century sharpened this tendency.

Rerum Novarum, which appeared in that century, was a major attempt at tackling a concrete social issue within this same scholastic tradition. There is a strong appeal to reason and natural law, but a well-laid biblical foundation is not that evident. This is still the Roman method. All the social encyclicals, without exception, illustrate this.

Vatican II did give a new thrust in its valuable document *Dei Verbum,* which reenthroned the Word of God at the center of the church's interior life, apostolate, and liturgy.[22] Though *Gaudium et Spes* seems to have initiated a new trend by adopting a christological approach to the social question,[23] its Catholic social teaching, as well as that of the subsequent encyclicals, con-

---

20. This polarization is clearly alluded to by Ignatius of Loyola in his "Rules for Thinking with the Church," *Spiritual Exercises,* no. 363. Yves Congar cites this Ignatian reference as a primary source of information on the two theologies.

21. Congar, *A History of Theology,* Doubleday, New York, 1968, 171–74.

22. Enzo Bianchi, "The Centrality of the Word of God," in G. Alberigo et al. (eds.), *The Reception of Vatican II,* Catholic University of America Press, Washington, D.C., 1987, 115–36.

23. David Hollenbach, *Justice, Peace and Human Rights, American Catholic Social Ethics in a Pluralistic Context,* Crossroad, New York, 1988, 4–9.

tinue the Roman tradition of being notoriously lacking in biblical radicalism. Despite the warning issued by Vatican II that even the magisterium is not above the Word of God but must serve it (DV 10), the Catholic social teaching of the Roman See — I exclude EN, which is not a social encyclical — has not given up the habit of making the Word of God serve its teachings.

An example: *Laborem Exercens.* This is the social encyclical that uses the Bible most, but uses it according to the worst of scholastic tradition! There, the whole "theology of work" is made to stand on a few sentences from the first two chapters of the Bible! The last section, which deals with the spirituality of work is a nice assortment of biblical references culled with the help of a Bible concordance and then woven together![24]

Thus, the doctrine of *abad* ("work," "slavery/service," "worship"), a central theme of the Jewish and Christian scriptures, runs through scripture like a thread holding together a unique social doctrine. It is at once an imperative word of God addressed to the whole of humankind and through it to the whole cosmos, something I have not discovered in any other sacred book. It is, however, sadly absent in the LE. Perhaps, this will be more evident to Roman Catholics, if they compare LE with Bastian Wielenga's little booklets *Biblical Perspectives on Labour* (TTS, Madurai, 1982) and *Labour: Service God or Mammon?* (ISPCK, Delhi, 1987). The author is a thoroughly Indianized Dutch professor of scripture, writing from a lived situation in India. It is a good sample of an Asian Catholic social teaching, where the Word of God seems to break forth from within the Indian social situation.

As I shall explain more fully in chapter 10, the whole package of "justice theology" in the Western Patriarchate, especially in its Roman form, is a biblical "confirmation" (*à la* scholasticism) of an extrabiblical theory (inadequate but by no means incorrect), whereas "liberation theology" in the Third World is the result of the actualization of the scriptures within the historical situation of the oppressed who hear and interpret the Word as addressed to them in the Basic Christian Communities and Basic Human Communities. The first brand of theology speaks to the rich nations and the powers behind them, who have not yet given any evidence of even attempting to pass through the needle's eye; the idiom of the second species of theology, on the other hand, resonates with that Word which, by a public agreement (or cov-

---

24. Commenting on these observations of mine, David Hollenbach, who read the first draft of this article, wrote the following in a personal communication, dated January 23, 1992: "...I think that your appeal for a really serious encounter with the Word of God in the development of social teaching is eloquent. Your observation about the use of scripture in the LE is very accurate. In fact the situation is even worse than you suggest. For example, in the section on the spirituality of work, LE gives a list of various professions mentioned in the Bible, with citations in the footnotes. Where it mentions the example of 'builder' as a form of work expressing a Christian spirituality in no. 26, the footnote reference is to Gen. 11:3...the building of the tower of Babel! I discuss some of this in chapter 3 of *Justice, Peace and Human Rights.*"

enant), is continuously exchanged between Yahweh and those victimized by the worshipers of Mammon.

A Catholic social teaching as a comprehensive but concrete response to the social question in Asia is now being formulated within the Basic Human Communities and other grassroots action groups that "actualize" God's Word in their historical context and also in the liberation struggle of various oppressed groups such as the Dalits fighting Indian casteism within and outside the Church,[25] or the *Minjung* of Korea,[26] and most of all, hopefully, women (Dalits of the Dalits and the Minjung of the Minjung, the ochlos of the ochlos).[27]

A Catholic social teaching that is biblically rooted reveals its submissive role of service before the Word of God in at least two ways. The first is that the community announcing it is self-critical; second, it consists of concrete options. These are the qualities that are conspicuously absent in the Catholic social teaching emanating from the See of Rome.

In the encyclicals, the Catholic social teaching is marred not only by a triumphalistic affirmation of its perennially valid teachings (MM 219–20; LE 3) but also by a conspicuous lack of autocriticism. We already referred to the absence of any reference to the colonialist connection of the early missions, which was widely recognized on the occasion of the controversial fifth-century celebration of Latin America's exploitation/evangelization.[28]

Moreover, should not the Roman church, in humble submission to God's forgiving Word, acknowledge and correct its own failings in the matter of social justice, dutifully pointed out by those who have been at the receiving end of it — e.g., acting as judge, accuser, and witness in the case of theologians who are eventually silenced, the injustices to the local churches in the appointment of bishops, the canonically recognized feudal structure within which episcopal authority is permitted to be exercised, the overreaction to criticism leveled against its bureaucracy, and most of all, its intransigent patriarchalism? Are these not a counterwitness to the grandiose declarations of the same church on the imperatives of justice?

The Western Patriarchate's unwillingness to confess its own sinfulness makes its version of Catholic social teaching suspect from a biblical point of view. Listen, for instance, to the ironic words with which it condemns "totalitarianism...in its Marxist-Leninist form" on the grounds that it

25. Cf. M. E. Prabhakar (ed.), *Towards a Dalit Theology*, Delhi, ISPCK, 1989.

26. Cf. *Minjung Theology. People as Subjects of History*, Orbis Books, Maryknoll, N.Y., 1981, revised edition, 1983.

27. Cf. V. Fabella and Sun Ai Lee Park (eds.), *We Dare to Dream*, Asian Women's Centre for Culture and Theology, Hong Kong, 1989.

28. L. Boff and V. Elizondo (eds.), "1492–1992: The Voice of the Victims," *Concilium*, 1990/6. See also E. Galeano, *Open Veins of Latin America: Five Centuries of the Pillage of a Continent*, Monthly Review Press, New York, 1973.

maintains that some people, by virtue of a deeper knowledge of the laws of the development of society or through membership of a particular class or through contact with deeper sources of the collective consciousness, are exempt from error and therefore arrogate to themselves the exercise of absolute power (CA 44).

We Roman Catholics have an eerie feeling that when we look through the broken mirror of Communist foibles, we see our own disfigured countenance. How salutary if that looking glass could help us acknowledge that we are no more immune to the effects of original sin than those outside the church! Would that such self-criticism and humble confession of our own sinfulness accompany also our strong condemnations of societies that restrict our "religious liberty" (EN 39)! For the non-Christians know how "free" they were when Christianity was the religion of the conqueror! If only we knew who we are in the light of God's Word, then our words, meant to teach God's ways to the nations, would serve that living Word rather than substitute for it!

The second weakness, as we noted, is that the Catholic social teaching of the papacy is busy with perennially valid general principles but lacks concreteness. The scriptures on the other hand educate us to discern here and now what God demands from us in a concrete historical situation. The scriptures present a definite option, as the authentic spiritual traditions of the church teach us (for example, in the "election" in the Ignatian Exercises). Since social praxis is part of the church's own spirituality, a social option has to be an integral element of it.

Vatican diplomacy which adapts doctrinal principles to concrete contexts in the face of ever-changing political climates has its own value in so far as the Vatican is a state constituting, according to its own canonical understanding, a moral person which is distinguishable from the other two moral persons: the Holy See and the Catholic Church.[29] Using its canonical language, we would plead that the Primatial See act as an independent moral person vis-à-vis the Vatican, and speak with a voice articulating the demands of God's Word in prophetic concreteness. John XXIII, Paul VI, and John Paul II have already indulged in certain independent acts — independent of that other moral person, the Vatican — though they were merely symbolic gestures restricted to the field of ecumenism. Similar acts in the socioethical field would require greater prophetic courage.

Such at least is also the way Basic Human Communities and other Christian cells of the Asian church act in given situations, allowing each viewpoint to emerge as expressions of a standpoint in the light of God's Word which is never vague or abstract.[30]

---

29. This thesis is valiantly defended in Jude M. T. Okolo, *The Holy See: A Moral Person. The Juridical Nature of the Holy See in the Light of the Present Code of Canon Law*, Rome, 1990.

30. The political theology that comes out of Basic Human Communities such as the Chris-

What we observed when discussing the Asian perspective is equally valid here: our task in Asia is not simply to fill in the missing (biblical) perspective so as to adapt Roman Catholic social teaching to our local context; rather, our task is to allow the Catholic social teaching of the Basic Human Communities to reach the rank and file of the local churches in Asia for their critical reception; in this way, Catholic social teaching can become a pan-Asian vision.

Such a process did occur in some way at BISA VII (the seventh session of the Bishops' Institute for Social Action) — BISA being "the Catholic social teaching Forum," so to speak, of the FABC (the Federation of Asian Bishops' Conferences). It was a very faint reflection of the precedent set by CELAM at Medellín.

TOWARD A CONVERGENCE OF THE THREE PERSPECTIVES

A convergence of the Third World, the Asian, and the biblical perspectives seems to characterize the Catholic social teaching that is seminally present in the praxis and reflections of the Basic Human Communities. In this context, I can only offer a few indications of what this means.

The basic fallacy in the Catholic social teaching of the Western Patriarchate in general (not exclusively of the Popes, but of other exponents such as Moltmann, Maritain, Vlastos, etc.) is the *non sequitur* which vitiates the three syllogisms central to the whole doctrine. I would formulate these three syllogisms as follows:

1. Image of God, therefore human dignity.

2. Human dignity, therefore human rights.

3. Rights, therefore duties.

The first syllogism is usually "proved" by appealing to the scriptures in the traditional manner of the scholastics. The basic text cited here is Gen. 1:26–31, which, however, does not support the first syllogism. The context of this text is the creation story narrated as a rescue operation analogous to the Exodus. It clearly equates God's likeness in man and woman with their cooption into God's own creative and liberative responsibility over the earth and its inhabitants. Adam and Eve are a corporate personality in whom all of us are called to be coresponsible with God for creation and human society. What is revealed in Gen. 1:26–31 is not the syllogism "*Imago Dei*=human dignity," as claimed in human rights theology, but the equation

---

tian Workers' Fellowship (CWF), Devasarana illustrates how concrete options made in the light of historical events and scriptural revelation generate a prophetic vision that is not reducible to abstract universals. Cf. *Sri Lanka Workers' Theology*, CWF, Colombo, 1977, and also the sociotheological postures adopted by *Christian Worker*, the Quarterly of the CWF.

"*Imago Dei*=our collective responsibility shared with God for the whole of creation." The overarching idea, in other words, is not so much our dignity but our accountability: "rule over" would mean take charge, be responsible!

It is this coresponsibility model (i.e., the covenant idea) that must permeate any Catholic social teaching; it alone must form the basis of any discourse on rights, not vice versa. It is not in terms of "rights" that the Book of Genesis describes the first violation of interhuman justice, but as a spurning of the obligation to be one's "brother's [and sister's] keeper" (Gen. 4:9). Besides, if rights are derived from human dignity, how could infrahuman creatures have any rights? The ecological question, in this case, does not find a consistent answer. But in the covenant model, we are coresponsible with God for the whole of creation, including humans.

Therefore it goes without saying that the second syllogism, too, finds no support in this biblical text. What is worse, the logic in that syllogism is not valid. Here, I find Ping-Cheung Lo persuasive in his refutation of that inference.[31] He also argues for two more "moral commodities" needed to make this world a warmer place to live in: (a) the principle of distributive justice based on basic needs and (b) the duty (or virtue) of love; the central issue is not one of first establishing *rights,* but of recognizing the prior realities and claims of *justice and love.*[32] In other words, our discourse on rights should begin not with talk of individual dignity calling for rights but with a covenant that calls us to love and makes us accountable.

Coming now to the third syllogism, we find it saddled with the incongruities issuing from the previous two. The rights discourse which Pope John XXIII introduces in a big way into Catholic social teaching has mixed up the question of duties derivable from rights (PT 28). It states, for example, that my right to my life implies *my* duty (rather than that of others) to protect my life(!), as Sieghart avers.[33] But Lo rightly points out that if I have such economic rights — that is a right to my own well-being — it implies, at the most, a duty for others not to mistreat me; it does not impose a duty on others to provide me with what I need to live well.[34] "Our worldview is such that all human beings are bound together by an implicit contract to help each other."[35] And this brings us back to the covenant idea of coresponsibility.

Could legal rights or the universal acceptance of the UN Charter serve as this contract? I think the Western Patriarchate, working within a secularized (dechurched) world, seems to think in this direction. The appeal to natural law and reason (with its already indicated logical flaws and superficial bibli-

---

31. Ping-Cheung Lo, "Are There Economic Rights?" *The Thomist,* 52/4, October 1988, 703–7.
32. Ibid., 715–16.
33. Paul Sieghart, "Christianity and Human Rights," *The Month,* February 1989, 48.
34. Lo, 714.
35. Ibid., 717.

cal props) are resorted to in Catholic social teaching presumably to reach out to the secular societies of the West.

But Asians still enjoy a cosmic religiosity beneath and behind the technocratic intrusions of the secular West and the "Communist" East. The West's discourse on human rights, moreover, has brought here its individualism (my right, our right, etc.) among various groups (e.g., industrial workers who fight for their rights in factories, with scant regard for the peasants and farmers who are victims of industrial complexes). Hence we should welcome Lo's conclusion that "the biblical idea of a covenant (with God and other human beings)" would provide the much-needed language about obligations.[36]

So language about obligations and duties needs to be watched carefully and critically, for it can easily be manipulated by the powerful in their own favor. Examples of this kind of manipulation are plentiful: the way codes of caste duties have been formulated by Brahmins or the way males in a patriarchal society have spelled out women's responsibilities or the role of the laity envisaged in the church's laws. Hence two things need to be clarified.

First, in any authentic Catholic social teaching, the UN's "rights Covenant" must be subsumed within the framework of the biblical covenant (partnership between Yahweh and the weak), wherein the obligations of the strong toward the weak constitute the proper divine order.[37] This, no doubt, is a paradigm shift in the West's way of thinking. Hollenbach seems to be calling for the same paradigm shift when he calls for "three strategic moral principles" to be incorporated into the discourse on rights: the priority of the needs of the poor over the wants of the rich; the freedom of the dominated over the liberty of the powerful; and the participation of the marginalized groups over the preservation of the order that excludes them.[38]

Secondly, an authentic Catholic social teaching must develop the obligations language within a socialist framework wherein a substantive, i.e., a participatory (rather than a merely representative or liberal) form of democracy is in operation. The obligations language serves the positive need for a socialist spirituality to be inculcated through proper education whereas the rights formula serves the negative need to set limits in a society of frail humans.

Regrettably, these two functions are interchanged in the current theology of social justice, in that the rights language has become the medium of "education for justice," while the obligations corresponding to rights are treated as legal limits to be imposed especially on the state. This order must be reversed.

The first function, as I pointed out in part II, is more consonant with the

36. Ibid. Lo doubts whether this idea has ever been proposed before. But liberation theology in the Third World has been doing precisely this in opposition to the West's language about rights. See chapter 10.
37. Cf. Sieghart, 49.
38. Hollenbach, *Claims,* 204.

third-world context and the religio-cultural ethos of Asia. The difficulties encountered by the Roman church to hold a religious discourse with the secular West do not exist here in Asia, unless, of course, the secular West is allowed to pursue its colonialist plans for a technocratic invasion of our continent. Therefore the language of the Roman Catholic social teaching which speaks from and to the secular West seems out of place in Asia.

If the Western Patriarchate is embarrassed by this biblical discourse of a God who rises in revolt with the oppressed victims of Mammon — that is to say, is embarrassed by the liberation language that the God of the Third World speaks — then it has forfeited its mission to proclaim what is unique in the Christian/biblical revelation: Jesus as the irrevocable defense pact between God and the poor.[39]

By contrast, Asian liberation theology in its various forms (Dalit theology, Minjung theology, womanist theology, third-world theology) contains a germinal Catholic social teaching which at least *attempts* to announce, through word and witness, this vision of Yahweh's Reign. The language of the Biblical Covenant which it employs makes sense within (even the nontheistic) oriental cultures because of its *cosmic,* i.e., sacral and ecological (as opposed to a *secular,* i.e., rational and profane) worldview, and because this worldview envisages a species of "religious socialism" which is reflected in the Asian religious propensity to derive our human dignity from our human obligations toward the cosmos and to *all* its beings.[40] This seems to be the Catholic social teaching paradigm almost taken for granted in some Basic Human Communities in Asia.

---

39. Pieris, *ATL,* 120ff.
40. Pieris, *Love Meets Wisdom,* Orbis Books, Maryknoll, N.Y., 1988, 14–16.

9

Faith Communities and Communalism

CONTEXT OF THE DISCUSSION

It is not by faith alone that faith communities live. As in other communities, their internal cohesion depends on many nonreligious factors such as economic solidarity, ethnic identity, language affinity, or political inclinations. Lest we overlook these nonreligious factors, which usually contribute to both community harmony and community conflicts, we do well to begin with a sociologist's descriptive definition of a community:

> Community implies having something in common. In the early use of the word it meant having goods in common. Those who live in a community have overriding economic interests which are the same or complementary. They work together and also play and pray together. Their common interest in things gives them a common interest in each other. They quarrel with each other but are never indifferent to each other. They form a group of people who meet frequently face-to-face, although this may mean they end up back-to-back. That people in such an area of social life turn their backs on each other is not a matter of chance. In a community even conflict may be a form of co-operation.[1]

In closely knit faith communities which constitute the larger national community, there seem to be "overriding economic interests" that bind their members together. In conflicts between faith communities or "communalism" (as such conflicts are known in our part of the globe), the aforementioned

First published in *East Asian Pastoral Review,* Nos. 3 and 4, 1989, 294–310. In its first version, it was a paper read at the Vidyajyoti Golden Jubilee Seminar on Faith Communities and Communalism held in November 1987, in Delhi, India.

1. Ronald Frankenberg, *Communities in Britain*, Penguin Books, 1966, quoted in Elizabeth J. Wilkins, *An Introduction to Sociology*, London, 1970, 314.

nonreligious "interests" must be identified. Though somewhat exaggerated, the observation that "their common interest in things gives them a common interest in each other" is not altogether far-fetched.

On the other hand, not every conflict is destructive, as Frankenberg remarks in the passage above: "In a community, even conflict may be a form of co-operation." Indeed it is conflicts that often help communities discover the nonreligious basis of communalism and discern the path to communal harmony. For example, in the sixties, Buddhists and Christians in Sri Lanka were involved in a bitter conflict which was advertised abroad as a Buddhist persecution of the church; advertised, obviously, by those who wished to collect money for Christian schools. The clash of "economic interest" that triggered this conflict was the disproportionately large percentage of schools owned by a Christian minority — a mere 7 percent of the national community — which meant that the Buddhist majority (64 percent) had to depend on such schools for a job-oriented education. Through these schools, the church exerted enormous sociopolitical influence on the nation. Yet she perceived the proposed schools take-over as a violation of a right rather than as the removal of a colonially acquired privilege. Eventually it was precisely the nationalization of the schools — an immediate fruit of Buddhist agitation — that forced at least a section of the church to acknowledge, albeit reluctantly, the harsh truth about the economic basis of her religious claims. In fact, as a result of this acknowledgment, there ensued in the next decade a relatively calm climate of dialogue and cooperation between the two communities. The conflict was not altogether destructive.

It is noteworthy that in this instance both parties appealed to their respective faiths as the basis of their struggle. The Catholic church in particular argued for a "Catholic atmosphere" in their schools, as a *sine qua non* for the preservation of the faith of Christian children, whereas the Buddhist suspicion was that schools owned and administered by the church had become an effective tool of Christian proselytism. Yet the socialists who forged the policy of the nationalization of schools claimed to have quite another motive: to provide a better distribution of opportunities for education by wresting the monopoly of higher education from the privileged class, a class with which the church had (and still has) strong links.

In a report read at a South Asian Regional Meeting of the Justice and Peace Commissions of the subcontinent, the Indian delegate made a similar observation regarding communal conflicts elsewhere in the region:

> It is in this context of the use of religion as a rallying point that communal riots are situated by many studies as competition for scarce resources and for political or economic leadership. The *Moradabad* riots, for example, have to be viewed mainly as competition between the traditional merchants who happened to be Hindus and monopolized the trade in the artisanal products manufactured mainly by Muslims and

the new Muslim merchants who tried to take control of these goods. In this context, both the Hindu and Muslim leaders used religion to rally their followers around themselves. Similarly, the *Bhiwandi* riots have to be situated within the context of the textile policy and the struggle for political leadership. Also the *Punjab* situation is viewed by many as an aftermath of the Green Revolution and the change in the relationship between the Jat landlords who happen to be Sikhs and the grain merchants who happen to be Hindus. The opposition of the RSS to the Chotanagpur tribals has to be seen not necessarily as an RSS-Christian conflict but mainly as an effort of the traditional vested interests, (the middlemen, the forest contractors, the landlords and others), to continue controlling the life of the tribals who are waking up to their rights as human beings. Similar questions can be asked about the *Nilackal Cross* controversy, the *Kanyakumari* communal riots and many other incidents concerning Christians.[2]

Hence we can hardly dispute Asghar Ali Engineer's contention that "religion is not the root cause of communal conflict; [religion] is rather a powerful instrument in the hands of those *interests* which seek to play their game through it."[3] It is an "unsociological approach" that has driven the secularists and rationalists to blame communalism on religion, argues Engineer, and warns that religious violence which is triggered by sectarian and doctrinal conflicts within a religion should not be confused with communal violence sparked by a struggle for political power and economic resources between the elites of the two faith communities.[4]

This analysis of communalism raises two related questions. If religious identity of the members of a given community serves as the focal point of communal hostilities that emerge from a clash of socioeconomic interests (more specifically, class interests), does it not mean that a religion entangled in communalism has put itself at the service of an *ideology* which makes that religion the motivational drive behind communal confrontations? This question is based on Marx's pejorative notion of ideology as "corruption of reason by interest." For any faith that marshals religious reasons to fortify unfair economic advantages or class interests of a given community is ideologically corrupt. We shall take up this question in the latter part of this paper, for it presupposes another equally significant question which must engage our attention first.

If religion lends itself to be a tool of ideology (or make ideology its tool), as will be shown later when studying the first question, is it not because

---

2. Report furnished by Peace and Justice Commission, New Delhi, 1987; pro manuscripto, courtesy SEDEC, Sri Lanka.

3. Asghar Ali Engineer, *On Developing Theory of Communal Riots*, Institute of Islamic Studies, Bombay, 1984, 2–3.

4. Ibid., 3.

religion, by its very nature, constitutes a psychosocietal inclination to maintain and develop the material and spiritual well-being of a community or to restore it when inimical forces (e.g., economic and other interests of another faith community) tend to diminish or destroy or even usurp it? In other words is not religion more than merely the ultimate concern of individuals seeking psychospiritual emancipation here and hereafter? Does not religion also mobilize the sociopolitical aspiration of its adherents toward building a community of equality, freedom, and fellowship?

The implication of this question is that religion is primordially a liberation movement, if seen in the context of its origin, though it does tend subsequently to be domesticated by various ideologies; that is to say, religion ever remains potentially liberative, even if actually subservient to nonliberative structures. We wish, therefore, to frame our discussion of communalism in terms of this observation. We shall first focus on religions (or faiths) as languages of liberation, i.e., languages of the Spirit (pp. 100–102). Then we shall see that this is so because a religion is the Memory of an Absolute Future, i.e., a memory of a Total Liberation (pp. 103–5). Finally we shall discuss the ideological contamination of that memory and the communalism that results from it (pp. 105–12).

FAITHS AS LANGUAGES OF THE SPIRIT

Language is not taken here in the nominalistic sense. It is not a mere medium for communicating an otherwise unrevealed event. Rather it is the *specificity* of a self-communicative event — presuming all events to be self-communicative. Language then is the specificity which is inseparable from that (self-communicative) event. In other words, language is the specific mode of "experiencing" reality — in this case liberation — and *consequently,* also the specific mode of "expressing" it. In this sense, each faith is a language of liberation, that is to say, a specific way in which the Spirit speaks and executes its redemptive intention in a given cosmic/human context.

The "Spirit" could be understood as the human or the divine Spirit. In nontheistic religions such as Buddhism, Jainism, or Taoism, it stands for the *given* human potentiality to speak, seek, and find total human liberation. But in the biblical and some other theistic traditions, this potentiality for the Absolute tends to be regarded as the divine Spirit operating immanently in the human person. In either case the diversity of tongues which defines the activity of the Spirit argues for religious pluralism, which, in turn, reveals, among other things, the following seven principles relating to the presence or absence of communalism among faith communities:

(1) No single language can claim to be better than another. We are not denying the fact that one faith community is more conversant with its own language than with another's and that it can both experience and express Reality/liberation better through its own idiom than through another. This

is natural and even necessary, since language is a particular community's specific mode of perceiving and pursuing the "truth that liberates." On that very account this specificity should not be mistaken for superiority. Such a mistake amounts to a sin against the Spirit and consequently a cause of communalism.

(2) One language does not mix with another. Neither *syncretism* (an amalgam of disparate elements) nor even a *synthesis* (a tertium quid absorbing the identity of each component) can ever be a safeguard against or a remedy for communalism. Rather, the practical way to interreligious harmony is a mutually corrective complementarity through reciprocal proexistence of religions, that is to say "symbiosis." This is how each language of the Spirit evolves further, thanks to its living contact with another, thus breaking through the language barrier. This is what we usually refer to as *inculturation*.

(3) No language should be allowed to absorb another. From what has been said so far, it follows that the worst form of communalism originates from a community that regards its own faith language as universal and makes use of economic and other advantages which it already possesses to convert that conviction into a sociocultural reality. This is what we normally refer to as proselytism, a chauvinistic reduction of religious pluralism to the uniform idiom of one's own religion.

(4) The rules of one language game should not be imposed on another. A very subtle way of neutralizing the specificity of another's language is to use it within the structure of one's own language, thereby distorting both languages. My contention is that each language game should be played according to its own rules. For instance, a Christian asking a Buddhist how nirvana could be realized without divine grace is as ridiculous as a hockey player asking a tennis player how many goals he shot in the tennis court. The Muslims asking themselves how ignorance (*avidya*) could be "sin" in Vedantic Hinduism can be compared to a cricketer trying to figure out why in the football court it is a fault to send the ball outside the boundary. The Buddhist or the Hindu who explains Christ's miracles in terms of psychic powers acquired through meditative trances is also guilty of a conceptual proselytism, that is to say, a forced conversion of one linguistic system into another.

(5) The specificity of each language implies an element of "chosenness." Specificity implies an election by the Spirit. The conviction of being specially chosen is therefore a justifiable feature in the self-understanding of any faith community. After all, a religion without a privileged identity will have no continuity, nor will it ever have its own contribution to offer to the other religious traditions. It is precisely this element of chosenness that accounts for the fact that even in its genuinely dialogical encounter with other religions, each faith invariably indulges in an evangelistic self-proclamation in the presence of other religionists. Every faith is *obliged* to manifest its specificity.

However, this irreducible distinctiveness, which each religion can trace back to its remote origins either through a revelation or to a discovery by its founder(s), lends itself to be ideologically vitiated into a form of pathological messianism: "my language alone is perfect; all must speak it" (i.e., mine is the only true religion; all must embrace it). This is a false conclusion and it violates principles 1 and 3 enunciated above. Rather, in keeping with these principles, the chosenness of one's own religion should be confronted with the equally inviolable specificity of other religions. Hence, all ideologies that corrupt the "election" concept into a species of religious bigotry should be detected wherever they are found as will be demonstrated below (pp. 105–12).

(6) True catholicity and ecumenicity consist of one's ability to speak or at least understand languages other than one's own. If the Spirit is a source of diversity in tongues, its activity alone ensures unity among them. To understand what the other speaks and to make the other understand one's own tongue is a pentecostal grace. In other words, as far as Christians are concerned (here I am employing an exclusively Christian idiom), the obligation to learn the basics of other religions, that is to say, the obligation to understand the language that the Spirit speaks in a neighboring faith community, is not an academic luxury of scholars but a pneumatological imperative constituting the ecclesial nature of the Christian *koinonia,* the implication being that no language, not even the Christian one, exhausts the totality of the Spirit's liberative self-communication.

(7) A faith language cannot be learned without a "communicatio in sacris." The obligation to learn the other's language contains within itself the obligation to acquire some knowledge of that religion's "originating experience" whose specificity constitutes that language. Following Raimon Panikkar's suggestion, we distinguish this originating experience (e.g., the exodus, Jesus' passover, the Buddha's nirvana, etc.) which gave birth to and specified the unique character of each religion, from the collective memory of that experience (oral and written traditions, myths and their ritual reenactments, lifestyle embodying moral convictions, and kerygmatic communications of the primordial experience through prophets, seers, sages, and witness communities). This collective memory is itself continually subjected to philosophical, cultural, and even ideological interpretations, which constitute the third level at which the primordial experience is communicated. Most of us dialogue at this third level, where the distance from the originating experience is greatest. It follows then that in order to understand the faith language of a neighboring community, that is to say to enter into its originating experience, one must necessarily consult the collective memory of that community; and this is what we mean by *communicatio in sacris.*

This brings us to the next step of our inquiry, namely, that religion, as a sociological phenomenon encountered in daily life, is essentially a memory of a "Total Liberation" or more precisely a memory of an "Absolute Future."

FAITH AS A MEMORY OF A FUTURE

The dream of a realizable future is at the root of every religious experience. When the Buddha abandoned the security and the comfort of his own palace and took to the forest in search of the Liberating Truth, he was actually renouncing the present order in favor of another that was yet to come. In a religious quest of this kind, it is the certitude of the future (in Christian terminology, "hope") that makes the renunciation of the present an adventurously joyful event. One does not suffer in giving up present securities when a longed-for future becomes the only certainty in one's life. This is what accounts for people's perseverance in painful and protracted struggles for liberation.

When, therefore, the Absolute Future is in some way experienced as the present moment of liberation (exodus, nirvana, Easter, etc.), it is *remembered* in terms of the categories of the past and communicated in a sociocultural idiom continuous with those categories. Thus the memory of that Future is stored up in a communication system further "specified," culturally interpreted, through the media available from the past. In other words, a set of kerygmatic formulas, liturgical enactments, moral codes, and lifestyles, often also a corpus of written material, not to mention oral traditions and social practices, begin to evolve as the media by which the Absolute Future (experienced by the founder or the founding community) is collectively remembered and thus passed on to successive generations. Hence, as a social phenomenon, religion is none other than this collective memory of an Absolute Future, a memory of Total Liberation which is realizable, at least partially, here and now.

This collective memory, in so far as it employs the categories of the past to anticipate the Absolute Future as the present moment of liberation, cannot operate in an ideological vacuum. The Absolute Future remains a pure illusion, an ever-receding horizon, an opium that renders us insensitive to the present disorder, unless that Future is translated into a visible social structure which is invariably dictated by an existing ideology.

The strength and weakness of an ideology lies in its quasi-dogmatic clarity with regard to the worldview and the social program it advocates. The strength and weakness of religion, on the other hand, is precisely the absence of such clarity, for, the Absolute Future defies dogmatic definition. The only clarity that religion seems to possess is with regard to the direction or the orientation toward the Absolute Future, something that ideology must appropriate in order to be liberative. But an ideology which is not continually corrected by that religious orientation toward the Absolute Future tends invariably to suffer from its "clarity" and consequently inflict its dogmas and clear-cut programs on the masses ruthlessly. If a religion has become dogmatic, it is because ideology with its cult of absolute clarity has overtaken it!

To sum up, religion without ideology is utopian; ideology without religion is despotic. Their dialectical collaboration, therefore, is imperative in our march toward total liberation. It is religion that decides which ideology is helpful or when exactly a helpful ideology has become harmful. Religion progresses toward the goals that define its essence — the Absolute Future — by continuous disengagement from ideological captivity.

For instance, when the Buddha envisaged the Sangha (the monastic community he founded) as an ideal society of greedless men and women, he also wished to offer it to humankind as a universally realizable future. But that Future could not have been "remembered" in history if it had not been embodied in the ideological categories of his time. We know that there were two ideologies available to him, namely, monarchy (emergent feudalism) and tribal socialism (a political model employed by his own clan). He clearly opted for the latter presumably because it seemed more consonant with the Future he wished to anticipate and register as a collective memory for our constant consultation. And yet, in course of time, as Buddhism began to spread under royal patronage in different parts of Asia, the Sangha — a good part of them — quite inadvertently absorbed the feudalist ideology as its theoretical and organizational framework. Only a constant recourse to the memory of that Future can redeem Asian Buddhism from this nonliberative ideology and reroot itself in the religious socialism of rural Asia.[5] Christianity is not without parallels in this matter. They are too well known to be listed here.

Another ideology — in itself neutral — that seems to embody our religious vision in Asia is nationalism which, however, *can* degenerate into ethnocentricism. The latter term is a euphemistic way of referring to communalism, a theory and praxis of placing the interests of one's own group as the criterion for evaluating the worth and, therefore, the rights of other groups. But nationalism (or patriotism) arises initially as a need to articulate one's own group identity against another group that is already ethnocentric. But nationalism can also outlive its purpose and fall into that same ethnocentricism which it aims to combat in others. In fact "decolonization" of many Asian countries has shown that religions (Buddhism in Sri Lanka, Burma, and Indo-China; Hinduism in India), operating through a nationalistic ideology to liberate the people from the colonizer's oppressive ethnocentricism, have themselves been exposed to the danger of communalism.

Iran is a unique example. The economic exploitation of Iran by the Western powers before and, especially, during the regime of the late shah, alienated especially the middle class (clergy and the bazaars), who associated Islam with their own national identity. This class, therefore, was able to

---

5. See my *ATL*, 43–45.

initiate and perpetuate the great revolution now associated with Khomeini.[6]
Should not nationalism (or any ideology for that matter), like the proverbial
banana tree, die once it has produced its fruit, to allow the next shoot to
sprout? Does not the Iranian situation suggest this? Does this not hold true
of Buddhism in Sri Lanka or Hinduism in India, where nationalism, which
was once liberative, has later made religion ethnocentric?

What we wish to underscore here is that religion, as the memory of the
future, has within itself a built-in mechanism to discern the enslaving and
emancipating character of ideologies and to disengage itself from even a
helpful ideology when it has ceased to be helpful. This process of discernment is not new to any religion. Each religion has developed, within its own
spiritual tradition, a *psychospiritual* process of discernment especially with
regard to an individual's unconscious self-deception. But Marx, who detected
the nature of (an enslaving) ideology as corruption of reason by interest, has
given us a sociological tool for discerning how economic interests of classes
corrupt faith communities to the extent of making them adduce religious reasons to justify a communal bias which has actually arisen from a struggle for
economic control. The few examples cited at the beginning of this paper are
amply confirmative of this observation. Religions are required, therefore, to
enlarge their traditional understanding of religious "discernment" by developing also a sociological perception of the ideology that stands at the root
of communalism.

This leads to a rather disturbing question. How can religion discern and
discard its enslaving ideological assumptions by consulting the (collective)
memory of the Future, if that Memory itself is ideologically contaminated?
In other words, are our sources of revelation, our scriptures, and our sacred
traditions, already vitiated by ideology? In which case, how can they be a
means of discernment?

IDEOLOGICAL CONTAMINATION OF MEMORY
AS A SOURCE OF COMMUNALISM

Feminists have already alerted us Christians, almost a century ago, that
our bible is infected with sexism. The patriarchal ideology has vitiated the
scriptures and the sacred traditions of practically all religions. The process of
purification, however, has begun and is now gaining momentum.

Here we are concerned with communalism, of which the worst manifestation is racism. Racism adds to communalism a further characteristic: that of
regarding other racial groups as humanly inferior and therefore not entitled
to rights and privileges associated with one's own group identity.

To put it bluntly, we wish to ask whether the bible and the church are

6. Ervand Abrahamian, "Iran's Turbaned Revolution," Review Article, *Third World Quarterly,* 8/1, January 1986, 341ff.

racist, whether the word of God and the tradition of the people of God are a religious or theological justification of racism.

The question was raised by Yves Congar more than thirty-five years ago.[7] His answer was an apologetic "no." Appreciating, as I do, his inclination to be autocritical, I wish to sum up his argument and offer the light of Vatican II's teachings on religious liberty. The six *norms* that I draw out of this critique are valuable for our assessment of communalism in South Asia.

In the first place he offers us a useful distinction between the *Jews* as a "race" and *Israel* as a "people." The bible, he insists, speaks of a chosen people and not of a chosen race. Moreover Israel was not chosen over and above other peoples, but for other peoples. There was no racial superiority intended in this election (Norm 1).

Congar concedes, at the same time, that some Jews did tend to present themselves as a race chosen for itself rather than a people for others. This was a racist self-understanding of the Jews and not the biblical view of the covenanted Israel. In fact, Congar suggests that this was a racist response on the part of the Jews after they had themselves been racially discriminated against. It is good to note here that an initial racist offensive against an ethnic minority or an ethnic majority can evoke in either of them a racist defensiveness. Such deviations must be seen according to the principle of cause and effect (Norm 2).

Coming back to Congar's thesis, we find him citing chapter and verse from the bible to prove the universalism of biblical faith. Then he goes on to defend certain biblical passages which have racist overtones. Here is a crucial passage from his thesis, which is at once enlightening and disturbing:

> However, there are also in the scriptures commandments to destroy members of other races in general. In the thousand years that elapsed between the command to destroy the Medianites, Canaanites etc., of which we read in the Book of Numbers, Deuteronomy or Joshua, and the somewhat similar measures taken by Ezra after the exile, much blood was shed. But it is clear and indeed stated explicitly in the Bible, that strange peoples and strange wives were never condemned to destruction as a result of race discrimination as such, but were so condemned because of the danger or the actual commission of idolatry. Nor was it racial prejudice, as such, which inspired so many of the measures for the protection of the line of the patriarchs and later that of Judah but rather the desire to remain pure for the carrying out of God's purpose which was, from Abraham to Mary through Judah and David, to fulfill the Messianic hope.

---

7. Yves M.-J. Congar, O.P., *The Catholic Church and the Race Question*, UNESCO, 1958, 28–38.

The theory that just because a people or race holds to a "false faith," they lose their human right to live is a religious justification of racism or a racist interpretation of religion (Norm 3). To me, therefore, Congar's is a dangerous explanation of the bible, and I presume that as one of the pioneer theologians of this century who inspired the church with a breadth of vision, he would today revise this apologia for Israel.

Not everything Israel did was right or divinely revealed. Hence we ask: Should we, as does Congar, argue that the bible was not racist because Israel destroyed members of other races purely on the ground that the people of these races adhered to a false religion? Should we not, rather, see in the behavior of this sinful but elected people — *populus justus simul ac peccator* — a dangerous compromise between racism and religion? Is not this racist ideology to be repudiated in terms of the axial theme of the biblical revelation which is one of "justice to the oppressed people" whatever religion they belong to (Norm 4)? This is the "canon within the canon" of the Jewish bible, which must be employed as a critique of ideologies (sexism, racism) that distort the Word of God. The same norm applies to the anti-Semitism of the New Testament!

The belief that those of another religion have no right to live because they are not human enough cannot reflect true religion; yet religion has been adduced as the actual motive for such racist persecution. In fact the church lived this heresy more than once in her own members. Congar cites, in this connection, the papal Bull *Pastorale Officium* (1538), where Paul III tried to persuade the Euro-Christian colonizers that the "Indians of the West and the South" are "human beings" (sic!) even prior to embracing Christianity and therefore, they should not be deprived of their freedom and their possessions and they should not be treated like animals that have no reason or reduced to slavery on the pretext that they have no part in the Catholic faith! This papal appeal not to regard non-European races as nonhuman because they were non-Christian indicates that the contrary belief prevailed among Christians.

However, the Christian violence against the Jews, the wars against the Moors, the crusade against Islam, the wars of the Teutonic Knights against the Balts and Slavs, and the struggle against the Turks, argues Congar, were not racist, as they were based "on the spiritual place of faith." But we ask, as Congar would today: Does religion justify crusading against other races in the name of religion? If it does, then such a religion justifies racism.

Finally, he makes a very significant observation about the Euro-Christian beginnings of racism. The first signs of national sentiments in Europe began to appear from the Carolingian times onward, while the church (of Rome), with its dubious notion of "universalism," did unfortunately suppress the ethnic particularities of other (national) churches; this provoked schisms that were therefore inevitably colored by national and racist sentiments. Examples listed by Congar (e.g., German nationalism in the Lutheran revolt against Rome) prove this sad experience. Was it not true that these ethnocentric tendencies were partially a reaction to an ethnocentric church that imposed its own national Christianity as a universal church (Norm 5)?

It is in the light of this false universalism (my church is the universal church, my culture is the universal culture, my language is the universal language, etc.) that we agree with Congar when he declares, with the support of some historians, that it was with the mercantile-missionary expansion of European presence (in short, with colonialism) that "racism" really came to settle down. We should not, therefore, gloss over the historical links between colonization and racism (Norm 6). We must reflect more on this connection.

In fact the Aryan myth of the Nazis began two thousand years before the Christian Era, with the Aryan invasion of India. These colonizers, like all colonizers, regarded themselves as the civilizers of the allegedly inferior races whom they could conquer purely because of their superior physical prowess rather than through cultural excellence. The Dravidian and tribal people of India were referred to disparagingly as *dasyus* by the Aryans. It is the Aryan colonizers who created the worst form of racism sanctioned by religion: *the caste* system, as two Buddhist scholars have noted.[8]

It is interesting to note, as these authors have averred, how the Aryans looked down upon the natives of India not merely for the color of the skin (*varna,* soon to be a synonym for caste) but also because their religion seemed so different from (i.e., inferior to) the Vedic version of it! Thus in the Vedas, the Sacred Writ of the Hindus, colonizers would sing to their God: "They do not perform sacrifice (such as we do); they do not believe in anything (that we believe in). *They are not human beings!* O destroyer of foes! *Kill them.* Destroy the Dasa race."[9] As late as in the last century, we hear Lord Acton resorting to the "Aryan heresy" in articulating the colonial imperialism of Christianity. He also refers to the mutual dependence of religion and culture among the orientals and advises the colonizer to civilize the Indians by destroying their (inferior) religion, and the missionaries to Christianize the Indians by destroying their (inferior) culture.[10]

When we turn to Buddhism, we are relieved to note that its scriptures are free of any ideology which denies other people's right to life on grounds of false beliefs. But wherever nationalism became the Buddhist ideology and Buddhism the national religion, such a tendency did manifest itself, though rarely. I want to give special attention to this matter, since it has become a much discussed theme in the context of the ethnic conflict in Sri Lanka. Let me begin with Thailand.

The "Thai Buddhist nationalism" summed up in the slogan "For King, religion and country" has led a prominent Buddhist monk, as late as in the 1970s, to declare "publicly and often, that whoever kills the opponents of the

---

8. G. P. Malalasekera and K. N. Jayatilleke, *Buddhism and the Race Question,* UNESCO, 1958, 30–31.

9. Ṛg Veda, X.22.8. quoted in Malalasekera and Jayatilleke, 30.

10. Malalasekera and Jayatilleke, 19–20, quoting *The Rambler,* May 1882, 534.

nation, religion and monarchy is not killing persons for 'such bestial types are not complete persons'; killing them is 'to kill the Devil (Mara); this is the duty of all Thais'."[11] Here, those not sympathetic toward the "Thai Buddhist State" are considered infrahuman creatures who can be so treated. This rabid species of nationalism, a clear departure from the Buddhist scriptural approach to religion and state,[12] is not generally articulated in such crude terms by the majority of the Thai people. But it can manifest itself when actual or presumed threats from the outside create the need to assert Thai Buddhist identity (see Norm 2 above).

The *Mahavamsa*, the Pali chronicle of the Sinhala people, records that already in the second century B.C.E., a war of liberation initiated by the Sinhala King (Dutthagamini) against a Tamil King (Elara) had caused the death of countless Tamils. But the dying Dutthagamini's remorse-stricken conscience is said to have been palliated by the thought — suggested, of course, by his monastic counselors — that after all these war victims were really not human beings, that is to say, not Buddhists; that only one of them was fully human because he had taken both the "triple refuge" and the "five precepts" of Buddhism, while another was half-human, as he had taken only the triple refuge. Dutthagamini's crime in such a massive war was thus reduced to a convenient minimum: the killing of no more than "one and a half human beings!"

This episode, obviously, is apocryphal, and is perhaps a later interpolation. But it does reflect an extreme and rare form of nationalism verging on racism sanctioned by religion. The South Indian invasions of the island, which generated among the Sinhala people an obsessive fear of extinction, is largely responsible for their distrust of Tamils (see Norm 2). The "Politics of Plunder," as this policy of aggression is called by some historians, had the Sinhala Kingdom as its frequent victim.[13] These, and especially the Magha invasion — the most atrocious of South Indian attacks on the island — have left an unhealed and unhealing wound in the nationalist conscience of Sinhala Buddhists, just as the July 1983 holocaust has left in the Tamil Memory a lasting hatred for the Sinhala people.

The Sinhala Buddhists have perpetuated their "dangerous memory" of Tamil aggression in their historiography. The events that led to the formation of this historiography have been carefully analyzed by Heinz Bechert, and his thesis has been condensed by Trevour Ling:

> Dutthagamini's liberation of Sri Lanka from Tamil domination during the latter half of the second century B.C. resulted in a wave of

---

11. Trevour Ling, "Kingship and Nationalism in Pali Buddhism," in Philip Denwood and Alexander Pratigorsky, *Buddhist Studies Ancient and Modern,* Curzon Press, London, 1983, 69.

12. See Ling, 65ff.

13. G. W. Spencer, "The Politics of Plunder: The Cholas in the Eleventh Century Ceylon," *Journal of Asian Studies,* XXXV/3, 405ff.

Sinhalese nationalist fervor which was given literary expression in the island's earliest known ideological historiography. This was the *Sīhala-aṭṭha-kathā-Mahāvaṃsa*, composed from various earlier sources which included *Purāṇa*-style genealogies and lineages of the sasana. It was in the form of verses in Pali and a prose text in old Sinhalese. This work, now lost, was made use of in the composition of the *Dīpavaṃsa* more than four centuries later (at some date just after 302 C.E.), a work of similar ideological purpose. Two other sources used by the compiler of the *Dīpavaṃsa* were the chronicles of the *Anuradhapura-Mahavihara* and *Abhayagiri-vihara*. The occasion for the composition of the *Dīpavaṃsa* was the glorious war of liberation from Tamil overlordship carried out by Vattagamini. The ideology which the *Dīpavaṃsa* served to reinforce was one which had been formulated in the earlier period of nationalistic enthusiasm, that is, "the inseparable connection of national identity and Buddhist religion" which, for the bhikkus, "resulted in a feeling of responsibility towards nation and state," a responsibility which they met by means of their historical writing, which magnified the notion of the Sinhalese Buddhist state, and in doing so contributed towards its preservation through the centuries. "Historiography thus effected long-term political results."[14]

Obviously the monk-historiographers have faithfully recorded the verdict of the Sinhala masses, when they refer to their own Sinhala hero by the popular nickname *Dutta-Gamini* (Wicked Gamini) and his Tamil rival as *Dharmistha Elara* (the Just Elara). This indicates that the Sinhala masses have never been racist! But in the course of time, the Dutthagamini-Elara war became mythicized into an ideological symbol of a later Sinhala-Tamil rivalry, which, in its most recent form, began only in the 1930s as a power struggle between the elite groups of each community. The masses, both Tamil and Sinhalese, have on the whole been free of racism.

Yet, the Sinhala Buddhist people have always entertained a profoundly rooted conviction of being — if I may use a familiar expression — "a chosen but persecuted people." Why chosen? Why persecuted?

The Sinhala people — later also the race — were the only people (race) in the subcontinent who (according to their self-understanding) conserved the ancient Indian Prakritic Buddhism, which gradually disappeared from India, and later even from among the Tamils of Sri Lanka. The Sinhalese alone saved it from extinction. The legends that associate the person of the Buddha with the history of this people and their country are a symbolic declaration of this "election." Besides, the chosen people actually became the chosen race because all other ethnic and racial groups abandoned the "Urbuddhismus" of Asia, which therefore became the sole possession of one race, one language,

---

14. Ling, 66, citing Bechert.

one culture (see Norm 1 above). This inseparable link between (the closest approximation to the original Prakritic) Buddhism and the Sinhala race is what constitutes the "Sinhala-Buddhist identity." Destroy the race, and you destroy the religion; and vice versa.

"Chosenness" becomes defensive when the element of "persecution" enters the picture. Internal strifes and external threats made the Sinhalese feel that they were an endangered race. Dravidian invasions from South India and later the "Christian colonialism" of the West instilled a xenophobia in their hearts. Tamils were seen in terms of their alleged "South Indian connections" and the Christians as those who served "Western" interests. Moreover, in the British period, the English-educated elite of Tamil and Christian minorities monopolized the civil administration of the country, while the majority race was underrepresented. The chosen race was a persecuted race!

Hence, the Buddhist revival, which began in the 1750s on a positive note as a renewal from within Buddhism, gathered momentum in the succeeding centuries as an anticolonial movement and took an antiminority turn by the 1950s when the Sinhala Buddhists staged a dramatic comeback into the politico-social arena of the country. The slogans such as "Sinhala only" or "Sinhala Buddhism" and the movement they represented were as pointedly anti-Tamil as they were anti-Christian. The Sinhala-Buddhist identity, which consists of many historically justifiable ingredients, as I have indicated elsewhere,[15] now assumed an aggressive form after centuries of suppression.

Regrettably, however, many important facts of history could not fit into the narrow framework of the Sinhala nationalist ideology. The first was that the Tamil and Christian masses were as much the victims of the colonial system as were the Sinhala-Buddhist peasants. In other words, the fact that the elite among the Sinhala-Buddhists have been as much a part of the oppressive system as their Tamil and Christian counterparts was not evident to the nationalist ideologies that ignored the class structure of their society. Finally, the obvious historical fact that the Sri Lankan Tamils were as much heirs to the land as the Sinhalese and that the former were driven to the South Indian shores in recent times only when their civic rights were threatened in the aftermath of the Sinhala revival was not discernible within the restricted perspectives of nationalism. Needless to say, in course of time Buddhism itself was diminished by the ideology it assumed.

This species of defensive nationalism reinforced the age-old perception of Sri Lanka as the Sinhala-Buddhist land, a blending of two concepts: the *Dharmadvipa* ("island of Buddhism") and *Sinhala-dvipa* ("the island of the Sinhalese" which in fact is what *Ceylon* literally means). The monks on the whole have consistently refused to grant that Sri Lanka is a multiracial, multireligious, and multilingual country. We might add in passing that the ar-

---

15. See A. Pieris, "Buddhist Political Visioning in Sri Lanka," Part III, *Towards the Sovereignty of the People*, CCA, Singapore, 1983, 140–43.

rival of the Indian Army, which evokes a "dangerous memory" in the Sinhala consciousness (memory of so many instances in the past when Indian soldiers came to "help" Sinhala kings and stayed back on the island to generate fear and disunity), only helped to harden and even militarize Sinhala-Buddhist nationalism.

CONCLUSION

The people who can truly purify a religion of communalist ideology are not the theologians or the exegetes or the religion hierarchs, but only the conscientized victims of that ideology. For only the oppressed know and speak the language of liberation, the language of the spirit, the language of true religion.

In the case of Buddhist nationalism, its extreme and violent forms cannot be removed merely by Buddhist reformers appealing to the pure doctrine of the *Tripataka*. Rather it is the victims of that ideology — some through political means, others militantly and even intransigently, who have made the point clear, just as Buddhist nationalism earlier assumed an aggressive stubbornness only as a reaction to other ethnocentric groups that threatened the Sinhala Buddhist identity through their colonial and mercantile domination (see Norm 6 above).

Even where the scriptures are concerned, the ideological purification is the task of the victims of that ideology. It is conscienticized women who have begun to cleanse the bible and the Christian Church of its patriarchalism. But in so doing, they appeal to the "canon within the canon" (Norm 4), that is to say the originating experience which gave birth to the bible: the election of the oppressed as God's partners in the liberation of all. Biblical sexism is being corrected by feminists who recognize their own oppressed character and engage themselves in a self-emancipatory struggle, as befits those "chosen" to be God's "co-redemptive" partners.

This holds good for racism, too. It is not religion in the abstract that can redeem its sacred writings from ideological presuppositions. It is the religion of those oppressed by the racist ideology that can cleanse the collective memory of a faith community — as the black Christians have been doing through consistently dignified affirmation of their chosenness.

10

Human Rights Language and Liberation Theology

The cloud of misunderstandings that has followed recent discussions on liberation theology in the official churches of the West cannot be dispelled fully without acknowledging that the two parties have been using two different theological languages, albeit within the same orthodox Christian tradition. Many first-world theologians committed to social justice follow their pastoral magisterium in using human rights language as a theological discourse whose primary addressees could only be wielders of power and the accumulators of wealth, including the governments of rich nations. Third-world theologians on the contrary take human liberation as God's specific language primarily addressed to and easily understood by the poor and the oppressed.

Unfortunately, this language difference is not respected. Thus certain first-world theologians tend to universalize and absolutize their paradigm, unmindful of its contextual particularity and ideological limitations. On the other hand, many activists and some theologians in Asia fail to make a "paradigm shift" when perusing the plethora of literature issued by human rights advocates from the West and liberationists from Latin America.

This essay is occasioned by this confusion. I would like to offer some reflections which I hope will promote a fruitful conversation with my colleagues both in the First and Third Worlds. With their critical response, I hope to arrive at some clarity, some day.

First published in Marc Ellis and Otto Maduro (eds.), *The Future of Liberation Theology: Essays in Honor of Gustavo Gutiérrez,* Orbis Books, Maryknoll, N.Y., 1989, 299–310; later republished in a paperback book also edited by Ellis and Maduro, *Expanding the View,* Orbis Books, Maryknoll, N.Y., 1990, 157–70.

THE HUMAN RIGHTS TRADITION: A BRIEF HISTORY

In origin and development, "the human rights tradition represents an almost Anglo-American phenomenon."[1] This movement reached its climax with the incorporation of the so-called Bill of Rights in the American Constitution. It was, undoubtedly, the most revolutionary event in constitutional history. The very idea that certain individual human rights should be invested with constitutional inviolability is said to be unprecedented in the history of political thought.

However, "without prior English development, *individual* rights could scarcely have developed to the level they did in the American law," says the American constitutional historian Bernard Schwartz.[2] Historians find the Magna Carta of medieval England (1215) a convenient starting point. The next convenient milestone would be the Petition of Rights (1628), followed by the English Bill of Rights (1689), which gave its name (not its contents, which were too meager) to the American Bill of Rights. For brevity's sake I omit here other intermediary events.

The Magna Carta was a monarchical document saturated with the language, the concerns, and the spirit of feudalism. It merely conceded certain rights to the barons in return for obedience. It was a royal bargain with feudal chiefs rather than the outcome of a common people's struggle for liberation. In 1965, the English playwright Arden wrote a play commemorating the seven hundred and fiftieth anniversary for this great charter and aptly titled it *Lefthanded Liberty!* Yet in some of its provisions, the phrase "any baron" seems to alternate with the more generic term *liber homo* (any free human). Such elements give these provisions an elasticity that the monarch may never have intended but that later human rights advocates found helpful. Thus the charter happened to contain "the germ of the root principal that there are *individual* rights that the state — sovereign though it is — may not infringe."[3] The Petition of Rights of 1628, in contrast to the Magna Carta, was not a feudal claim of privileges. The battle for parliament's independence from the crown was the context that gave rise to it. It started with the Protestation of 1621, and this struggle climaxed with the fundamental rights of English persons becoming a positive law by way of a parliamentary enactment. Herein, "the almost superstitious reverence Englishmen feel for their law" and their "legal conservatism" were made use of by a group of "common lawyers who rewrote the history on parliamentary lines in the House of

---

1. William R. Garrett, "Religion, Law and the Human Condition," *Sociological Analysis*, 47, 1987, 21.

2. Bernard Schwartz, *The Great Rights of Mankind: A History of the American Bill of Rights*, Oxford University Press, New York, 1977), 25; italics added. This is the source I follow in writing this section of the paper.

3. Ibid., 3.

Commons who built up the body of rights and precedents alleged to be the immemorial heritage of the English People."[4]

History showed that superstitious reverence for the law was not effective even among the English. A law-enforcing machinery was never built into the parliamentary acts, which therefore remained merely declaratory. Charles I, the king of England, did not bow down to this act of parliament. It is the crown that ruled. Thus the achievements of 1628 were null and void from a constitutional point of view — a lesson the Americans learned to avoid in their declaration of rights.

It is true that the so-called levelers — religiously motivated radicals in the parliament — tried to bring a more fundamental concept to the fore: (what we might anachronistically call) people power as the primordial source of authority to which even the parliament should bow and which alone can countercheck any form of arbitrary government. Their document — the Agreement of the People — after a series of debilitating amendments, fell finally to the fate of all previously written declarations. It had no binding power. The whole exercise was no more than a mere dream. And there was Oliver Cromwell, who would not let it become history.

Only against this background can one recognize the revolutionary character of the English Bill of Rights of 1689. King James II had dissolved the parliament in July 1688 and five months later fled from the kingdom after throwing the Great Seal (the symbol of constitutional continuity) into the Thames. In the absence of a crown to legitimize a new parliament, a body of responsible persons assembled in an unprecedented manner to form a self-legitimized parliament and offered the throne to William and Mary, subject to the conditions laid down in the Declaration of Rights — better known as the Bill of Rights — which passed as a regular act of legislature. According to the bill, the parliament was to be freely elected by the people and was to enjoy complete freedom of speech uninhibited by court or crown. The revolutionary nature of this document has earned it the title: the Second Great Charter.

Yet, the English Bill of Rights, Schwartz warns us, was rudimentary compared to the American one; for the former contained much fewer rights than the latter, and was ever subject to interference by the legislature.[5] The American Bill of Rights, with its more complete list of individual rights, succeeded in immunizing itself constitutionally against any such interventions from successive governments or court, whereas the English Bill of Rights did not have enforcement machinery built into it. Thus, the American Constitution has immortalized the inviolability of the human person in terms of a series of basic, "God-given" rights.

---

4. Ibid., 9, referring to Pocock, *The Ancient Contribution and the Feudal Law,* 1957, 48.
5. Ibid., 1.

THE "SECULAR-HUMANIST" AND "RELIGIOUS-CHRISTIAN" CONTRIBUTIONS TO THE HUMAN RIGHTS THEORY

The major influential factor in the development of the American Bill of Rights is what Garrett calls the "human rights tradition," which, he complains, is too easily confused with something quite different, the "natural rights tradition," as he names it. In presenting Garrett's valuable insights,[6] I am compelled to make use of his terminology. In the subtitle above, I have called these respectively, the religious-Christian and the secular-humanist streams of the one human rights tradition. I shall switch back to this terminology after developing Garrett's insights.

The movement that climaxed in the American Bill of Rights could be viewed as a confluence of these two streams of thought. But a sociological analysis has convinced Garrett that the natural rights tradition is overrated as an influential factor; the human rights tradition was largely responsible for the development of the American ideal.

Garrett's analysis of the natural rights tradition begins with medieval Europe. The immediate context was the phenomenon of papal absolutism, which tried to absorb secular monarchy into its own hierocratic structure. The defensive posture adopted against this papal hierocracy was twofold. The first reaction produced the "dualist school." It revived the ancient "divine right theory of monarchy." It saw both pope and king as two independent recipients of divinely conferred authority in their respective spheres of competence, spiritual and temporal. The other defensive posture was adopted by the "natural law school" with leanings toward the Aristotelian theory of nature and society, a theory gaining currency among intellectuals. It looked for a secular basis for political authority, to free it from all ecclesiastical interference. Their appeal to "reason" and "natural law" was equally aimed at the dualist school in order to safeguard humans from the dangerous consequences of the state claiming God-given, inalienable rights over persons.

There was, in the course of time, a *populist view* emerging from these conflicts. In the divine-rights school, this meant that God grants political power to the king through the people. This same theory, applied to the papacy, resulted in the "conciliar movement." In the natural-law school, however, it took the guise of a social-contract theory, which received a more sophisticated articulation later in Locke and Rousseau.

The human rights tradition differs from this European ancestor on many counts, Garrett maintains. First of all, it was an exclusively *Anglo-American* phenomenon. In England, it was associated with the lower-status levelers (as opposed to the Independent Party, which was made up of the gentry); in America, the main actors were Roger Williams and Isaac Backus, with the

---

6. Garrett, "Religion, Law and the Human Condition."

Baptists and Separatist Congregationists serving as the social carriers of the tradition.

Secondly, it was essentially a *religious* movement in neat contrast with the natural rights tradition, which had a clearly marked secular thrust. It was particularly nurtured by a piety expressed through a variant form of Calvinistic theology. To me the implication seems to be that, here, the inviolability of human rights is based on a "divine origin," so to say, and this makes the individual the only "sacred" component of any given society.

The third difference, in Garrett's list, is that the human rights tradition was a *populist* movement, both in England and in America; its social carriers were the "lower-status folk" and its ideologues, for the most part, were not even university trained. This explains the widespread support that the American Bill of Rights received from the common folk in the colonial states. The natural law theory, by contrast, was a movement of intellectual theoreticians, from the lawyers and philosophers of medieval Europe to the founding fathers of the American dream.

Finally, the motivational points of departure are diametrically different in the two traditions. The natural-law theory aimed at protecting the sovereignty of the secular state from ecclesiastical encroachments, whereas the human rights tradition, especially in America, began as an effort at safeguarding the "freedom of conscience" — that is, *individual religious liberty* — against a secular state trying to impose an official religion (in this case, the Church of England) on the consciences of all. In fact, almost all the rights (speech, assembly, property, and the like) were derived from this basic concern for religious liberty.

Obviously, the two movements, despite radical differences, converged in the demand for total separation of church and state. The "experts" who framed the Bill of Rights and the "people" who greeted it with an overwhelming approval arrived at the same conclusion from divergent points of departure. The two streams have joined together to form one river: a great human rights tradition. It has flowed beyond the confines of the North American continent, thanks to the UN Charter of Rights.

HUMAN RIGHTS LANGUAGE AS A PARADIGM
OF HUMAN FREEDOM IN WESTERN CHRISTIANITY

The human rights movement — I am now shifting back to my original nomenclature, leaving that of Garrett — has been shown to be a convergence of a secular-humanistic and a religious-Christian tradition. In appropriating this tradition as a theological discourse on social ethics, both the radical reformed movements in Protestantism and the progressive thinkers, including popes, within Roman Catholicism were merely yielding to an ancient Christian propensity to combine humanistic reason with biblical revelation — that is, a universally valid and transcendent *theoria* with the concrete tenets of Christian faith.[7]

In fact, according to one scholar, " 'human rights' is not a biblical construct;" it is one of the "nonscriptural categories" that, in confrontation with the scriptures, give rise to the Christian discourse on human freedom. "The biblical communities functioned with a conception of rights, though they would not recognize the terminology of natural rights or human rights," for the manner of stating universal human claims in terms of a comprehensive and compartmentalized list of rights reflects a typically Western mode of perception.[8]

The human rights movement is, in other words, the West's specific contribution to the understanding of human liberation. It is the spiritual nucleus of Western culture, the quintessence of the Western ethos. It is the ideological substance of which the Western democratic order of social relationships is constructed. Understandably, therefore, all political organs of the West — both governments and the NGOs (non-governmental organizations) — could hardly perceive, proclaim, or promote the values of freedom and fellowship except in terms of individual rights.

The Western church absorbed this language in the very process of contributing to its development and to its eventual refinement. This church gave the human rights tradition a solid biblical basis, by rooting it in the revealed doctrines of creation (every human is created to the *image of God*) and redemption (every human is an object of God's redemptive intervention through Jesus' *atonement*). Accordingly, it is God who has *gratuitously* endowed each individual with a transcendental and inviolable dignity so that the "autonomy," which the secular-humanist tradition (of the natural rights school) claimed for the human person in terms of inalienable rights, takes the guise of a "theonomy" in the social teachings of the church.[9]

With this type of theological reasoning, the Western Patriarchate tried to refine the rights tradition in three interconnected areas. The first revolves around the phenomenon of "individualism," which has now come to be the hallmark of Western spirituality and is the most pernicious outcome of enthroning individuals where formerly kings ruled with divine authority. A team of North American sociologists, led by Robert N. Bellah, have monitored "the classical polarities," or more bluntly, the contradictions of American individualism; they describe one of them as "the commitment to the equal right to dignity of every individual combined with an effort to justify inequality of reward, which, when extreme, may deprive people

---

7. Max L. Stackhouse, "Public Theology, Human Rights and Mission," *Human Rights and the Global Mission of the Church*, Boston Theological Institute, 1985, New York, 13–21.

8. Stephen Charles Mott, "The Contribution of the Bible to Human Rights," in *Human Rights and the Global Mission*, 5–6.

9. Ibid., 7–8.

of dignity."[10] The church resolved this contradiction — theoretically, of course — by presenting the human person not as a self-enclosed unit dissociated from the human community, but as a dynamic member of society intrinsically related to other members of that society even in the exercise of rights.

The other inadequacy springs from the close ideological nexus that this individualism maintains with the liberal democratic tradition of the West. The church consciously steered clear of both individualism and collectivism by distancing itself from this liberal democratic ideology — as well as from Marxism, which rightly insisted on the inseparability of personal freedom and social solidarity.[11] Although it repudiated Marxism, the church was certainly influenced by the Marxist critique of liberal democracy and of individualism, and also by the Marxist thesis that economic freedom is basic to political freedom.[12]

Thus we come to an important distinction that Christianity's "public theology" introduced: the distinction between *economic* rights (to food, shelter, work, health care, and social security), which Marxists lay stress on, and *civil* and *political* rights, which are the foundation of Western democracies (freedom of speech, belief, assembly, association, habeas corpus, due process, etc.).[13] By affirming them both as inseparable and as equally essential, the Catholic social teachings in particular have not only critically accepted the Marxist distinction, but also partially appropriated its critique of the Western tradition of rights — namely, that this tradition concentrated on political rights, without basing them on the foundation of economic rights. This is the third area in which the Christian rights theory corrected the human rights tradition of the West. The most powerful statement of recent times in this direction is the North American Catholic Bishops' Pastoral, "Economic Justice for All."[14]

As Hollenbach has argued, social doctrine still continues to be developed in the Christian community and he has himself suggested "three strategic moral priorities" that all liberation theologians would endorse, though from quite another perspective: (1) the needs of the poor take priority over the wants of the rich; (2) the freedom of the dominated takes priority over the liberty of the powerful; and (3) the participation of marginalized groups takes priority over the preservation of an order that excludes them.[15] This is indeed a revolutionary stance; if carried out, it would overturn the ideological

---

10. Robert N. Bellah, et al., *Habits of the Heart: Individualism and Commitment in American Life*, University of California Press, Berkeley, 1985, 150. See also 28–35.

11. David Hollenbach, *Claims in Conflict*, 21.

12. Ibid., 83.

13. David Hollenbach, "Both Bread and Freedom: The Interconnection of Economics and Political Rights in Recent Catholic Teaching," in *Human Rights and Global Mission*, 31–34.

14. "Economic Justice for All: Catholic Social Teaching and the U.S. Economy," *Origins*, NC Documentary Service, 16/24 1986, 410–55.

15. Hollenbach, *Claims*, 204.

framework of Western democracy. For such a shift in policy implies a radical structural change that goes beyond the "social democratic conception with the welfare role of the state" as advocated by other Western theologians who wish to combine the "freedom rights" of liberal democracy with "benefit rights" of socialist systems.[16] Liberation theologians too are asking for a structural change in opposition to the Western democratic model. Can the Catholic human rights tradition, even in the radical form envisaged by Hollenbach, meet the demands of liberation in Latin America and other third-world countries? This is the issue I take up next.

THE LIBERATIONIST THESIS VERSUS THE HUMAN RIGHTS DISCOURSE OF THE WESTERN CHURCH

I was intrigued to note that there is no entry on *individualism* in the extensive index of the Hollenbach classic — *Claims in Conflict* — which is the most comprehensive and critical exposition of the Western church's social teachings. I was equally intrigued to note Hollenbach's own surprise at the absence of any entry on *human dignity* or on *human rights* in the extensive index of the Gutiérrez classic, *A Theology of Liberation*. As Hollenbach suspects, the liberation theologians abandon the rights language because that language, in their minds, is associated with the "static and individualistic notions of the human person."[17] These omissions in Gutiérrez and Hollenbach are a clear index of the language difference between the first-world theologians concerned with human rights and the third-world theologians steeped in the liberation struggle.

The two paradigms differ primarily in the way they combine the secular-humanist and the biblical-religious components of their respective theologies. In the West, the human rights theologians not only ground their natural rights language in the doctrine of the human person extracted from the Bible, but they also employ that language as a critique of the Bible, detecting the absence of scriptural references to many rights, such as freedom of religion or freedom for women, even though such rights could eventually be deduced from the biblical principle of "the dignity of the human person."[18]

In the liberationist paradigm, the secular-humanist contribution comes from socialism, which includes the reality, if not also the ideology, of class struggle,[19] whereas the biblical foundation it seeks for its praxis is not a transcendental principle extracted from the Bible — as is the case with human rights theology and Catholic social teaching — but the *foundational experience* that forms the axis of biblical revelation: the election of the oppressed

---

16. Mott, "The Contribution," 11.
17. Hollenbach, *Claims,* 179, n. 2.
18. Mott, "The Contribution," 11.
19. Gustavo Gutiérrez, *A Theology of Liberation*, Orbis Books, Maryknoll, N.Y., 1973, 26, 27, 30, 90, 91, 111–13, 274.

as God's covenant partners in a liberation praxis initiated by God. This foundational experience is the "canon within the canon," which is the critical principle that judges the biblical contents internally. Unlike the human rights theologians who "critique" the Bible from a human rights perspective, the liberation theologians subject the whole corpus of Catholic social teachings and human rights theology to this critical principle of biblical revelation (and would perhaps question the right of anyone other than the oppressed to speak of human rights!).

Thus, according to Gutiérrez, even *Populorum Progressio* seems to be entrenched in the Western developmental model of human growth. The first comprehensive use of the language of liberation, according to Gutiérrez, is found in the message delivered by eighteen third-world bishops in response to that same papal encyclical; this language resonated in Medellín and became its central and all-pervasive concern.[20] And, if Puebla was a step back from Medellín, was it not because the Catholic social doctrine permeated by the human rights language was trying to regain lost ground in Latin America?

I find it quite significant that Gutiérrez not only makes absolutely no use of the human rights language, as Hollenbach has already noted (see above), but has also ignored the whole human rights movement, as if to say that it has no relevance in a Third World context. This movement, as I described it in the earlier part of this chapter, began from an elitist concern, not from the underside of history, as is made evident by the nature of the major events that contributed to that movement from the Magna Carta to the American Bill of Rights.

The implication of this observation is not that the human rights movement has no global message but that it constitutes the mood and method of a theology that continues to speak from elitist and conceptual heights and presupposes Western democratic structures, whereas liberation theology is born out of a struggle that in some way is directed against those same democratic systems and their domination in the Third World. Hence, one cannot gloss over the contextual, ideological, and methodological discrepancies that separate the two theologies.

This may be why the American Bill of Rights has not merited even an adverse comment in the pages of *A Theology of Liberation*. The United States of America is mentioned there only about three times; and in each instance, this gigantic paragon of Western democracy is made to appear as the major hindrance to Latin America's sovereignty! In Gutiérrez's references to liberative initiatives recorded in history, the great American independence struggle is conspicuously absent, whereas the French Revolution (which was, in fact, inspired by it) receives an honorable mention, as does also Russia's October Revolution. He counts these two among "the great revolutions," which, at least tentatively, "wrested the political decisions from the hands of the

---

20. Ibid., 33–35.

elite" — that is, from the "elite" who claimed they alone were "destined" to rule.[21]

Does this mean that for Gutiérrez the American Revolution is not really an example of a "people's struggle," since it had not "wrested the political decisions from the hands of the elite?" I would hardly contest the fact that the social carriers of the human rights movement (the religious, populist stream of it) in the British colonies of North America were the lower-status folk, as Garrett (quoted above) has cogently argued. But in the wider context of colonization and in the perspective of liberation theology, it was a battle of the elite and not a *colonized* people's struggle against the domination of *colonists;* indeed it was a case of colonists wrenching for themselves the "privileges, liberties, and immunities" of English citizens — that is to say, the colonists' acquisition of "Englishmen's rights."[22] The colonists were (European) "emigrants" who — according to John Adams's boast — were the real "author, inventor, and discoverer" of American independence.[23] Neither the black slaves imported by the colonists nor the colonized natives marginalized by the same colonists were the immediate beneficiaries of this revolution. Thus, to the liberationist it is not a meaningful model, even though it remains the crown and glory of the human rights movement in the Western democratic tradition.

And yet, no liberationist would deny the fact that the human rights language is the West's own indigenous way of communicating the gospel of justice to the rich and the powerful. Nor would third-world theology stand in the way of Western theologians forging a third way between capitalism and communism, even if that might sound abstract.[24] For that abstract idea has crystallized into a "public theology," which has, at least *theoretically,* corrected three major defects of the human rights tradition — individualism, liberalism, and neglect of economic rights, as indicated above.

Although one would be skeptical about a mere idea generating a change in social structures, one would still respect the great philosophical tradition of Western theology that succeeds in clarifying issues conceptually. Hence when the church appropriates radical ideas as basic to Christian message, it is bound to express them with prophetic clarity. When this happens, a sigh of relief is heard in third-world churches. That certainly was the case when the news of the U.S. Bishops' Pastoral Letter on Economic Justice reached our ears in Asia! Though reformist and tame,[25] it is the only language the Western church knows to speak.

---

21. Ibid., 46; see also 28.

22. Schwartz, *The Great Rights,* 27.

23. Ibid., 29.

24. But Hollenbach ("Both Bread and Freedom," 32) argues against the accusation that human rights theology is abstract.

25. See Leonardo and Clodovis Boff, "Good News of US Bishops' Economic Pastoral and Bad News Left Unmentioned," *National Catholic Reporter,* 23/28, August 28, 1987.

As long as this theology speaks to the rich and the powerful in the West and in the westernized enclaves of the Third World, it is within its own right, and the only enemy it will encounter will be political liberalists and Christian fundamentalists. But it draws the wrath of liberation theologians only when it becomes a tool at the service of the Western church's ecclesiastical colonialism in the poor countries. This is the concluding argument of my analysis.

HUMAN RIGHTS THEOLOGY: A TOOL OF ECCLESIASTICAL IMPERIALISM IN THE THIRD WORLD?

Ecclesiastical imperialism is the tendency of one church to regard all others as its extensions and to make its "particular" theology "universally" obligatory. This is but an ecclesiastical version of the ethnocentric dogma: "my culture is the modern universal culture." The human rights theology as it appears in the social teachings of the Western churches tends to be used in this manner.

Eminent and much respected theologians join the official church in this campaign, though not with bad faith. They criticize black, feminist, Latin American, and Afro-Asian theologies for being mere particularized perspectives claiming to be theologically comprehensive, but quite firmly believe that the human rights theology is based on transcendent universal principles valid for all situations.[26]

Although this universal principle ("dignity of the human person") is invoked against all other theologies, the ultimate criterion, I suspect, is a matter of *ideological* preference.[27] The human rights theology is ideologically tied to the Western democratic model of social organization; but liberation theology accepts critically the socialist paradigm, which includes also the *reality* of class struggle. Therefore, at the root of the argument against liberation theology there is more ideology than theology at work.

The history of the Roman Church's social doctrine can be cited in support of this. For instance, two Popes who laid the foundation for the church's social doctrine, Leo XIII and Pius XI, may have had many biblical, theological, and philosophical arguments against the Marxist theory of class struggle. But, as Hollenbach observes with scholarly candor, their rejection of the class struggle idea, in reality, came from "the close links between the church and the classes which were the targets of Marxist attacks." Moreover, "these links prevented the papal tradition from understanding important aspects of the Marxist social analysis."[28] It is such ideological links that prevent both the pastoral and the academic magisterium of the Western patriarchate from re-

---

26. E.g. Stackhouse, "Public Theology," 17.
27. Here I understand ideology as I have defined it in chap. 3 of my *ATL*.
28. Hollenbach, *Claims,* 52.

specting the particularity and therefore the validity of another local church's theology.

The Vatican's reaction to liberation theology cannot be explained otherwise, as a careful analysis of this excerpt from Ratzinger illustrates. Explaining his own congregation's second instruction on liberation theology, he says:

> Catholic social teaching accordingly knows no utopia but it does develop models of the best possible organization of human affairs in a given historical situation. It, therefore, rejects the myth of revolution and seeks the way of reform, which itself does not entirely exclude violent resistance in extreme situations, but protests against the recognition of revolution as a *deus ex machina* from which the new man and new society are one day inexplicably to proceed.[29]

Here one local theology posing itself as "Catholic social teaching" refuses to recognize that the shift ("conversion") from sin to grace in the order of relationships is a qualitative jump; the "myth of revolution" is rejected in favor of "reform." But the scripture scholar and Ratzinger's collaborator in *Communio*, Norbert Lohfink, has inquired into the biblical roots of liberation theology and come to quite another conclusion: The revealed notion of liberation is distinguished from the nonbiblical approaches to social questions (1) by treating the poor as *the* poor — that is, a people oppressed as a class — and therefore also (2) by advocating a radical opting out of that oppressive system rather than resorting to reformist solutions, and (3) by believing that God takes full responsibility for this radical change[30] (notwithstanding Ratzinger's suspicion of *deus ex machina*). In that case, "Catholic social teaching," which, according to Ratzinger, is called to "develop models of best possible organizations of human affairs in a given historical situation," cannot a priori preclude a third-world church's option for a social system that conforms to the biblical principle enunciated above, or impose on a third-world church the West's reformist model of human rights theology as if it were "catholic" (universal). That would be an ideological imposition of the Western church on other churches.

It is this "ecclesiastical imperialism" that liberation theologians wish to combat, and not necessarily the human rights theory or the public theology that appropriates it, or the ideologically ambivalent principle about social models that Ratzinger enunciates.

The most critical area of conflict therefore revolves around the ideologically interpreted biblical foundations of the two theologies. Liberation theology does not speak of a "transcendental principle" extracted from the

29. Joseph Ratzinger, "Freedom and Liberation: Anthropological Vision of the Instruction 'Libertatis Conscientia,'" *Communio*, 14, Spring 1987, 70.

30. Norbert Lohfink, *Das Judische im Christentum. Die verlorene Dimension*, Herder, Berkeley, 1987), 132–34.

Bible and then "applied" to concrete situations. Such a manner of theologizing is indigenous to a Christian culture that employs philosophy as *ancilla theologiae*. Liberation theology does not explain reality philosophically; it analyzes reality sociologically. Hence, it is not concerned about a "transcendent principle" (biblical or otherwise) that "integrates" various conceptual dyads such as "individual and society," "economic freedoms and political freedoms," "liberal democracy's anticollectivism and Marxist socialism's anti-individualism." Liberation theology is engaged, not with reconciling conceptual opposites, but with resolving social contradictions between the classes.

Let me, therefore, reiterate that the biblical basis of liberation theology is not a transcendent principle derived from reason and confirmed by the Bible but the very foundational experience that gave birth to the Bible, a canon within the canon, by which the Bible itself is criticized internally. This foundational experience is the election of the oppressed class as God's equal partners in the common mission of creating a new order of love, a mission that can be shared by anyone who becomes one with God by being one with the oppressed class. Each concrete situation that reveals a new class of oppressed — women, minorities, and the like — is a continuation of this biblical revelation.

In this scheme, the transcendental and universal principle of "the dignity of the human person" fades away into a larger picture: God's election of the oppressed as God's cocreators of the kingdom and God's co-redeemers of the world; it is not an ontological status conferred by grace through creation and atonement, as in human rights theology, but an elevation of the oppressed, insofar as they are a class, to the status of God's covenantal partners engaged in God's project of liberation. Thus in partnering God, they have learned to use the language that the rich and the powerful refuse to speak or understand, the language of liberation, the language that God speaks through Jesus.

The human rights language is a language that may persuade the rich and the powerful to share their riches and power with the poor and thus gain access to this covenantal partnership. In that sense, the human rights language has a pedagogical value for liberation theology. In fact, Sobrino seems to use it as a means of communicating this message to the churches of the rich nations.[31]

When the secular humanist tradition, which discovered the role of the proletariat in the construction of the new order, coincides with the aforementioned biblical foundation of liberation theology, the "socialism" appears to be "the best possible organization of human affairs in the given historical situation" — to use Ratzinger's words. The past failures in the socialist experiments could serve as guideposts rather than as barriers, if only the powerful ideological blocs of either side do not interfere — as Russia did in Vietnam

---

31. Jon Sobrino, "The Divine Character of Human Rights," *COELI Quarterly* (Brussels) 43 (Fall 1987), 19–27.

and the USA in Nicaragua — and if the church does not side with one or the other of these superpowers, but allows the "foundational experience" of the Bible to become a social reality.

This theology is diametrically different from the human rights theology of the Western Patriarchate, but considers itself as a local theology, which, however, confronts the human rights theology on ideological grounds. This healthy confrontation is neutralized when the human rights theology parades itself as the universal theology valid for all churches. The tendency in the West to extol Christian institutions that follow the human rights tradition,[32] and to condemn missionaries who opt for the liberation schema,[33] contributes to this species of ecclesiastical imperialism. Most episcopal peace and justice commissions in Asia stay at the human rights level; if they change their stance in favor of the liberation scheme, they could be disbanded by the hierarchy, as the Australian experience warns! This way, human rights theology is *used* as the tool of ecclesiastical imperialism.

My concluding remark is directly addressed to the human rights theologians in the very language they have created: Respect the God-given inalienable *right* of every local church, especially in the Third World, to evolve its own theological discourse. Any tendency to universalize the social teaching of the Western patriarchate and impose it on others is a violation of the autonomy of the local church. Even in the struggle for justice, let justice be done to the creativity of the third-world theologians who have initiated a "neat break" from the cultural domination of the Western church even in social ethics; it is the *caesura* (radical rupture from the West) that Karl Rahner, voicing our concerns, advocated fearlessly as the *conditio sine qua non* for the birth of a truly universal church.[34]

---

32. Max L. Stackhouse, "Militarization and the Human Rights Tradition in Asia: Implications for Mission Today," in *Human Rights and Global Mission*, 86.
33. Ibid., 87.
34. Karl Rahner, "Toward a Fundamental Theological Interpretation of Vatican II," *Theological Studies*, 40, December 1979, 716–27.

11

Inculturation in Asia
A Theological Reflection on an Experience

THEORETICAL CONSIDERATION

"Inculturation" — the word as well as the concept — has been subjected to a long, drawn-out debate. Though missiologically relevant, this discussion is too theoretical to be engaged in here. Hence, the reader is kindly invited to peruse chapter 12 below: "The Problem of Universality and Inculturation with Regard to Patterns of Theological Thinking." It can serve as a theoretical supplement for what I intend proposing here as a "theological reflection on an experience." In this reflection, I give the word "inculturation" a special meaning. If we agree on this meaning provisionally, we may be able to arrive at some tentative conclusions.

Inculturation as Aggiornamento

Let me make it clear that inculturation is not an archaeological exercise of returning to Asia's cultural past but an awakening of the church to Asia's present realities. Inculturation, in other words, is a neologism that has gradually replaced Pope John XXIII's catchy term *aggiornamento. Aggiornamento* was really a summons to reeducate the church, rank and file, in the languages and idioms of the people that it had been so far speaking to in an obsolete tongue. The presupposition was that the church had not walked with the Spirit (Gal. 5:25), but had lagged behind; it had failed to communicate the Good News in the language of the *Magister Internus* who instructs every person born in this world with the things pertaining to salvation.

Attuning the church once more to the Word that illumines everyone who comes into this world (John 1:9) is what *aggiornamento* seems to have meant for Pope John. In other words, it was a summons to the church to return

First published in *Jahrbuch für Kontextuelle Theologie*, Verlag für Interkulturelle Kommunikation, Frankfurt, 1994, 59–71.

to its pentecostal origins and relive the primordial mission with which the church came into existence: that of speaking in such a way that all nations understand its message each in its own native tongue (Acts 2:8).

The church had somewhat deviated from its pentecostal origins. What Pope John XXIII meant by *aggiornamento* was a new Pentecost. And that precisely is what we mean here by inculturation. That was also the primary purpose for which the Council was convoked. This is why we have to take a pneumatological approach to the question of inculturation.

A Pneumatological Approach Means "Primacy of the Word"

A pneumatological approach does not amount to a discourse on the Spirit. For the Spirit is not the object of any discourse; s/he is the subject of all discourse. The Spirit speaks and is not spoken about. What the Unspoken Speaker (*Pneuma*) utters about the Unspeakable One (*Theos*) is speech itself, the illuminating Word of Revelation, the sure means of Salvation and the sole path to transformation: *Logos/Dabar/Hodos/Mārga/Tao/Dharma/Vac*. It is the great discourse of the Spirit heard and recognized by any person who walks with the same Spirit. However, what reveals, saves, and transforms is this Word itself, not our "words" (e.g., Christ, Lord, and other human categories) by which we describe it.

Jesus Christ is he whom Christians recognize as the Word that has been seen, heard, and touched with human senses. Today he continues to be visibly and palpably available in the flesh and blood of those whom he himself has designated as his vicars on earth: the little ones, least of his brothers and sisters, the nonpersons and nonpeoples of his earth, the victims of nations.

In Asia, the slaves of Asia's unjust social institutions and movements (feudalism, caste, bonded-labor, agro-industries, ethnic wars, etc.) are the voiceless transmitters of this Word. Listening to that Word and obeying it involves a process of learning the language of the Unspoken Speaker who resides and works in an eminent manner in the people who continue in our own times as the paschal body of Christ. Such learning we call inculturation.

Inculturation and Evangelization

The paradox of evangelization is that these very vicars of Christ are also the principal addressees of the Word. To them, the Good News is to be preached first, and through them to the others. Thus evangelization in Asia is an exchange between the Spirit in the Powerless ones and the Spirit in the church; that is to say, between the Unspoken Speaker that is heard in the oppressed who are mostly non-Christian but are Christ's proxy on earth by the fact of their being oppressed, and the same Unspoken Speaker that stirs up the church from within to become the voice of Christ. In short: the church's claim to be Christ's vicar on earth is challenged by Christ's claim to have chosen the poor as his vicar on earth. This bilocation of the Spirit is the fruit of our own sin and was not the intention of Christ.

The disciples to whom the words "Whoever listens to you listens to me" were addressed by Jesus were people who had given up all for the sake of the Kingdom. They were poor either by birth or by option. It was they whom Christ summoned to be his disciples and addressed as "little ones"; it was they who rallied around him and took over his place and continued his mission by living and proclaiming the paschal mystery. It was they who were entrusted with the authority to be pastors and teachers.

But in the course of time, the successors of this nuclear church and the poor of this world became two separate bodies, each with a claim to be the vicar of Christ or the body of Jesus. The challenge of the two claims — the church's and Christ's — is met only through the right type of evangelization. Such evangelization is the exchange between the church evangelized by the poor (a church that educates itself to become once again the vicar of Christ or the voice of the Spirit by becoming the church of the poor) and the poor evangelized by the church (the poor recognizing their covenant partner in Jesus).

Now inculturation is the first part of this process, namely, that by which the church takes up this challenge and is evangelized by the poor and requalifies itself to be the evangelizer of the poor. This species of inculturation is a difficult process which is nevertheless the absolute condition for evangelization as there is no short-cut available. Thus our notion of inculturation can be defined as follows: Inculturation is the costly faith-response by which the church — as a community that claims to be the voice of Spirit — recognizes this voice in the Asian [body of] Christ, the vast suffering peoples of Asia, wherever it is heard today, and responds to it in obedience so that the church may become Good News to them as Jesus was, in the freedom of the Spirit. This is the thesis on inculturation which I wish to develop in the following pages.

Freedom of the Spirit

The question is often asked in Asia why the church was so slow in this matter and even hostile to inculturation during the last four centuries. Even today, there is no widespread enthusiasm about this need in the churches of Asia. One reason for this may be the confusion regarding the word and the concept of inculturation, as mentioned at the beginning of this discussion. But our attempt at a fresh definition is not going to make it easier. What is proposed here carries with it our natural dread of the cross, the cost of having to give up the comfortable ways of the past. For the plunge into the paschal mystery of people's struggles (inculturation as we understand it) involves social conflicts.

I wish to concentrate here on one significant aspect of this great failure, namely, the tendency of the church to replace the Spirit as the speaker. The church is inclined to compete with the Unspoken Speaker. It is tempted to raise a counterplatform which is at variance with the pulpit which the Unspoken Speaker has placed amid the "least brothers and sisters of Christ." This is what makes us indulge naively in an aggressive discourse (misnamed evangelization) which has not been preceded by a process of humble learning (i.e., inculturation).

Is it surprising that slogans such as "Accept Christ for your salvation," "Christ is the Answer," "Open your hearts to Christ," and so on have irritated many religiously sensitive non-Christians in Asia in recent times? Only the Spirit can speak the Word that opens the heart. Wherever evangelization amounts to ranting without listening and learning (i.e., without inculturation), the Word gets drowned in the din of our own many words.

There is one good criterion of discernment in this matter. The Word is universal, and if our word is the Word that the Spirit utters in the nonpersons of Asia, then the nonpersons should recognize the voice of the Spirit in us. Do they? The answer to this question would be a good criterion to go by.

The Criterion

Let me reformulate the two aspects of this criterion:

a. The poor have to be the social location of inculturation (if inculturation is the process by which the church is evangelized by the poor, i.e., educated by the Spirit);

b. Social conflict (the cross/calvary; the paschal mystery lived with and amid the poor) is the inevitable sign and proof of an inculturated church, i.e., a church that has so fully become a vicar of Christ in and through the poor as to be a sign of contradiction.

For only when the paschal mystery is enacted until the climatic moment of apparent failure before the powers of this world will the Word we preach truly coincide with that which reveals itself to the nations: "Truly he is the Son of God" (Mark 15:39b).

When, like Peter, we prevent Christ from entering the arena of social conflict (the way of the cross) and like Peter cannot understand the reproof "Get behind me, Satan" (Mark 8:33), which means, "I lead you, not you me" — it is then that we separate ourselves from the scene of the conflict, as Peter did. Peter was not found among the crowd that looked helpless at Christ's mock trial, but was conspicuously seen in conversation with the servants of the persecutor in his very courtyard. Peter was in the wrong place. Hence the great betrayal.

This is what happens when one mixes up God's program of action with that of the powers of this world, as Jesus forewarned Peter: "Your mentality is that of the World, not that of God" (Mark 8:34). The social location (the Galilees of Asia) where we opt to be and the social conflict (the Calvaries of Asia) resulting from that option are the very stuff of which inculturation/ evangelization is made.

The Spirit that speaks in the Asian poor has given this Word to many noble Christians who have individually responded to it with courage; but the church as a whole is not one continuous body with the Asian Christ but offers a diminished Christ. "Get behind me...I lead you, not you me" is the Word we hear from the Christ of Asia. The church and, *a fortiori,* the magisterium, are never above the Word; they are at the service of the Word (*Dei Verbum* 10). The Word must lead us, not the other way around. The Spirit who prompts the things of God must be given the freedom to speak and to be heard.

CONCRETE ILLUSTRATIONS

A *True Parable*

Let me exemplify this with a true parable. In the late 1960s when I was discovering the Word in Buddhism, studying for my doctorate under the guidance of Buddhist monks, I had a visit from Shree Charles de Silva, a great Buddhist scholar, poet and litterateur, linguist and philologist, and member of the editorial staff of the Sinhala Encyclopedia. He was as much known for his learning as for his humble and simple living in conformity with the teachings of the Buddha. He was universally admired as a paragon of *alpecchatā,* the Buddhist equivalent of evangelical poverty.

As we became friends — it happened so quickly! — he shared with me the text of a drama (entitled *Paramapuda,* "Supreme Sacrifice") which he had composed. It was on the passion and death of Christ, the paschal mystery as he had understood it. I became curious to know why he thought of such a "plot" for one of his literary works. Here is the explanation:

He had heard much about the "Passion plays" enacted every Lent in Negombo, the Catholic stronghold in Sri Lanka. Perhaps as a scholar who had to supply the Sinhala Encyclopedia with words and customs peculiar to the Catholic subculture he had an academic interest in the Catholic theater coming down from the time of the Christian missionaries. Perhaps there was another type of interest, too. These plays usually seem to be long, drawn-out, and boring for mere spectators but could be devotionally moving for simple participants; and my Buddhist friend, being a religious scholar, went there probably as a spectator-participant.

The impact of the play on him, however, was disastrous. "I was not impressed by the Christian performance of Christ's paschal story (*paskusirita*)." These were his exact words; they were an understatement which meant that he was thoroughly disillusioned. Yet these words are profoundly theological. "The Christian performance of the mystery of Christ," he confessed further, "was not worthy of Christ."

What he insinuated — namely, that the church's enactment of the paschal mystery was a meaningless farce — opened for me a new program of theological search, as I shall indicate later.

The Word Communicates Even through Bad Media

And yet, the Word, by its very nature, refuses to be muffled too long. The voice of the Spirit could be distorted when passing through the church's Public Communication System (sacraments, lifestyle, preaching, customs, etc.) and the Word often may not be correctly heard because of our bad performance; but still the Word is Word, and it still makes sense to the simple and wise Asians who have an inner affinity with the universal Spirit that speaks in all of us. Such people hear the Word in the Spirit and are inspired to give it back to us in its new-found fullness. This is what I meant when I said that inculturation/evangelization is an exchange of the Spirit bilocated in the church and in the Asian Christ.

In fact, this devout and intelligent Buddhist friend saw the grandeur of the Word. What shocked him was the literary ruggedness in the script, the rhythmic rudeness of the chanting and the overall failure to communicate the noble message. Having been confined to a Catholic ghetto for centuries, the Sinhala Christian community seemed unfamiliar with the language and the idiom of the Buddhist environment in which it had lived for so long. They were talking to themselves even if their message was meant for all who are outside their ghetto.

The irony is that this kind of drama (*nadagam*), despite its allegedly Christian-missionary importation to the country, had received much refinement in the hands of great contemporary artists such as Ediriweera Saraccandra (a Christian converted to Buddhism) and had reached a very sophisticated level of performance in the country today. But the Christian drama does not seem to have been touched by this progress in the rest of the country. It repeats every year faithfully the crude version of a few centuries ago. It has got stuck in the past.

That was why this sensitive Buddhist scholar decided that something worthy of Christ, something that allows Christ to speak to the Buddhist heart, must come from his own pen. He said he was driven by an inner impulse to do so. He went home and began to write a Passion play that would truly communicate the Word that was Christ.

I was deeply moved by the text; on reading through it, I felt that the Sinhala culture in me and the Christian faith in me simultaneously discovered the Buddhist in me hearing a Word that was ever ancient and ever new. My emotional reaction to it and my aesthetic appreciation of the style and content of the play became a source of great encouragement to my friend, so that he decided to write also a Christian play.

These plays (including a translation of Oscar Wilde's *Salome*) are a watershed both in the history of Sinhala literature and in the history of Christian literature: in Sinhala literature, because of its Christic content; in Christian literature, because of the Buddhist cultural idiom that makes Christ shine in Asian splendor. I have already been studying the christology that emerges from this play. I have also learned the way the Unspoken Speaker pronounces the Word here in Asia, the accent, the intonation, and the innuendos which make us think differently from other churches.

Listening before Talking

Since then I began to engage many non-Christian friends in the work of telling me and the church what the word "Christ" should mean in Asia. Since then, the old missionary practice of preaching Christ to Asia has been reversed, at least at Tulana Research Center. Here the question "Who do you say I am?" is addressed to Buddhists who are sensitive to the Unspoken Speaker, to the Spirit that is not tied down to any dogma, rite, or law.

Asia has not been allowed to educate the church in listening and following the Word, since the church has been talking the whole time. Even now, it is talking loud and irritatingly to the non-Christians to accept Christ. "Which Christ?" is the counterquestion. To that, the non-Christians who have an inner affinity with the Spirit can supply a creative answer.

On our walls, here at our center, a few Buddhist artists have expressed their understanding of Christ, in oil, stone, and clay. Let me select three of them for presentation.[1]

What Is Unique and Universal about Christ?
Three Pictures by Ven. Hatigammana Uttarananda

The first three pictures I describe here are by a Buddhist monk, Ven. Hatigammana Uttarananda Thera, who had been at the helm of a movement for ethnic justice in Sri Lanka and the editor of a journal that reached the hands of the young and the old in the universities and the Buddhist monasteries of the country. His life and his thought were inspired by the aspirations of the marginalized groups with whom he identified himself, so much so that in 1989 at least six hundred of his confreres were liquidated as subversives. The artist is now a refugee in Europe.

I give this background of the artist in order to identify which kind of Asian is qualified to speak of Christ, which kind of non-Christian person vibrates with the Unspoken Speaker.

He spent a few months reading the scriptures and studying my collection of Christian art with the intention of holding an exhibition of paintings on Christ and the Buddha. The suggestion was that the artist does not duplicate in his Christian paintings what is already found in Buddhism. What is unique to Christianity was the object of the search. It was finally decided that the picture he would do for me was of Jesus washing the feet of the disciples (John 13:1–17). Here, in a life-size cement embossment, the artist brings out Jesus as the voluntary Slave of his sisters and brothers.

---

1. In the address given in Aachen in March 1994, I presented slides and color photos of these pictures. Here I can only describe them to the best of my ability.

Jesus: God of slaves — the slave of God. The cultural background against which the artist has envisaged the scene of foot-washing is the *sanghika-dane,* the sacred meal of the Buddhist monks. Offering a meal to the monks is a meritorious act celebrated as a religious rite. The monks come in procession to a home with their begging bowls, and as they are received into the residence, a servant of the host pours water and assists them in washing their feet.

The artist depicts the disciples as a mendicant community coming in single file to Christ's home, all holding their begging bowls. Jesus the host does not employ a servant to help in the washing of the feet. He is himself the servant, with towel around his waist, washing Peter's feet from a basin of water. In the hills from which this monk-artist came, the servants take off their turban (a towel covering the head) when they see their master and tie it around their waist as a sign of subservience. Jesus the host is also the servant of his own disciples, with the towel tied around his waist. This is shocking. In fact Peter is shown with a *mudra* (a stylized manual gesture, used in oriental dramas) meaning "Don't do it, I don't like it." Another disciple is depicted with a *mudra* indicating that something strange is happening. Against the culture of servants and masters, this artist has brought out the revolutionary change of values that Christ's gesture creates.

Also highlighted is the presence of women in Jesus' household, one woman of low caste and another of high caste. Unwittingly, the picture helps to translate Paul's classic saying (Gal. 3:28) in a new way: in the Word, there is no discrimination between male and female, between high and low caste, and between Christian and non-Christian. Christ is the name we give to a *universal* word not unknown to our people.

Thus something that has also appeared *unique* about Christ has been discovered for us by this monk: that Jesus makes sense in Asia only when he scandalizes the feudal society by manifesting himself as the one who becomes the slave of the slaves of this earth. Since then, my reading of Philippians 2:6–11 has not been the same. The whole doctrine of incarnation can miss the real issue at stake if our theological exercise revolves around the futile attempt at reconciling intellectually the divine and the human natures in Jesus. Rather, the Incarnation is the scandalous agreement (covenant) between God and slaves, embodied in Jesus who sided with the nonpersons as a sign and proof of his divine nature. This covenant, so unique to Christians, is precisely the point of the Kerygma.

This is unique to Christianity in that it proclaims a God who lives and dies a slave on a cross reserved for the *humiliores* that create social conflicts. This fact was anticipated in the passover in Egypt when God accompanied the slaves to freedom; and this God has become a slave in Christ, both in life and, especially, in the manner of his death. The washing of the feet has been singled out in this embossment as something unique to Christ. Evangelization which ignores this dimension ignores what is inalienably distinctive in our faith. The non-Christian recognized this feature as something not duplicated in other religions.

Also the church's enactment of Christ's paschal mystery becomes a ritual farce if this uniqueness is not witnessed to. Our sacraments are unintelligible rites, not only because they are mere translations of a Latin ceremony, but because they are not related to the drama of the Asian poor. "It is a Passion play not worthy of Christ."

The judge on the side of the victim. The second picture, an oil painting by the same artist (Uttarananda), shows the role of Christ vis-à-vis the woman caught in adultery. The innocence of the woman (declared free by Jesus: "Neither will I accuse thee") and the hypocrisy of the male society that sexually abuses the woman and later stones her are powerfully contrasted, while only the palm of Christ shown in the classical *abhaya-mudra,* the manual gesture that indicates the message "fear not" (*a-bhaya*) is shown raised high over the crowd, with a nail mark to show that it is Christ's rather than the Buddha's. From that manual gesture comes forth a powerful message about who Christ is: the fearless defender of the victims of social discrimination and religious hypocrisy and the safe sanctuary of the outcasts.

Why this waste of innocent blood? The third picture captures in oil and canvas the events that took place in July 1983: the holocaust of innocent Tamils on the streets of Colombo. The artist was so shocked that he organized a whole movement of monks against ethnic injustice. The Tamils who died were usually the most harmless and extremely poor people such as the shoe-repairers on the roadside, the street vendors, the estate laborers, and so on. Judas's question raised against Mary Magdalene's generosity is now directed to Christ by the artist: *Why?* Why this waste? The pitcher of wine tilted flat on its side, allowing the contents to flow freely on the ground, and the refusal of the apostles to drink from the chalice of innocent blood express the artist's question: Is there no other way of saving humankind?

Here the Buddhist asks a very serious question about our atonement theory. We are accustomed to ask the misleading question "Why did Jesus die?" and we answer, "He died for our sins." Surely, he did not die of old age or disease! Could a more complete answer be ever given to that wrong question? The monk is making us ask the proper question: Why was Jesus murdered? This is the question which, when answered, brings out the liberational thrust of the paschal mystery.

Christ, the Word: Two sculptures by Kingsley Gunatilleke

Pietà Lanka 1989. The Pietà Lanka has taken the shape of Mother Lanka identified with the image of Mary holding the dead body of Christ. The body is not that of the renaissance man as in Michelangelo's Pietà, but a picture of *natura morta*. The cross on which the youth are killed is formed by the military tank (state terrorism) and the lamppost (youth militancy). The reference here is to the youth insurgency both in the Tamil North and in the Sinhala South.[2]

The lamppost has taken the shape of a cobra, a symbol of a dangerous force that can be tamed. Legend has it that a cobra coiled beneath the Buddha to keep him from the mud and covered him with its hood to protect him from the rain. Buddha's policy was one of taming perilous forces rather than antagonizing them. Youth militancy (Tamil as well as Sinhalese) represents a dangerous force that can serve Mother Lanka if its demands for justice are met. But state terrorism can never be tamed.

This sculpture has frozen in cement and stones the events of 1989 when thousands of youth lost their precious lives in a brutal conflict with the state forces. The sculptor saw in Jesus a Word of challenge and hope that speaks through these events. Mother Lanka and her youth are made to announce the paschal mystery which we call Christ-event.

Christ: the ever-growing Word.   Jesus, the child, learning from and questioning the Past (Luke 2:41–52), is the theme of a large mural relief made of baked clay. Clay is a fragile medium, but once dried up with the breath of the wind and the warmth of fire, it lasts forever, argues the artist. One is reminded of Adam the "mud-man" who came alive by Divine Breath, now only a little less than God (Psalm 8).

The artist, Gunatilleke, has been dialoguing with me on Luke 2:41–52 for nearly two and a half years. The final sketch was made last year. In August 1993 he started making the mural. After it was complete, the clay slabs collapsed to the ground. He made a second attempt in September. It collapsed again. Then he consulted an astrologer and found an auspicious time, and began work for the third time with fresh slabs of clay. The structure was made inside the house so that he could sleep there without distancing himself from the work of his hands. More love and care was needed if the clay should collaborate with him. Besides, the theme was too deeply religious to take lightly. He realized that nature rebelled against him because he was not religious enough in handling such a profound theme.

When he finished Moses' character, he was burning with warmth inside. He lived every character that he depicted in this mural, the great teachers of the world: the Buddha, Mahavira, Krishna, LaoTse, Confucius, and of course the great Greek trio, Socrates, Plato, and Aristotle (said to be the Gang of Three who influenced the dominant stream of Christian theology!). The unknown and unsung women teachers who have been erased from memory by the male society which wrote our history were also represented: a Greek woman and an Indian woman in the form of Tara Devi.

---

2. Initially the militant youth would tie to a lamppost the dead body of a person together with the placard announcing the crime for which he was killed.

The Holy Family steals the show from Moses and the Buddha. Mary's face shows pain mixed with annoyance, for Jesus has acted rather independently. Her hands show the "controlling" and "protecting" attitude of an overanxious mother. She is the symbol of the church, as Luke meant her to be. Jesus' two hands say everything about the Word that he claimed to be: The left hand demonstrates his refusal to be controlled by parental anxiety. "Mind your business, Mother, and leave me alone to do mine. For I have my own mission that your God and mine has bestowed on me. I shall obey you and be under your jurisdiction, but it is good that you know that my mission comes from above and you cannot interfere with it.[3]

The right hand makes a gesture of inquiry: learning and questioning. He grows not only in age, but wisdom and grace, too. The whole history of human search for truth and freedom is a sacred temple in which the Word is being formed in the exchanges of many holy and learned people who have served humankind with their sacred findings. It is a dialogue in the Spirit.

Here we have the finest thesis on the primacy of the Word over the church, and also on the nature of the Word as something/someone growing.

The Christ Whom We Wish to Know with and from the Asians

Jesus as the discourse of the Spirit is not a polished sentence that has dropped from the sky; it is a word that grows in history as it receives meaning from other words and gives meaning to them, until it becomes woven into one coherent discourse together with others, a communication through which the Ultimacy of the Unspeakable One and the intimacy of the Unspoken Speaker become reconciled. To reach the end of that process, the church has to monitor with all Asians of goodwill the growth of the Word whom we have recognized in Jesus.

The Spirit is this incessant and cumulative process of salvific communication by which the Word (Jesus) is ever growing toward its final and all-comprehensive expression: the Total Christ, as Christians call it. The church cannot keep away from this activity of the Spirit. Much listening, learning as well as questioning in the presence of the Asian masters of yesterday and today — *ecclesia discens* — and dialogue with contemporary Asians who have inner affinity with the Universal Word, is the sure way the church can learn the language of the Unspoken Speaker in contemporary Asia. This process is called inculturation.

---

3. There is a small inscription which the artist has incorporated into the mural, saying that this whole scene reflects the nature and the mission of the Tulana Research Center [vis-à-vis the institutional church]!

12

The Problem of
Universality and Inculturation
with Regard to Patterns
of Theological Thinking

APPREHENSIONS ABOUT THE THEME

The theme of this chapter has been formulated for me by the editors of *Concilium* in the key words contained in the title. But this theme, as well as its formulation, is fraught with many methodological difficulties which I have discussed at length elsewhere.[1] In brief, they are as follows:

1. The very word "inculturation" presupposes a theory of culture and religion which certain forms of emergent Asian theologies reject as a misconception of the Asian reality and an anachronistic imposition of a first-century Mediterranean experience on contemporary Asia.

2. Besides, the phrase "inculturation of theology (or of liturgy)" presupposes a concept of universal theology (or a universal liturgy) that exists by itself in a noninculturated form waiting to be particularized in a given context.

3. Furthermore, the first initiators of inculturation had misconceived their own theology, ecclesiology, liturgy (and now christology) as something universal to be inculturated, thus giving fuel to the charge of Euro-ecclesiastical imperialism.

4. Finally, there is also the great unfinished debate about the real or apparent antagonism between inculturation and liberation, and a well-founded

First published in *Concilium* (1994/6), 70–79.

1. Aloysius Pieris, *An Asian Theology of Liberation,* Orbis Books, Maryknoll, N.Y., 1988, 37–42, 44–45, 51–58, 109–10 etc.; and also in my recent article "Inculturation: Some Critical Comments," *Vidyajyoti: Journal of Theological Reflection,* LVII/II, November 1993, 641–51.

fear among liberationists that the inculturationist model is advertised and advocated by certain interested parties whose secret agenda is to thwart the march of liberation theologies.

Aware of these difficulties, I shall evaluate the current theological scene from the cultural perspective I know best.

THE INDIC CULTURAL CONTEXT

The Indic culture in which I live my received faith in Christ entices me to evaluate my equally received theology in terms of the dialectics between theory and praxis (*vidyā-carana*), between a view of life and a way of life (*darśana-pratipadā*), between the salvific Reality and its moral imperative (*dharma-vinaya*), between the sovereign truth and the sovereign path which include each other (*āryasatya-āryamārga*), and so on.

Now, this manner of perceiving soteriology as a mutually inclusive dyad of "seeing and doing" imparts its dialectical character to the task of "speaking" about that which is at once "seen as the ultimate truth" and "sought as the ultimate goal." The basic ingredients of theology are seeing, doing, and speaking. Religious discourse is speech prompted by the perception of a truth-goal and marked by the struggle to arrive at it. All other speech is purely speculative and soteriologically inconsequential.

Christian "theo-logy," seen from this perspective, seems to be a religious discourse (*logos*) addressed to, by, and regarding *theos,* who is both the ultimate truth and the ultimate goal. It is a systematic discourse and a disciplined speech commensurate with that truth-goal. This discourse (*logos*), no doubt, is inherent in the very reality of the truth-goal (*theos*). This is the basic axiom on which Christian theology is founded.

THE CONSTITUTIVE DIMENSION
OF THE CHRISTIAN DISCOURSE

The question of theology as discourse in the Christian context presupposes the following datum of faith: that the truth-goal is identified as the Unspeakable One (*theos*/God) who becomes speakable only as the speech (*logos*) uttered by the Unspoken Speaker (*pneuma*/Spirit). The Spirit is the subject, not the object of discourse. All discourse about the Unspeakable One is the revelatory word uttered by the Unspoken Speaker.

Furthermore, this speech is also the medium by which *theos,* our source of salvation, becomes accessible to us. To put it more clearly, the word of revelation is also the medium of salvation and the path to intimacy with the Ultimate. Thus all theology revolves around this word-medium-path; it alone is speakable and therefore spoken. Being speech, it is theology itself, seminally.

This word-medium-path has been available to all tribes, races, and peoples of all times and all places. It has been recognized by various names (*Dharma, Mārga, Tao,* etc.), giving rise to many forms of discourse.[2] It is too profound to be exhausted by one single utterance — be it our human utterance or even that of the Unspeakable One. For both these utterances — the human and the divine — are emitted by the breath of the same Unspoken Speaker who speaks in God and in people or, more accurately, in nonpersons covenanted with God.

THREE THEOLOGICAL PATTERNS

The belief that Jesus of Nazareth is the enfleshed historical manifestation of this word-medium-path turns Christian theology into a christology. Such naming, however, is not a condition for salvation demanded by the Word which, being universal, operates even among those who do not recognize it by that name. It is the word-medium-path that saves, not the name one gives to it. Naming, which belongs to theology, cannot be universal.

Now, the theandric speech recognized as "Jesus" by Christians is not merely an explanatory word (*logos*), but also one that is creative (*dabar*) and directional (*hodos*). For the breath by which it is voiced is the Spirit of wisdom, the Spirit of love, and the Spirit that blows all words toward the mystery of ultimate silence.

Regrettably, therefore, Christian theology has sinned against the Spirit by dividing her discourse into three separate theological idioms. For want of better terms, let them be known as the *logos* model, the *dabar* model, and the *hodos* model of theology.

LOGOS MODEL:
PHILOSOPHICAL OR SCHOLASTIC THEOLOGY

Logos is reason and rationality. If we prescind from the Johannine synthesis of *logos* and *dabar* — something rare in current theological thinking — we are left with a theology that insists on the all-pervasive role of intelligibility. Jesus of Nazareth is the primary explanation of God and creation. He is the one who makes sense of what is otherwise meaningless.

In this view, salvation is knowledge of God; theology is the explanation of revelation. "I believe that I may understand" (*credo ut intelligam*). My mind must satisfy itself in understanding God with the help of revelation. Faith is a gift of knowledge that allows the intellect to give its assent (*assensus intellectus*) to truth(s) explained by those who have received the divine guarantee to teach such truth.

---

2. See Chapter 10 of my *Love Meets Wisdom: A Christian Experience of Buddhism,* Orbis Books, Maryknoll, N.Y., 1989, especially 131–35. See also *An Asian Theology of Liberation* (n. I), 62–63.

Love results from knowledge. Knowledge may culminate in love, but that love is affective knowledge. The final salvation is a beatific vision enjoyed by the human mind elevated to the new level of understanding. Contemplation of the mystery of God is the goal of Christian existence; action (both social action of an "ethical" order and ascetical practices of a "spiritual" order) is a stepping stone to that goal. The anticipation of this final salvation here on earth is infused knowledge, which contemplation is.

Theoretically speaking, even obedience (i.e., action in conformity with the Word) comes after an understanding of the Word. In theory, therefore, the government (*imperium*) of a Jesus-community belongs to the domain of the intellect. When the community learns collectively the will of God, it is moved to obey it. The will follows the intellect (*voluntas sequitur intellectum*). This is how St. Thomas understood obedience.[3] He represents the noblest moment of the *logos* movement after which it was overtaken by the decadent scholasticism of later centuries. For, in the decadent form, an emphasis on knowledge that generates power seems to have vitiated community-government into a one-party rule. The following three observations are, therefore, relevant:

1. Rightness and wrongness in the formulation of truth are crucial to this theology. Dogma-heresy dialectics play an important role in maintaining the purity of truth. Authority is the result of possessing truth rather than of being possessed by truth. The power to rule is associated with the privilege of knowing the truth. An infallible authority guarantees the possibility of such knowledge for all. The Word of God may be, theoretically, above the teaching authority in the church (*Verbum Dei,* no. 10), but in practice it has to be interpreted as the true Word by that infallible authority. For there is a magisterium which has the power to interpret the Word and demand assent to *that* Word as interpreted by it.

2. The word-medium is believed to be entrusted to knowledgeable persons. In their consecrated hands and in their hallowed mouths, this word can be a medium of transformation or transubstantiation. The sacraments are speech uttered by these privileged persons, rather than speech of the Unspoken Speaker. In Greek Orthodox theology, on the contrary, the transformation (*metabole*) is rightly regarded as an *epiclesis,* that is a "manifestation (of the transformed matter) by the Spirit"; but here, in *logos* theology, such change of species is "caused" by the "words of institution" uttered by the aforementioned persons.[4]

3. The liturgy is so organized as to exhibit this power-principle operating in the church. A Eucharist revolves around this person, with special dress (and in some cases with a special headgear and a wand of authority). Such

---

3. As explained in Herbert McCabe, O.P., "Obedience," *New Blackfriars,* June 1984, 280–86.
4. See Alexander Schmemann, *The World a Sacrament,* London, 1965, 52–53.

4

persons preside over the ceremonies, where the eucharistic species as well as the community seem to be under their control. The Word is not the focus of the celebration. The cleric who handles the Word is the one who dominates the liturgy. At his words, the species change; God's people bend their knees and receive what he confects for them. The Eucharist as celebrated according to this theology is the symbol of how the power of knowing the Word exercises power even over the Word.

Such is *logos* which is not *dabar.*

THE *DABAR* MODEL: LIBERATION THEOLOGY

The *dabar* pattern of theology moves in another direction altogether. The word-medium is not merely a speech that displays authoritative knowledge, but an utterance that creates and transforms. The theological task is not just to "interpret" the world philosophically but to "change" it.

Speech, in this case, is not a rational explanation but a happening, an event. Here, therefore, history and revelation meet. The word of salvation is continually heard in history — not only in the history of Israel and of Jesus, but in the continuing history of the world. *Extra historiam nulla salus.* To obey the Word is to partake in the *epiclesis,* to share in the Spirit's work of manifesting, here and now, a transformed world.

Hearing the Word does not primarily coincide with understanding it; rather, the Word heard is the Word obeyed. It is the execution of the Word that brings understanding of the Word. Praxis is the first formulation of theory. *Doing* the truth leads to discerning the path — a procedure that would sound incongruous in *logos* theology.

Hence there can be no authority above the Word. The one who is faithful to the Word — the prophet — is the one who has authority to announce it. The Word shows its power in the prophet; the prophet has no power over the Word. Kerygma has priority over the cult. The prophet's word is prefaced by "It is the Lord who says." It is not a given infallibility that guarantees his or her credibility, but the transforming effect of the Word visibly evident in the prophet's life (personal witness) and in other readable signs of human wholeness by which the prophet anticipates the new order (miracles of healing). The Word announced is the Word attested in this twofold manner. Hence prophetic authority is not magisterial (in the sense in which the word "magisterium" has developed in the *logos* stream of theology) but martyrial.

All prophets — from the First Testament prophets beginning with Moses, down to Jesus and his precursor in the Second Testament — were persons who entered the history of their people at the risk of courting dangerous social conflict which in many cases culminated in premature death. After Jesus, the cross has now become the symbol of this social conflict and the final proof of martyrial authority, for it is on the cross that the Word triumphs, both as revelatory and salvific; it is there that prophetic authority is finally vindicated.

In various liberation theologies, this active participation in the transformation of history through the *via crucis* constitutes the *fons et culmen* (the source and summit) of Christian life — in contrast with the Second Vatican Council's emphasis on the liturgical celebrations as the source and summit (of a historical struggle). The paschal mystery is primarily enacted in the sociohistorical context of the liturgy of life. This means that "formal prayer" — both as private devotion and as communal worship — is, respectively, a personal interiorization and an ecclesial celebration of the liturgy of life. This shift of emphasis illustrates the difference between the *logos* model and the *dabar* model of Christian theology.

THE *HODOS* MODEL:
THEOLOGY AS SEARCH FOR WHOLENESS

The word-medium in the *hodos* stream of theological thought is essentially a path, a process, a journey. It could be viewed as an ascent to a mountain, or a descent to the depths of the mystery, or perhaps as inward journey toward the interior of one's own castle. Sometimes it is described as a series of steps leading to a summit (*scala perfectionum*). Accordingly, the pilgrims could be categorized in terms of their position in the path: *incipientes, proficientes, perfecti.* The trajectory is itself designated progressively as the purgative, the illuminative, and the unitive ways.

The God-experience itself in God-talk appears to be a graduated path in which "moral life" is the first phase leading to "spiritual life," which, in its turn, is once more seen as two stages: the "ascetic" stage, in which one's personal effort to move toward the goal is registered intensely in the soul; and the "mystical" stage, in which the magnetic pull of the goal is so overwhelming as to minimize the gravitational drag of the early ascesis.

This way of considering morality as the necessary minimum and spirituality as an ascent toward a higher stage (counsels of perfection?), and of dividing spirituality itself into a lower form of active struggle and a higher form of passive absorption, is typical of a *hodos* theology that identifies the goal of the path as "perfection in formal prayer."[5] This manner of defining spirituality tallies with the *logos* theology, according to which action is transcended by mystical knowledge gained through formal prayer.

Another school understands spirituality in terms of a struggle to bring God's Reign on earth through apostolic labor, that is to say, through an effort to transform the world sociospiritually in response to God's will.[6] This spir-

---

5. By "formal prayer" is meant the type of prayer which is characterized by a special method and structure, a regularity in time and a definite place. See Giacomo Lercaro, *Methods of Mental Prayer,* London, 1957, 1ff.

6. Thus in the *Spiritual Exercises,* no. 189, Ignatius of Loyola insists that conformity with

ituality, which proliferated from the sixteenth century onward, speaks in an idiom that is not quite consonant with *logos* theology. But, as Lozano seems to insinuate, the authentic Christian tradition is one in which the goal of the spiritual path ought to be what he calls apostolic mysticism.[7] The newly emerging *dabar* theology seems to have an inner affinity with this "activist" model of *hodos* theology.

Whatever the conflict between the two trends, one thing is clear: the path, once taken, becomes less and less the focus as the journey progresses; the goal becomes the all-pervading concern. Thus, Teresa of Avila seems to have wondered why Jesus the man tends to disappear in the process of her gradual union with God. Merton suggests the answer: Jesus is not the goal but only the way to it.[8] To be one with Christ is to be fully in the path, and therefore goal-consciousness must gradually supersede the path-consciousness.

In the body of the *Exercises,* Ignatius of Loyola, too, is quite insistent on the role of Jesus as the way to be followed, but ceases to mention him in the climactic, contemplation of union with God. This is, presumably, because Christ is the medium with which one becomes identified in the course of the journey; thus, through Christ, with Christ, and in Christ, the exercitant stands face to face with God, the Father-Mother-Lover-Friend-Coworker. *Hodos* theology scrupulously safeguards the mediational character of Christ.

This is *a fortiori* true of the church and its institutions, which serve as guideposts and pilgrims' rests that one must leave behind as one moves along the path. Hence, there could be (as there have been in the past) conflicts between the practitioners of a *hodos* theology (mystics) and the cultic magisterium that has its roots in a *logos* theology.

A (PARTICULAR) THEOLOGY
AS THE (UNIVERSAL) THEOLOGY?

Yves Congar has cited the *Ignatian Exercises* (no. 363) and other works of that period such as Juan Mair's to demonstrate that there were two theologies in vogue even as late as the beginning of the modern period: "positive theology," which reflected the affective spirituality of the Fathers, and "scholastic theology," which was an intellectual and apologetical affirmation of the Cath-

---

the will of God is the measure of progress in the spiritual path. Hence the various spiritual exercises (which include formal prayer) are mere means of acquiring indifference, i.e., a detachment from one's own selfish pursuits, a discerning mind which alone is capable of discovering God's will, and a willing heart to embrace it. Ignatius defines the *Exercises,* not as a school of prayer, but as a spiritual gymnasium wherein one trains oneself to undertake apostolic labor, i.e., get involved in the work of God's Reign.

7. John M. Lozano, "The Theology and Spirituality of the Apostolic Life," in J. M. Lozano et al., *Ministerial Spirituality and Religious Life,* Chicago, 1988, 35ff.

8. See Thomas Merton, "The Humanity of Christ in Monastic Prayer," *Monastic Journey* (ed. Patrick Hart), Kansas City, 1977, 87ff.

olic doctrines against the heretics.[9] These two correspond to the *hodos* and *logos* models we are talking about here.

It would seem that certain monastic (i.e., positive) theologies such as the Antiochean version taught in the *Congregazione Casinese* could not survive the Council of Trent.[10] After Trent, *logos* theology dominated the Western patriarchate within the framework of the Latin jurisprudential scheme of guilt and justification.

Jean Leclerq tried his best to retrieve from oblivion the much forgotten monastic theology[11] which was certainly a *hodos* (i.e., positive) theology. In the Jesuit Constitution, Ignatius, too, insisted that positive theology should be taught over and above the scholastic type.[12] But the Jesuits, in their preoccupation with apologetics, tilted heavily toward scholasticism and ended up with highly speculative theological pursuits at the turn of the nineteenth century. With that deviation, the *Spiritual Exercises* too became highly intellectualized.[13] It is in this century, thanks to five decades of research, that the theology of the *Exercises* has been rediscovered as a positive theology.

With regard to a reintegration of *dabar* theology, however, we are still very backward. It had been abandoned since the time Christianity was "inculturated" in the Greco-Roman world. It yet has to be reabsorbed into the mainstream. The contrary idea that the *dabar* model needs the supplementary support of a strong intellectual *logos* theology has been worked out into a persuasive thesis, strongly emphasizing the West's literary tradition in which "the Word has become Spirit" in the scientific study of texts.[14]

Hence this word of caution about the "power-generating knowledge" which results from a *logos*-minus-*dabar* development of thought; it manifests itself both in the secular domain with its scientism and technocracy, and in the religious (Christian) world where cultic control coincides with "the power of knowledge." A white-robed clerical elite operating in scientific laboratories and in religious sanctuaries amply testifies to the effects of a neo-Gnosticism derived from a *logos*-current of knowledge that has been divorced from the *dabar*-stream of loving action.[15] Could Peukert's

---

9. See Y. Congar, *A History of Theology,* New York, 1968, 171–74.

10. See B. Collett, *Italian Benedictine Scholars and the Reformation,* Oxford 1985, chaps. 4–8; also "The Benedictine Origins of a Mid-Sixteenth-Century Heresy," *Journal of Religious History* (Sydney), 14/I June 1986, 17–18.

11. Jean Leclerq, *The Love of Learning and the Desire for God,* New York, 1961, 189–231.

12. *The Constitution of the Society of Jesus* (ed. and trans. George E. Ganss), St. Louis, 1970, no. 351, 446, 464.

13. E.g., the former Jesuit General John Roothaan's treatise *De Ratione Meditandi.* See J. Roothaan, *Exercitia Spiritualia S.P. Ignatii de Loyola: Versio Literalis ex autographo Hispanico notis illustrata,* Ratisbonae, 1923, Appendix II, 460–528.

14. See John C. Meagher, "And the Word Became Spirit," *Continuum* I/3, 1991, 4–29.

15. For a more precise formulation of this observation, see chapter 6, above, pp. 50–62. See also Langdon Gilkey's remarks appropriated and commented upon in A. Pieris, *Love Meets Wisdom* (n. 2), 10, 28, 113.

Habermas-based "Theology of Communicative Action"[16] be interpreted as an (unconscious?) attempt at restoring the *dabar* dimension of Christian discourse within the traditional *logos* theology, even though this terminology is conspicuously absent in his exposition?

INCULTURATION AND LIBERATION

The metacosmic religions of non-Semitic Asia seem to follow a twofold trend, like Western Christianity. On the one hand, there is a *hodos* model of religious thought and practice reflecting the mutuality between truth and the path. This tradition has its personal embodiment in the figure of the sage, the guru, the mystic, and is available today in the ashrams or their equivalents. On the other hand, Hinduism, Jainism, and Buddhism have also produced a highly speculative brand of scholasticism thanks to centuries of sectarian debates.

It is not surprising, therefore, that the Asian spirituality of the Christian ashrams resonate with the *hodos* stream of Western Christianity, just as Christian intellectuals who have been nourished by *logos* theology have tried to construct an Asian theology using Hindu-Buddhist philosophical speculation.

This twofold trend in "inculturation" is in conflict with "liberation" theologies such as Minjung theology in Korea, Dalit theology in India, and Asian feminist theology in general, which have their roots in the cosmic religiosity of Asia. These theologies reject the inculturationism of the ashramic and the philosophical models as anti-liberational.[17] For the Asian liberation theologies, unlike these two "inculturated" versions, have appropriated the *dabar* idiom of the Semitic tradition of Asia. Herein lies the conflict between inculturationists and liberationists.

This conflict cannot, therefore, be resolved until a comprehensive and holistic approach is adopted in Christian discourse. An all-embracing christology (call it universal if you like) is one that weaves together all three aspects of Christian discourse: Jesus as the *word* that interprets reality, the *medium* that transforms history, and the *way* that leads to the cessation of all discourse. Sophia?

---

16. Cf. Helmut Peukert, *Science, Action and Fundamental Theology: Toward a Theology of Communicative Action,* Cambridge, Mass., 1984, 143–245.
17. A. Pieris, "Does Christ Have a Place in Asia?" chapter 7 above, 65–78.

13

Whither the New Evangelism?

The mainline churches have recently been affected by a new evangelistic fever. They seem to believe that their Christian identity has blurred and their mission consciousness has weakened during recent decades. Among the many reasons adduced, two are singled out: excessive concern with non-Christian religiosity; and, secondly, unwarranted compromise with post-Christian secularity. Hence the talk about "new evangelism," "reevangelization," "Evangelization 2000," or "The Decade of Evangelism." This seems like a last-minute bid, at the end of two millennia, to redeem the world, and Christianity itself, from the imminent threat of extinction.

The occasion for this fervor is the fast approaching year 2000. It is the bimillennial jubilee of the birth of Christ and of Christianity, calling for an honest assessment of the past; it is also the dawn of another millennium, summoning the churches to revitalize themselves and renew their mission. In this new excitement, the old tension between dialogue and proclamation is felt more and more.

Lest some think that I want to resolve this tension with too much facility, let me first state my credo: (1) Evangelization is our top priority today. (2) But we have not proclaimed the Good News in an integral manner during the last two millennia, judging from the situation of the world and the church today. (3) Therefore, we need to launch immediately an integral evangelization — an evangelism in which the proclamation of faith and the promotion of justice are integrated. (4) Integral proclamation is not mere talk, but word made credible by visible signs of transformation such as miracles of human wholeness in a broken world. The ministry of the Word and the ministry of Healing, taken together, constitute evangelism. (5) The goal of this evangelism is conversion; conversion to YHWH's program of liberation referred to in the gospels as the Reign of God. (6) The cross of Jesus Christ is the standard under which we can ever hope to partner God in bringing about this Reign of God. (7) This implies that we must continually retell the story of

First published in *Pacifica* 6, 1993, 327–34.

Jesus to ourselves and others — rewriting the gospel for our local communities. (8) The story of his birth and life, his words and deeds, his assassination and victory, must be made to reveal not only what God says and does through Jesus, but also who Jesus is.

With this declaration I hope I have confessed my orthodoxy and, perhaps, established some credibility. But having done this, I also have to point out that it is often the evangelical wing of the churches that has failed most in this matter. Hence let me spell out what integral evangelization means today.

INTEGRAL EVANGELIZATION

The phrase "integral evangelization" was coined by the Jesuits. In one of their major assemblies (the 32nd General Congregation) held in 1978, they rediscovered their missionary identity by reformulating their evangelical vocation. Let me repeat this formula, as it also may give you an idea of my own context: What is it to be a Jesuit? It is to know that one is a sinner, yet called to be a companion of Jesus ... to engage, under the Standard of the Cross, in the crucial struggle of our time: the struggle for *faith,* and that struggle for *justice* which it includes.

The phrase "integral evangelization" began to be used later to indicate this manner of including the promotion of justice as an integral part of the proclamation of faith. You know as well as I do that many Jesuits have been engaged in this "integral evangelization," and not a few of them have even crowned their lives with violent death on the cross of Christ. El Salvador immediately comes to our mind.

Yet there was and still is some uneasiness about the formula itself, though not certainly about integral evangelization. The formulation quoted above received its inspiration from the Synod of 1971, at which the bishops of the Roman Catholic Church declared that the promotion of justice is a constitutive part of preaching the gospel. However, according to certain third-world Jesuits, such a formulation is couched in western categories of faith and justice and therefore does not forcefully express what integral evangelization is. While I am writing this article, some of my Jesuit confreres in various parts of the world are busy studying the problem afresh. Therefore let me use this forum to present to you what I have always seen as a biblical way of formulating integral evangelization, a formulation that makes sense in an Asia that is predominantly non-Christian.

A NEW FORMULA

The formula I wish to propose consists of the two basic axioms or principles found in biblical Christianity. Jesus, both as message and person, can hardly be encountered, and much less proclaimed, except in terms of these two axioms; they are: (1) (Jesus is) the irreconcilable antinomy between God and Mammon; and (2) (Jesus is) the irrevocable covenant between God and the poor.

I have often tried to spell out the implications of these two axioms for an Asian theology of liberation.[1] Here I shall show that any form of evangelism which ignores these two axioms distorts both the *image* and the *message* of Christ, and it is this distortion that we must set right by means of a new evangelization. I also wish to show — citing a recent Roman document hailed by non-Roman churches — that the new evangelization we hear about today in the mainline churches is the total negation of the integral evangelism which I am about to spell out in terms of the two principles just mentioned.

The first principle (allegiance to God and rejection of Mammon) constitutes the spirituality of Jesus and consequently the spirituality of his disciples; the second principle (YHWH's partnership with the weak ones of this earth) is what the mission of Jesus is about and, therefore, what also describes the mission of his apostles. The first axiom is announced as a program of spirituality in the Sermon on the Mount by Matthew and in the form of blessings and curses in Luke, and it is demanded as a condition for discipleship in all the call narratives. The second axiom is the assumption behind Jesus' own mission-manifesto proclaimed in the words of Isaiah at the synagogue of Nazareth and in Christ's judgment of nations at the end-time. The first axiom enunciates what we are called to be, as disciples of Christ; and the second spells out what we are sent out for, as apostles of Christ.

A NEW EVANGELICAL VISION

If we are faithful to these two inseparable dimensions of our Christian existence, we, the little flock of Christ, may soon discover our authentic God-given role in Asia in the context of its profound religiosity and its scandalous poverty. But it requires great courage to make this discovery, as it implies a total change of mentality, a massive paradigm shift, a true conversion to an entirely new way of seeing ourselves as well as the Asian reality.

So let me offer my thesis:

> The spirituality of discipleship revealed in the first axiom is the common denominator between Christianity and all nonbiblical religions in Asia; whereas the mission given to us in the second axiom is conspicuously absent in the Scriptures of other religions, and therefore it imparts to us our specific evangelical identity not shared by the nonbiblical religions.

Interreligious solidarity, then, is not optional, but the obligation of the whole church to stand, together with non-Christians, on the common plat-

1. See Aloysius Pieris, *ATL*, and *Love Meets Wisdom*, Orbis Books, Maryknoll, N.Y., 1988.

form of evangelical poverty, that is, the renunciation of Mammon; for only from that platform can the church announce with authority, the specific message entrusted to her: "Jesus is the covenant between YHWH and the nonpersons of this world." Liberation theology is, in fact, the elaboration of this specific mission.

Thus you see, interreligious collaboration and liberation theology are each a constitutive part of an integral evangelism in Asia. I insist on this because the new evangelism in many churches — certainly in the Roman Catholic church — is a subtle attack on both the evangelical role of other religions and the prophetic evangelism of liberation theology.

THE COMMON PLATFORM

The spirituality of the Sermon on the Mount is variously formulated in various religions and cultures as an ideal to be achieved. There are both theistic and nontheistic versions of it. Renunciation of Mammon, or "voluntary poverty" to use a classical Catholic term, makes sense in most cultures in Asia in a manner it unfortunately does not in the Christian West (despite all the talk in the West about converting Asia to Christ).

The liberative core of most of these religions consists of the basic teaching that the Truth sets us free from being tied to things that cannot give us that freedom. This is what *vairagya* means in Hinduism or *alpecchatā* means in Buddhism, and it is what is implied in the common ownership of land and property as advocated in the cosmic religiosity of tribal and clan cultures, echoing the social organization perceived in the Book of Judges or in the early Christian "Communism" described in the Acts of the Apostles.

Take a nontheistic religion like Buddhism. Obviously it does not speak of a liberator; but it does speak of a final and total liberation — *nirvana.* Using apophatic language, nirvana is defined in terms of what it is not: it is not acquisitive or accumulative (*alobha*), it is not hateful, vengeful, or unforgiving (*adosa*), and it is not naive, heedless, and unperceptive (*amoha*). Put in positive terms, the experience of this freedom is a combination of selfless love, forgiving love, and wisdom. This experience has driven some Buddhist mystics, both male and female, to burst into ecstatic psalms of joy which now form part of the Buddhist scriptures. This joyous freedom is the pearl of great price before which everything else loses its fascination. This spirituality is still available in Asia as a flickering light rather than a blazing fire.

If this liberating spirituality — a non-Christian version of the Sermon on the Mount — is gradually being extinguished, it is precisely because of the wave of capitalistic techniculture that has begun to shake the religious foundation of our cultures. The market economy (which thrives on the quest for profit) and consumerism (which plays to our accumulative instinct) have enthroned Mammon where, once, the human person and the human community, as well as the earth on which we live, were the sole beneficiary.

Is a Christianity which failed to check this tide in the West capable of being more successful here in Asia? Not unless it accepts the "evangelical role" that other religions can play in summoning the church back to the spirituality of Jesus! Can there be a new evangelism in Asia? Not without restoring the basic ingredients of Christian discipleship in our local churches and preserving them in the cultures around us with the help of our non-Christian co-pilgrims!

Mahatma Gandhi is said to have claimed that the church was not a disciple of Christ because it did not practice the Beatitudes. The irony was that Gandhi practiced them to the letter. Thus discipleship, it appears, is possible outside the church. Gandhi's scepticism about the church's evangelistic intentions has now become a permanent challenge — what credibility do we have to preach Christ if we refuse to be his disciples? With what authority do we dare to evangelize non-Christians, who may already be disciples of Christ, if we ourselves depend on Mammon for our missionary expansion?

WHITHER NEW EVANGELISM?

I shudder to think that any church that claims to be the spouse-body-servant of Christ would launch a mission campaign in Asia on the strength of massive quantities of money. What can I make of my own (Catholic) church recently holding an international seminar on evangelism for a couple of thousand invitees in Manila, in a building that is usually hired only by extremely rich multinational corporations? Who supplies the money for the church's "Evangelization 2000"? Those who provide the money are also the ones who set the agenda of evangelization. Evidently, the advocates of this new evangelization are hell-bent on liquidating the two things we consider absolutely essential for integral evangelization, namely, interreligious dialogue and liberation theology.

The recent encyclical *Redemptoris Missio* makes dangerous reading. Its redactors have clearly emphasized the need to convert the whole of Asia to Christianity. But the Christian discipleship that it advocates is not what we have just been considering; it is not something available outside the church; regrettably, it is absent in that very part of the church that wants Asia to be Christian. The encyclical deplores *our* Kingdom theology and insists on the missiology of ecclesiastical expansionism, on the so-called *plantatio ecclesiae,* or church-planting, model.

Many other churches have welcomed this encyclical as timely and boldly evangelical. In Sri Lanka it is the only encyclical that was immediately translated into the vernacular. It has now become a manual of the Pontifical Missionary Society, whose aim is to increase the membership of the church by the year 2000. Has no one detected the hidden agenda in the introductory paragraphs of that encyclical?

There one sees the ghost of a church that has lost its grip on the West, precisely because it has failed to practice and preach the spirituality of God's Reign enunciated in my first axiom. It now wants to have a grip on the Third World, where the majority of Christians live. The new evangelism advocated in this encyclical seems to have a clear goal — to create many churches in the Third World, that is to say, to erect many dioceses under bishops appointed by the center. This could be an easy way for Euro-ecclesiastical control of the people of the Third World. But, power, control, and manipulation are not supposed to be present in God's Reign. Is there a covenant with Mammon in this evangelical program?

What is more, this new evangelism completely ignores the specific mission entrusted to the church, one that truly defines our Christian identity before other religions.

OUR SPECIFIC MISSION

To make disciples of nations — that is the mission Jesus entrusted to us. Each nation must be baptized into a spirituality of nonacquisitiveness and nonaccumulativeness which guarantees a healthy, ecologically balanced sharing of our resources. Absence of greed is freedom from Mammon. It is the dawn of God's Reign. For at the end time — which begins now — all nations are judged by the victims of that nation: "I was hungry . . . depart from me. . . . " Christ is Jesus plus all the little ones who have been deprived of the blessings of the earth. Jesus and the oppressed in their covenanted togetherness is the Christ, the Victim-Judge of Nations (Matthew 25). Have you ever heard of an ecumenical council making this christological declaration?

Chalcedon gave us too little of the mystery of Christ when it tried to reconcile the divine and human in Jesus. God's becoming a human being was not a puzzle for the New Testament writers, however much it puzzled those who came after. All that God created was good; the whole creation is God's body. God did not find it demeaning to be human. God could have become a flower without lowering Herself. So, at Chalcedon, we solved a nonproblem by debating about the hypostatic union in philosophical categories which sound nonsensical when translated into Asian languages.

Perhaps the doctrine of incarnation should not have depended so much on that single Johannine sentence "The *logos* was made flesh." The hymn in the Letter to the Philippians (1:6–11) shows that what is degrading for God is not so much God's becoming a human being but God's becoming a slave of human tyrants. Humanity is beautiful because it is the finest creation of God, the fruit of sin. I personally believe that this christological hymn was composed in the communities of converted slaves, the principle addressees of the Good News.

Incarnation cannot merely be the hypostatic union between divine and human natures, but the covenantal identification of God with the slaves of this earth. Jesus as the God of slaves and the slave of God is a proclamation that the Greeks never thought of. Which "evangelist" today means this when he or she says "Jesus is the Lord"? It is only an apostle of Christ that believes and proclaims the doctrine that God calls the victims of our greed to be God's trusted and equal partners in ushering in God's Kingdom. God does not choose the oppressed because they are sinless but because they are oppressed. But they become holy only when they accept this covenantal partnership and respond to the call of God. To evangelize the poor is to summon them to rise from their complacency and fulfill their role in the coming of the Reign of justice and peace. Latin Americans call it conscientization.

To sum up, integral evangelism consists of two inseparable processes. The first is the evangelization of the church by the poor; the aim would be to reconvert the church to discipleship so that she may have the authority to undertake the second task in the evangelizing process, namely, the evangelization of the poor by the church; this consists of awakening the poor to their evangelical vocation vis-à-vis the Reign of God.

WORD AND SIGN

What I have written here is only a word, a word I hear the Spirit speak to the church. It should now be *our* word. No word, however, is credible without a sign. The only sign we can give is that of Jonah. It is a matter of going underground and emerging, in the way Christ did. The church is too visible as a tower of power. It is too prestigious a body to be sullied by any association with the invisible God of the oppressed.

This adulterous generation seeks a sign that makes the church glitter in the eyes of the nation. Exhibitionist messianism which glories in miracles of healing is a concession to Mammon. (See how Mother Teresa is used by the media, to advertise Christian charity at the expense of the poor.) It is time for the church to bury itself in the midst of the invisible nonpeople of our land, by giving up prestigious institutions through which we are hooked on to Mammon worshipers. The cross is the price fixed by the rich who refuse to be evangelized by the poor. If one day we truly take up this cross as a body and go underground and pay that price for the sake of our intimidated masses, that day the world will see the miracle it is yearning to see, a church which has been evangelized by the poor, and, therefore, a church that has become Good News to the poor, as Jesus was.

14

Interreligious Dialogue and Theology of Religions
An Asian Paradigm

Interreligious dialogue, like all else, is having its own way in Asia and reveals its own theology of religion. This has to be seen against the background of what transpires in the Western patriarchate in the same field of theology. Here I will focus on one particular model which has created tension between the two magisteria that function dialectically in the church today: the "academic magisterium" of the theologians and the "pastoral magisterium" of the bishops and in particular the bishop of Rome. They differ in their responses, but they begin their theology of religion by asking almost the same question.

Their starting point as well as the frame of reference is the issue of "Christian uniqueness" and/or the "uniqueness of Christ." The influx of oriental religions into the West (not only through Asian emigrants but also through conversion movements) as well as the West's secular democratic tradition, which respects pluralism and religious freedom amid growing secularization and de-Christianization, creates a certain amount of apprehension among concerned Christians about the concomitant crisis in traditional Christianity. To assert itself as a living force, Christianity has to rediscover its identity as well as reformulate its inalienable role in society. Thus the question of specificity and uniqueness — a euphemism for absoluteness? — of Christ and his religion becomes the pivotal point of the Western patriarchate's theology of religion.

EXCLUSIVISM, INCLUSIVISM, AND PLURALISM

Today the academic magisterium in the West has developed this theology in terms of three significant categories: exclusivism, inclusivism, and

Published in *Horizons,* 20 (no. 1, 1993), 106–14.

pluralism. In the first category are those who perceive their own religion as exclusively salvific; the Christian version of it is reflected in the adage *extra ecclesiam nulla salus*. Hence conversion of others to their own faith is a religious imperative that invokes love and compassion for the unredeemed as the driving motive for direct evangelization.

The inclusivists would situate the Salvific Absolute (e.g., Christ) in their own religion, but hold it to be secretly operative in other religions, which thus become indirectly salvific. Other religionists are saved insofar as they are potentially Christians (awaiting *fulfillment* in Christianity) or anonymously Christians (needing *explication* of their true identity in and through Christianity). The goal of dialogue is to complete the incomplete, in the first case, or name and recognize the implicit discipleship, in the second. The third school — pluralism — attributes to each religion its unique role in salvation, rejecting as almost irreligious any attempt at co-opting the other's religion to one's own paradigm of soteriology.

The pastoral magisterium, also concerned with the uniqueness of Christ and Christianity, is apprehensive of both inclusivist and pluralist trends. I see *Redemptoris Missio* as a countermove against these two approaches which may have diminished the old missionary spirit in the church. The conversion of Asia to Christianity is specifically mentioned as an urgent missionary task. Non-Christians are urged to "open the doors to Christ"; furthermore, the physical expansion of the church (*plantatio ecclesiae*) is stated to be the practical aim of mission. The renewal of this zeal for conversion of the world, it is hoped, would rejuvenate the contemporary church. The preoccupation with the contemporary challenge to the belief in the uniqueness of Christianity and of Christ has probably predetermined the encyclical's subtle regression to a preconciliar (exclusivist?) approach to other religions.

In Asia, the Western Mission started in the sixteenth century with the exclusivist theology. Gradually, the two versions of the inclusivist approach, namely, that of fulfillment (later taken up by Vatican II) and that of explicitation (current in the postconciliar decades) came into vogue in Asian theological circles. Understandably, those Asian theologians who condemn both exclusivism and inclusivism as imperialistic get easily thrown into the third slot. They are labeled pluralists. It is not surprising that Asians themselves often employ these categories of the Western patriarchate to describe their own theological stance — so ubiquitous is the Euro-American thought in the Christian enclaves of Asia, and so contagious too!

I am embarrassed when I am asked in classrooms and in public forums whether I am an inclusivist or a pluralist. The reason is not that I dismiss the paradigm that gives rise to these categories as wrong, but that I have found myself gradually appropriating a trend in Asia which adopts a paradigm wherein the three categories mentioned above do not make sense. For our starting point is not the uniqueness of Christ or Christianity, or of any other religion. *A fortiori* such a concern would never be a hidden agenda in any interreligious dialogue that may engage us. Furthermore, interreligious dialogue itself is not a conscious target pursued as something desirable per se, as it is a luxury which the urgency of the sociospiritual crisis in Asia would not permit.

What then is this Asian paradigm? I would describe it in terms of three overlapping concerns which do not receive any emphasis in the Western approach. The first is the acknowledgment of a third *magisterium,* namely, that of the poor; the second is the *liberational thrust* that defines our theology of religions; and finally, the social location of this theology is the *Basic Human Communities* (BHCs).

My intention is to present the new paradigm by spelling out the implications of these three concerns.

THE THIRD MAGISTERIUM

The poor (the destitute, the dispossessed, the displaced, and the discriminated) who form the bulk of Asian people, plus their specific brand of cosmic religiosity, constitute a school where many Christian activists reeducate themselves in the art of speaking the language of God's Reign, that is, the language of liberation which God speaks through Jesus. Neither the academic nor the pastoral magisterium is conversant with this evangelical idiom.

Some members of the two official magisteria here in Asia did make an all too brief — perhaps a merely symbolic — effort to enroll themselves in this school in 1986, in preparation for the seventh session of the Bishops' Institute for Social Action (BISA VII), which discussed the "religiosity of the Asian poor." These "exposure programs" ended with a powerful declaration, which was, of course, prepared by the theologians and approved (after discussion) by the bishops.

After a few days of learning, these two magisteria (I too was a part of them) thought they should teach something about it to the rest of the church. We are programmed to do very little learning and a lot of teaching. The real purpose of this exercise, which a few exemplary bishops and theologians have not forgotten, *was to persuade the twofold teaching office in the church to be in a permanent learning relationship with the poor of Asia.*

As one of the resource persons working out those exposure programs, I was able to pick up seven *liberative* features from the "cosmic" religiosity of the poor, though it cannot be said that what I say here in any way replicates the bishops' statement.

1. The poor have a distinctively this-worldly spirituality. They cry to heaven for their daily needs. To those of us who have all our material needs met, they may appear materialistic. For their *life's basic needs* — something to live on (food), something to live by (work), something to live in (shelter), something to live for (decent human setting) — color their prayer life and their spirituality.

2. Secondly, in these needs, they do not have Mammon at their beck and call, as most of us do. So in their utter helplessness, they *totally depend on God.* Hence theirs is a God of rice and curry, a God of shelter and clothing, a God of marriage and children, in short the only God of this life and, of course, the only God of their life. This total dependence on God is their spirituality.

3. It is also to this God that they *cry for justice.* In many Asian cultures there is a divine manifestation (often in female form) which is concerned with retribution or restitution already here on earth rather than in some post-mortem state of existence.

4. Their "this-worldly" approach to God and religion, however, is not *secular,* but *cosmic.* The difference is crucial. The secular is the nonsacred or the areligious world vitiated by the acquisitiveness-consumerism cycle; the cosmic is a blend of the sacred, the womanly, and the earthly, making that vicious cycle physically impossible except when and where the secularizing process (brought by capitalist technocracy) moves into that world, with the following *consequences.*

5. In the cosmic spirituality of the poor, *women* often find some space to express at least symbolically their state of oppression. In contrast, the meta-cosmic religions (including Christianity) are more inextricably entrenched in patriarchalism.

6. The constant awareness of earthly needs, and the faith in various cosmic forces which determine their daily life, make their spirituality *ecological.* The involvement of the oppressed classes of women in eco-movements (e.g., the chipko movement in India) is therefore a distinctive feature of feminism in certain parts of Asia.

7. The most powerful idiom of communication in their religious tradition is the *story.* Human liberation, which constitutes their only religion, is the story of a God among his/her people. The world is the sacred theater. The epic, the narrative, and the drama are media very sacred to the masses.

These ingredients of the *cosmic religiosity* of the poor have somehow or other entered the theological world of Asian Christians, especially among the liberation theologians and feminists (hence our second concern which determines our theology of religions).

THE LIBERATIONAL THRUST
IN THE THEOLOGY OF RELIGIONS

For too long a time we Christians have dialogued too exclusively with the metacosmic religions (i.e., the so-called higher forms of Hinduism, Buddhism, Taoism, Islam, etc.) and tried to create a theological language to communicate our common experience of the Absolute. Cosmic religiosity (i.e., tribal and clanic religions, as well as the popular forms of metacosmic religions, e.g., popular Buddhism, popular Hinduism, popular Christianity, etc.) was looked down upon as an immature and infantile stage of spiritual development.

This approach has resulted in a distorted view of the Asian religious ethos. One aspect of this distortion is the underestimation of the liberative potential of cosmic religiosity. As I have substantiated elsewhere in my writings, many great social transformations in Asia have taken place thanks to the involvement of tribal and other groups known for their cosmic religiosity. Their "this-worldliness" as well as their faith in a God of justice, far from being an opiate (as some Asian Marxists thought), has often been a stimulant in revolutionary situations whenever it is mobilized in an appropriate way.

Today, we are happy to observe that, in the common struggle against poverty and destitution of the masses, many adherents of metacosmic religions (Buddhists, Hindus, Muslims, and Christians) have learned to reinterpret their beliefs according to some of the *liberative elements* in the cosmic religiosity of their co-believers who belong to the poorer classes. Thus a reinterpretation of the sacred scriptures of metacosmic religions along a liberational thrust is noted among the exponents of various faiths, who have been involved with popular movements, for example, Sulak Sivaraksha in Buddhism, Swami Agnivesh in Hinduism, Ali Ascar Engineer in Islam, to name a few.

Christianity too has begun to appropriate this trend, not in seminaries or in houses of religious orders, but in Basic Human Communities, where the magisterium of the poor is taken seriously. Hence I cannot speak of the liberational thrust that Christianity has received from the cosmic religiosity of the poor without entering into a discussion of the social location of such theologizing: the Basic Human Communities.

THE ROLE OF BASIC HUMAN COMMUNITIES

The Basic Human Community is not a group that has come together for interreligious dialogue. Dialogue is not an end in itself. Nor is there any preoccupation about one's religious identity or uniqueness. The origin, the development, and the culmination of the activities of a BHC is, ideally, the total liberation of the nonpersons and nonpeoples. It is within the process of this ongoing liberative praxis that each member of the BHC discovers the uniqueness of his or her religion. My religious identity is not something I seek and find through academic discussion; it is something that the other religionists impart to me. It is the process of naming and recognizing both sin and liberation as experienced and acted upon by us in a BHC that we acquire for one another our respective religious uniqueness.

Let me recount a concrete example of something I have experienced more than once. In the course of a seminar which I conducted in July 1989 for Buddhist, Hindu, Christian, and Marxist members of a BHC (i.e., the Christian Workers' Fellowship) I was drawn into a very lively exchange with one of the participants from a Buddhist-Marxist background. He was Sarath Mallika, who nine months later died a martyr's death by the hand of a Sinhala extremist. We were discussing the liberational thrust of the scriptures of various religions.

Sarath's interventions centered on what he thought was unique to biblical Christianity. He acknowledged that rationalist literature which he had read as a young man made him see the Bible as a fairy tale. But he pointed out that, in their common struggle and the common reflections which each had on the other's religious literature, and in the sharing we had at that seminar, he had discovered that the concept of "God" which motivates Christians to liberationist activity is radically different from the concept of God which the Buddha is reported in the Pali scriptures to have rejected as absurd and chimerical. As a Marxist coming from a Buddhist background, he could not accept the idea of God, but "if I ever have to believe in a God, this is the only one worth believing in," he confessed. I responded: "To believe in any other god, as most Christians do, is idolatry."

But What Is Unique about Christian Theism?

"This is the first time I have heard of a God *who has made a defense pact with the oppressed*," he declared. And the Christian participants came to realize that what is unique about their religion is that *Jesus whom they follow is this pact!* We further realized that we Christians tend, unfortunately, to duplicate the institutional aspects of other religions in Asia and thus compete with them rather than preach and practice that which is our unique mission.

In the ensuing discussion, it became evident to the Christian members that if they do not confess that Jesus is God's defense pact with the nonpersons of the earth, "there will be no eternal life in them." Thus, this Buddhist-Marxist activist and prospective martyr who had labored tirelessly for the workers of a sugar factory and had learned from the "little ones" of the earth their language of liberation was eminently capable of capturing the liberative essence of the Gospel for all of us.

To sum up: the Christians in BHCs are given their identity and are made to discover what is unique about Jesus by the non-Christians and that, too, in the context of a common liberational concern.

This discovery was a recurrent experience in many such encounters in many such groups, so that one begins to see why an Asian theology of liberation proclaims God as the One who is reached only through the mediation of the (mostly) non-Christian poor, and equally proclaims that Jesus is this mediation. Such a kerygma does not clash with other religions and does not compete with them for adherents. But it does clash with the official catechesis of the church.

The Common Spirituality and the Credibility Gap

But there is a *conditio sine qua non* for Christians to live out their unique-ness and be recognized as Christians: their *credibility*. And this depends on how far the Christians join the other religionists in that which is the only common denominator between religions, namely, the spirit of nonacquisitive-ness or the renunciation of Mammon (which, in theistic terms, amounts to a total reliance on God); it is the evangelical poverty proclaimed in the Ser-mon on the Mount as constitutive of discipleship. It is the basic spirituality of God's Reign, which is also the spirituality of Jesus who precisely on that account can become at home in most Asian cultures, if only he so appears in the belief and behavior of his Asian followers!

The much-desired Christian credibility, however, is threatened by every form of financial and ideological subservience to Euro-ecclesiastical power bases. Most Asian churches, consequently, find it difficult to exercise their twofold evangelizing role: (1) to experience solidarity with non-Christians by witnessing to the *spirituality common to all religions* (i.e., by practicing the beatitudes); (2) to reveal their *Christian uniqueness* (i.e., to proclaim in Jesus as the new covenant by joining the poor against Mammon's principalities and powers that create poverty and oppression).

The churches, instead, take refuge in a more convenient kind of unique-ness which they spell out in terms of the theandric (God-Man-Savior) model. This makes no sense in many of our cultures where it often evokes the image of one of the many cosmic forces rather than of a personal and absolute Creator-Redeemer. Moreover, this model, utterly untranslatable into some Asian languages, suffers also from an ontology before which soteriology (concern for liberation) fades into insignificance.

But the aspiration for a liberator — a God of this *life,* a God of *justice,* and a God who can transform this earth into the garden of delight it was originally intended to be — such aspiration of the poor, so clearly expressed in their cosmic religiosity, is spurned as a futile dream by some adherents of metacosmic religions, who propose in its place another kind of "future world" which coincides with some kind of an "acosmic Absolute."

Which of these two is purely utopian? As for interreligious dialogue ac-cepted within the ecclesiastical set-up, one wonders whether it resonates also with the cosmic religiosity of the poor or only with the metacosmic spirituality of the elite. Are not the Christian Ashrams also guilty of this onesidedness? Finally in terms of its organized charity, does not the church organization find it more convenient to gain control over the poor than to join them in their struggle for emancipation? These are the questions raised in the BHCs.

But some BHCs also operate as non-government organizations (with Western aid) and thus fail to witness to the common spirituality (opted pov-erty), so that their struggle with the poor runs the risk of being ineffective in their proclamation of that which is unique to their religion: that Jesus is Good News insofar as he is also YHWH's irrevocable answer to the cry of Asia's (mostly non-Christian) poor.

Wherever the Christian members of BHCs make themselves one with the poor in their total dependence on God (opted poverty as common spirituality), and thus qualify themselves to proclaim the new covenant between God and the poor (Christian uniqueness), there Jesus comes out convincingly as God's story in the lives of the covenant partners (the Asian poor) rather than as a subtle combination of natures and persons.

As Marinus de Jonge has admitted in the epilogue of his brilliant description of the "Early Christian Responses to Jesus,"[1] the characteristically Christian way of communicating Jesus to others would continue to be through drama, narrative, and poem. This is the idiom of cosmic religiosity. The story of God's public agreement with the poor to embark on the common task of transforming this world into the new heaven and new earth that God and the poor are dreaming of together is a story the Asians would never refuse to hear; and it is the story that Christians fear to narrate. And yet that story is Jesus.

The New Categories

Now, one might rightly ask: where do exclusivism, inclusivism, and pluralism fit in here? If categories are needed at all in this new paradigm, my suggestion is the following three: syncretism, synthesis, and symbiosis.

Syncretism is a haphazard mixing of religions: something of a cocktail which changes the flavor of each constituent under the influence of the other. That really does not exist among the poor, but is attributed to them by "observers" (some theologians and some sociologists). *Synthesis* is the creation of a *tertium quid* out of two or more religions, destroying the identity of each component religion. This, of course, is a personal idiosyncrasy of certain individuals, or groups of individuals.

What happens in the BHCs is a veritable *symbiosis* of religions. Each religion, challenged by the other religion's unique approach to the liberationist aspiration of the poor, especially to the sevenfold characteristic of their cosmic religiosity mentioned above, discovers and renames itself in its specificity in response to the other approaches. What I have been describing as Christian uniqueness in the BHC experience reflects both the process and product of a symbiosis. It indicates one's conversion to the common heritage of all religions (beatitudes) and also a conversion to the specificity of one's own religion as dictated by other religionists. You may call it interreligious dialogue, if you wish.

---

1. This is the subtitle of his *Christology in Context,* Westminster, Philadelphia, 1988.

Part III

Spirituality and
Authentic Human Liberation

15

The Spiritual Dimension of Change

Spirituality is our innate orientation toward God insofar as it is consciously cultivated and translated into a way of life. But this God-relatedness, even prior to becoming a spirituality, manifests itself as a *coincidentia oppositorum* (coincidence of opposites), an unusual blend of two antithetical inclinations programmed into us at the moment of creation: our creatureliness, which humbles us, and our creativeness, which exalts us.

THE BIPOLARITY OF CHANGE AND THE EPICLESIS

This bipolarity springs from the fact that our God-relatedness is based on creation, namely, that we have both *God* and *nothing* as our absolute beginning (2 Macc. 7:28), so that the possibility of both divinization and annihilation is built into our system. If God and dust are each our origin (Gen. 2:7), are they not also our twofold destiny (Qoh. 12:7)? "Earth to earth, ashes to ashes, dust to dust in the sure and certain hope of the resurrection to eternal life," the church declares at our graveside.

Indeed it is the ability to keep ourselves in touch with the dustward and Godward orientation of our human existence, that is to say, the conviction that we are at once nothing and everything (Ps. 8:1–5) which authenticates our spirituality.

This ambivalence can lead to much confusion, as the history of spirituality attests. Some medieval mystics who were groping for words to express this experience were accused of Manichaean dualism and, as in the case of Margaret Porette, even burned at the stake! Many of them (Mechtild of Magdeburg, Julian of Norwich, the author of *The Cloud of Unknowing,* and others) seemed to advocate self-annihilation or "noughting" of the soul for the purpose of "deification" or "alling."

First published in *The Way,* January 1988, 34–41.

In fact, the dynamics of the Ignatian Exercises lie precisely in fostering the soul's spiritual growth along this binary path of creatureliness and creativeness. The one evokes a deep sense of shame, self-effacement, and many degrees of humility; the other spurs the exercitant to a chivalrous participation in the adventures of Christ the King.

This bipolarity which ensures spiritual transformation is not an invention of the mystics. It can be traced back to the gospels, e.g., the dialectics of living and dying (John 11:25; 12:24–25), losing and finding (Matt. 10:39), and decreasing and increasing (John 3:30). There is also the Pauline spirituality of noughting the "I" for the alling in Christ (Gal. 2:20), and Jesus' own cyclic movement from *pleroma* to *kenosis* to *pleroma* sung about in one of the earliest Christian hymns (Phil. 2:6–11) and celebrated annually in the church's slow-motion unfolding of the liturgical cycle from Advent to Easter.

This whole sequence of the liturgical cycle is, in its turn, epitomized in the Eucharist, which schools us in the art of crumbling to dust and rising to life. The brittle wafer of bread that breaks to bits between our fingers and the weakness of the wine which time turns into vinegar and vapor are the fruit of our labor, but also the symbol of our own dustness. With them, however, we too are transubstantiated gradually into the body of Christ by the creative power of the Spirit invoked upon them and upon us. This is the *epiclesis,* the "Spirit dimension" of change.

The *epiclesis* is the highest manifestation of our creativeness operating in the depths of our creatureliness. God's creative word, in which the Spirit hovered over the primordial waters to bring forth life (Gen. 1:27), breathed life into mud to make it human (Gen. 2:7), descended on Mary to plant and nurture the theandric seed of life (Luke 1:35), and raised the mangled body of Jesus from the limbo of death (Rom. 8:11)...indeed that creative word which calls down the Spirit can be uttered by the human heart to change all cosmic dust into the body of Christ.

This creative word is Love. Love which is coextensive with God (1 John 4:16) has been generously poured into our hearts (Rom. 5:5; Tit. 3:6) and is that very love by which we love one another (1 John 4:7–13); it therefore defies death by its power to call the Spirit on all that is frail and feeble. When our own crumbling and pouring (2 Tim. 4:6), sweating and bleeding, aging and dying becomes a nourishment *for others,* like the sacramental bread and wine, then we have uttered the creative word. The *epiclesis* that christifies all that crumbles to dust, including ourselves, is love. Not to love, then, is a sin against the Spirit who transforms the face of the earth. Stoic cynicism about sociopolitical change, ecclesiastical narcissism that precludes God from non-churchly activities, and heresy hunting which does not allow error to take its own time to tell the truth it is trying to say — are all a defeatist concession to our creatureliness and a vote of no confidence in the creativity of human life.

On the opposite side are those who fear to accept their creatureliness. They refuse to die. They cling to life only to lose it all. The incapacity to retire gracefully from positions of authority, from the stations of life and from life itself, or the stubborn refusal to accept changes that threaten one's personal convenience is the old temptation to be like the creator (Gen. 3:5) without acknowledging one's creatureliness. This suicidal hungering for the fatal food which creates a lethal thirst for deathless perpetuity (Gen. 3:2–4) is the total negation of the Eucharist which quenches our hunger and thirst forever (John 6:35–38) and promises eternal life only to those willing to die.

Eucharist is bread and Spirit together; so too, the christification of the world is possible only through the conspiracy of both creatureliness and creativity. The mystic and scientist Teilhard de Chardin identified these impulses as two energies — tangential and radial — whose dialectical interaction accounts for the epochal formation of that cosmic-human-divine continuum called Christ, a formation that converges toward and radiates from one single theandric nucleus: Jesus in whom God becomes the dust of which we are made, the dust which is subsumed by him into the bosom of God.

Put more precisely, these dustward and Godward movements of creation conspire to bring to fruition the yet incomplete process — the axial change of all ages — of Jesus becoming the *pleroma* which is Christ. The implication is that Jesus who is wholly Christ (*totus Christus*) is not yet the whole of Christ (*totum Christi*) which he certainly will become only when all are christified in him.

To use a graphic simile, we, his body, are still held back by our creatureliness, reluctant to leave the cozy and comfortable womb of death and darkness, while he, our head, is already out of the womb ("firstborn among the dead") struggling to pull us out into the light by the power of the Spirit which animates the whole body, head and members, so that our eucharistic acclamation could very well be: "Jesus has died, Jesus is risen, but Christ will come again when we have died and risen with him!"

Obviously, this grandiose view of christogenesis is granted to us only when we stand with him on Thabor. Were we to come down to the "high-tech" society below, we might meet quite another perception of the phenomenon of change.

GODLESS CHANGE AND THE CHANGELESS GOD

Those who crusade against Hellenistic stoicism contaminating the Christian faith, including Martin Luther, have taught us to sing: "Change and decay all around I see. But thou who changest not, abide with me." His intention was perhaps to contrast the fickleness of the human heart with God's steadfast love. But the words, as they sink into the depths of our being through repeated singing, could elicit from us a stoic response to the world around. The infinite chasm that yawns between creation which is "change and decay" and the creator who "changes not" makes us subscribe to a spirituality that invites us to anticipate, here and now, our eschatological fulfillment in a Being that knows no becoming.

It was within such a theological framework that Cardinal Ottaviani strove to be *semper idem*, "always the same," like the God of Aristotle, the Immovable Mover! Never to change was also the ideal he proposed for the church! Thus, our pilgrimage on earth is not to end up in a permanent city that would replace this impermanent one, as St. Paul would have us believe (Heb. 13:14), but in an unchanging *state* of beatitude; the Risen Lord's gift to us would not be an incorruptible body in place of our corruptible one, as the same St. Paul hoped (1 Cor. 15:42), but one that would neither change nor decay.

Indeed should change be so neatly equated with impermanence and perishability? Surely, change is robbed of its spiritual or rather, its Spirit dimension if God is expelled from it. Outside a changeless God, all is going to be godless change!

This notion of change has been challenged by the process theologians. The scope of this article is too modest and practical to include their vision. Suffice it to note that one of them, Teilhard de Chardin, did not allow God and change to cancel each other in our minds. With him we perceive change as christogenesis, we see God and dust *becoming* each other, Creator and creature *growing* one into the other, so that we can truly sing a new canticle to the Lord:

> Change and growth all around I see
> Change Thou who changest all, grow now through me.

Regrettably, Teilhard lived all his life on Thabor and did not live long enough to see his ecstatic vision obstructed with biosphere pollution, his dream of a gradual amorization of the world shattered by the imminent threat of its pulverization, the Christian participation in the recapitulation of all things in the person of Christ challenged by a counterprocess that reduces even persons to things at the service of Mammon. Yet without his vision we cannot initiate a counterculture that can redeem our generation from technocracy. We need Thabor.

It is more in keeping with the theme of this chapter to focus on the fact that, contrary to his prediction, the old theory of the changeless God has survived long enough to produce its ghost: godless change. What I pick up here for discussion is the current behavioral pattern which operates on the unformulated principle that change is the antidote to that dreadful disease which our high-tech society has produced: boredom.

Like any unexamined assumption which tacitly justifies a social practice — "ideology" as Marx would call it pejoratively — this practice too discloses its absurdity only when formulated into a theory. Hence our question: is change in itself the remedy for boredom? Rather, is not boredom itself the result of a misconception of change? After all, does not continuous change bore us as much as changeless continuity? Read a few pages of a dictionary: how tedious it is to find the subject change with every new word!

In fact boredom cannot be correctly diagnosed unless the nexus between change and *routine* is first established. Aspects of the postconciliar effort for renewal illustrate how "change," which is introduced as a remedy for routine, can itself be so routinized as to make one seek routine for a change! When, for instance, the triteness of a tradition, the immutability of an institution, or the repetitiveness of a ritual begins to bore us, we turn to change as the remedy. So changes are made in the rules and rites and roles of religious groups, but *life* which is "change and growth" remains unchanged, i.e., *dead.* The innovators themselves cannot keep up with their own urge to change which, in any way, brings spiritual boredom and bankruptcy.

Though not as widespread as the alarmists have claimed, this species of renewal helped the traditionalists to justify their infantile regression to the status quo and the semper idem. Some Catholic seminarians who sought holy orders in the Lefebvre sect are known to have claimed that they were so fiercely tossed by the waves of renewal on a sea of incessant change that they finally found their anchor in the clarity of the past, the security of the rite and the regularity of the pre-Vatican II seminary.

The error behind this confusion is to oppose regularity and repetitiveness to change, when in fact they are integral aspects of it. It is also assumed that the biblical faith's unilinear movement of history must correct the "cyclic" or repetitive conception advocated in other religions. This contrast is too neat to be true. Besides, a unilinear movement can be simultaneously cyclic like the wheels of a moving car. In fact the whole liturgical cycle we referred to earlier demonstrates that even the church, in her "life in Christ" (this is what liturgy means in Vatican II) captures the rhythmic movement of the cosmos, the moods and seasons of nature. It is this cosmic liturgy that the Hindus have perceptively visualized as a cosmic dance, dynamic and repetitive. The ancient Vedic expression for the cosmic order is *rta* which is etymologically related to the English word *rite.* Therefore, routine, rhythm, regularity, rite, and repetitiveness cannot be divorced from change which is also growth. Change is not necessarily the antithesis of routine and routine is not necessarily the source of boredom.

What causes boredom is the disorientation that occurs when we stampede against this cosmic order, ignoring the rhythm of nature, out of step with the changing beat of the cosmic dance, technologically distancing ourselves from nature's cyclic movement toward Christ, her personal Center. Conversely, being and acting in conscious harmony with this rhythmic process of christogenesis is true contemplation. It is faith seeking an understanding of the Spirit dimension of change.

It is, therefore, a false diagnosis of boredom that allures the victims of technocracy to seek "peak experiences" in order to break the monotony of the plateau of daily life, a *change* that lifts them above the ordinary. If the chemical inducement of such "changes" — the "altered states of consciousness" as they are respectably known — are not indulged in by Christian believers, there are other drugs of a spiritual nature available to them. In contrast to Newman's contentment with just enough light to see the next step in the life of faith, some of us prefer extraordinary illuminations which would exempt us from that faith. Thus, such gifts of God as the charismatic movement, oriental mysticism, shrines of saints and centers of healing are resorted to with an obsessive craving for the ecstatic and the miraculous. Is it not a wicked generation that seeks such signs (Luke 11:29; John 4:48)?

After all, did not the "peak experience" on the Red Sea, God's stupendous intervention on behalf of his people, lose its impact within a few days of desert life? Did not their enthusiasm sink below zero and their songs of praise turn into psalms of plaintive murmurs as the weariness of walking through the wilderness began to irritate them? Did not the boredom of the desert delete from their memory all traces of their miraculous past? A miracle does not solve the problem of faith, warns Rabbi Kushner, any more than a sumptuous dinner could solve the problem of hunger for long.

> So God changed his tactics. Instead of a spectacular miracle once in a generation, He provided the Israelites with water to drink, manna to eat and shade to rest in, everyday...they experienced the goodness of God and the fullness of life in the everyday unspectacular miracles which made their lives bearable...a few small experiences of the meaningfulness of life everyday will do more for our souls than a single overwhelming religious experience.[1]

Such small experiences can hardly be possible where speed is the rule. Like the frames of a filmstrip that fascinate us by the velocity with which they move past our eyes, it is the hurry and haste of our high-tech world (now intruding into the urban societies of developing countries) that keep us from enjoying the individual "stills" of life, each of which, to adapt Kushner's words, is an "everyday unspectacular miracle which makes our life bearable."

We are seduced by what one might call our "highway spirituality" (each individual rushing to his or her spiritual destiny, whatever that be, ever fighting against time) so that even a simple thing as our lunch (is it not as much a sacrament of life as a biological need?) turns out to be "a hurried refuelling, the equivalent of an auto-racer's pit-stop," whereas it could really be "an opportunity to savor the miracle that dirt, rain, seeds and human imagination can work on our taste buds." And Kushner concludes: "We just have to be wise enough to know how to recognize the miracle and not rush headlong past it in search of 'something important.' "[2]

---

1. Kushner, H. S., *When All You've Ever Wanted Isn't Enough: Search for a Life that Matters*, Pan Books, London, 1987, 144.
2. Ibid.

To recognize this miracle is to recognize the Spirit dimension of change. That "something important," if there is one, is the peak experience that awaits us, the *pleroma* of Christ that lures us to take the small strides that make up the long leaps of his cosmic dance. An old Italian song instructs us on how to have our eyes on the peak in the horizon and dance toward it without missing the miracles of every moment:

> Se tu corri, non potrai vedere
> Le cose belle che stanno intorn'a te;
> Se ti fermi, non potrai salire
> La vette bianca che sta di front' a te.

This can be translated, if somewhat missing the beauty of the Italian, as: "If you rush, you will miss the beautiful things around you. If you're stuck, you'll never reach the dazzling peak in front of you." Or as Paul said: "Since we live by the Spirit, let us keep in step with the Spirit" (Gal. 5:25).

16

Religious Vows and the Reign of God

Every God other than Yahweh — the state, the capital or even the church — is tyrannical by nature. When such gods usurp Yahweh's throne, the obligation to restore the humanum to the center of the world falls on the "little ones of God" who dare to proclaim: "we have no king but Yahweh." They would do this not by mere words but by a lifestyle which discloses their inner surrender to God's will (evangelical obedience) as well as their open rejection of riches, which compete with God to win human allegiance (evangelical poverty). In Yahweh's communities, therefore, chastity — conjugal or celibate — is the sheer joy of being totally open to God; it is the aesthetic experience of being unconditionally obedient and absolutely poor. In that sense alone is chastity prophetic. The nascent church was one such community. In it, God who is Love was the sole rule of life. So the slaves of other gods declared in wonder: "Look how these Christians love one another!"

If indeed the option for God is necessarily an option against Mammon, as Jesus emphatically declared (Matt. 6:24), then *obedience* to God who calls us to be poor and religious *poverty,* which makes us free to obey God, are mutually inclusive. As a matter of fact, initially, they were two inseparable and even indistinguishable dimensions of the Kingdom spirituality so clearly set forth in the Sermon on the Mount and demanded in the call narratives of the gospels. It is much later that they branched into two distinct vows which, together with celibacy as the third, have now entered our definition of religious life.

Going along with John Chrysostom's well-known animadversion that the renunciation of family life was about the only thing that set the monks and nuns apart from other Christians, I shall treat poverty and obedience as the basic Christian commitment and celibacy as a specific feature of religious life.

First published in *The Way, Supplement* 65, Summer 1989, 3–15.

Note, however, that in base communities, both Christian and trans-denominational, conjugal spirituality has become a respectable alternative to celibacy. Furthermore, in these "contrast societies," as we shall call them, chastity — conjugal or celibate — seems to derive its authenticity and prophetic character from two other options: from an opted poverty that is capable of challenging the prevailing order of Mammon, where the consumerism of a minority maintains millions in misery, and from a radical orientation (obedience?) toward an Ultimate Concern identified as the humanum which clamors for attention in the poor and the oppressed.

The religious who wish to rediscover their mission as contrast societies on the fringes of church and society should be made to realize that they risk being superseded or even displaced by these new communities if they do not realign their specific vow of chastity to the prophetically dangerous implications of the two basic vows. This concern remains the theological perspective from which I propose to spell out in what follows the general principle already enunciated in the very first paragraph of this chapter.

POVERTY AND OBEDIENCE: THE PROPHETIC VOWS

The seed-idea that germinates into various species of monastic and religious life at critical periods of the church's growth goes further back into history than we are willing to concede. The hermits and wandering ascetics who protested against Rome's imperialized Christianity were only a particular form which this seminal idea assumed in history. The idea of religious life did not originate with them. This is equally true of the circles of virgins and ascetics that appeared even earlier. They can distort our perception of religious life if the seed-idea which they incarnated is not recognized and named.

Not even Jesus, I dare say, was the originator of this idea. He did certainly envisage a community which would embody the Kingdom that he preached and epitomized in his own person. In fact, several Kingdom communities of Jesus people began to mushroom immediately after his resurrection and served as the vital nucleus of the local churches that grew out of them, although the way they practiced the Kingdom spirituality is not as clearly documented as we would like it to be. The point I wish to make here is that such communities were not so much an innovation on the part of Jesus as they were the fulfillment of his lifelong effort to revive Yahweh's ancient dream of a contrast society, a society where only Yahweh and no other god would reign, a human community governed by love. This is what the phrase "Kingdom of God" meant for Jesus. The humanum that Jesus embodied could continue as a palpable reality only when his followers proclaimed to the world in word and deed: "we have no king but Yahweh."

When Yahweh's sovereignty is allowed to be challenged by other gods, human rulers emerge as a "powerful" class. Now, *power,* unlike "authority," is appropriated only by accumulating *riches*. Authority, on the other hand, is rooted in one's willingness to renounce power, a refusal to count on riches. By riches one does not mean only material possessions and money; various spiritual acquisitions such as knowledge and education, political acumen and resourcefulness, prestige and the right connections are as capable of generating power as do material possessions and money. In other words, there is a subversive conspiracy between power and riches; Jesus names it Mammon.

Mammon is the source and sustenance of social structures in which the powerful control the beliefs and behavior of their fellows. They either dethrone God, as in atheistic states with totalitarian governments; or divinize money as in antitheistic systems such as capitalism; or invoke God as the "authority" behind their "power," as often happens in the church. This last mentioned theo-ideology used to be known as the "divine right theory of kingship" and was invoked by medieval kings and popes against each other in their struggle for power. Many religious institutes have tried to create alternative models of obedience and government as a corrective to these feudal structures of the church.

Ignatius of Loyola, for instance, wished to enrich the church with a contrast society where Yahweh would reign unchallenged, or as he would put it, a religious order where God's greater glory was the only thing that mattered. He would therefore have sounded naive to his contemporaries when he declared right at the beginning of the Jesuit *Constitutions* that "discerning love" had to be the sole guiding principle in such a society! But to serve the church with his new vision, that is Christ's vision, he had to acquire a little space within the pyramidally structured governmental system of the Roman Communion. In doing so, he did incorporate the monarchical ideology, but with two revolutionary modifications. First, he had presented a new concept of kingship, that of a leader who derives his authority from powerlessness, whose leadership consists of service even unto death. This ideal King is obviously the Jesus of the *Spiritual Exercises*, i.e., the Jesus of the gospels.

Secondly, he tamed the monarchical form of government by introducing the structure known as *congregatio generalis*, one form of which was in vogue among the Benedictines. Ignatius may not have been aware that its remote ancestor was conciliarism, the antimonarchical movement which opposed the papal absolutism of the Middle Ages. The fact, however, is that in this manner, the elective principle was made to control the monarchical so that God's greater glory would not succumb to human ambition.

In such a community, leadership amounts to mediating the entire group's constant submission to God's will (obedience) by creating an atmosphere of honest detachment (poverty) so that no ideology ("corruption of reason by interest" — Marx) would compromise God's liberating and humanizing presence in that community. This is what the much worn-out word *discernment* really means: "obedience through poverty." It means communal listening to God and recognizing God's voice in a chaos of conflicting messages.

In fact, *obedience* literally means "listening," from the Latin *obaudire*. The word *hypakoe*, in the Greek spiritual tradition, conveyed the same sense; listening to (the word of) God. Since, however, God's word is not merely an expression of God's will, but also its execution (Isa. 55:11), listening includes doing: the word is not heard if it is not executed (Luke 6:46–47; 11:28).

Such is the obedience that constitutes Christian discipleship and guarantees almost a blood-relationship with Jesus (Matt. 12:48–49). This is the origin of Jesus people among whom Yahweh alone reigns and Yahweh alone is obeyed.

Regrettably, we have invented another concept of obedience which is at variance with Yahweh's sovereignty: hypotage or submission, that is, the ascetical practice of bending one's will to the "authority" (but in reality, to the "power") of a human ruler, for example a religious superior, a bishop, or a pope, who claims to have a privileged contact with God by virtue of the institutional position he or she holds. But, as Lozano reminds us, the New Testament always understands obedience as *hypakoe* (listening) and never as *hypotage* (ascetical submission).[1] Even the so-called "evangelical counsel of obedience," believed to differentiate the religious from other Christians by means of a special vow of submission to a human superior, finds apparently no support in the New Testament.[2] Is it again a case of humans encroaching on Yahweh's domain?

How then is authority to be exercised in Yahweh's community? Let us make a brief survey of the experiment Yahweh tried out in the second millennium before Christ. It all began when the God of Israel lodged a protest, through Moses, against Egypt, a superpower that thrived on slave labor. The conspiracy between riches and power had allowed the few to turn the many into beasts of burden. Yahweh wished to prove to the whole of humankind that equality, freedom, and fellowship, in short, the humanum, can reappear in the world only where Yahweh and no other god is allowed to reign.

And so God called a people. But even before the people heard God's call, she heard theirs (Exod. 2:23–25). God is not only the supreme Caller, *ho Kalon* as the Greek Church named her; she is eminently a listener, a God inclined to obey the summons of an oppressed people. But listening implies execution of the other's wish; God did not merely hear their cry for help, but also opted to make their cry his own. God would not only deliver them from the inhuman, that is the antitheistic system, but would partner them in founding a contrast society which would serve all generations as a mem-

---

1. J. M. Lozano, *Discipleship: Towards an Understanding of Religious Life,* Claretian Center for Research on Spirituality, Chicago, 1980, 226–27.

2. Ibid., 242–43.

ory of the future, a future to be realized by the whole of humankind![3] This
was a vow, a covenant, a public agreement between God and the poor. Thus
was sown the seed-idea of religious life, perhaps for the first time in known
history.

If this is the prototype of religious life, as indeed it is, then a few dangerous conclusions have to be drawn before we proceed any further. First we
note that the rich and the powerful are hard of hearing. Only the poor and
the powerless are able to obey God. Consequently, it is only the little ones
and not the big people who can found communities of Yahweh. Finally it is
those who are oppressed and those who have rendered themselves powerless
in solidarity with the oppressed that are qualified to speak in God's name and
prophetically announce to the whole of humankind what kind of future God
is planning for them. If they speak with God's authority, it is not because
they have usurped God's place through riches and power, but because their
powerlessness and poverty have put them into a covenantal intimacy with
God. They alone know Yahweh.[4]

That is why Yahweh began his experiment in the hilly region which,
not without significance, lay between Egypt and Babylon, two superpowers which needed lessons in politics and economics! For Yahweh inspired
her covenantal partners to impose legal barriers against any accumulation
of riches, lest it lead to a concentration of power in the hands of the few.
Precautions such as periodic cancellation of debts (Deut. 15) were political and economic options taken to ensure "that there would be no poor
among [them]" (Lev. 15:4–5), which is to say that there would be no rich
among them!

The sharing of all resources in a spirit of religious poverty and the consequent distribution of responsibility which facilitated collective obedience to
God are truly humanizing features conspicuously absent where Yahweh is not
free to rule. That is why these little ones of God had no human ruler above
them (Judg. 19:1). It is not surprising that this society was able to produce
so many charismatic leaders, the so-called "judges," who distinguished themselves as the servants of God's people. They refused to be treated as kings
because they dared to believe that Yahweh alone was their King (Judg. 8:22–
23).[5] Even death came easy for a leader who had vowed to be the people's
slave so that God alone would reign among them (Judg. 16:27–30). This
new concept of leadership as service would be taken up afresh, centuries

---

3. The liberative core of any religion is a memory of a future, as I have explained in
chapter 9.

4. For an insightful analysis of the economics of Yahweh's ideal society, see Norbert
Lohfink, *Das Judische im Christentum: die verlorene Dimension* (Herder, Freiburg, 1987),
107–15.

5. The observations made on the period of Judges, substantially, and the reflections on
the contrast society of Yahweh in Palestine I owe, partly, to the Sri Lankan biblical scholar,
Shirley Wijeysingha, whom I assisted in conducting a study session on this theme in March
1989.

later, by Jesus the "servant-king," washing the feet of his disciples (John 13:1–20).

Yahweh's experiment, not totally unsuccessful, was indeed a rebuke to the two superpowers. But how long would it last? Will her people once more look back to Egypt with nostalgia? Will the developed nations around be a source of temptation for them? Indeed they knew that slavery was more convenient than freedom! Why not choose a human ruler to act as God's vicar on earth, just as once earlier they allowed a golden calf to be their god?

Alas, the people who were chosen to teach the rich nations the ways of Yahweh soon began to ape the ways of those very nations! With Solomon's gigantic building program (1 Kings 9:15–28) and extensive militarization (1 Kings 10:26), the Babylonian/Egyptian model began to replace that of Yahweh. The rulers swam in wealth and had slaves to work for them (1 Kings 10:14–29)! They would not listen to the prophets, who only irritated them. The leadership of service that characterized Yahweh's community during the period of Judges gave way to a power structure that so assimilated the Babylonian ideology that Yahweh allowed her adulterous people to experience it in Babylon itself!

When Jesus arrived on the scene, Rome had become the new Babylon. The aristocracy (the rich Sadducees) and the high priests (who were accountable to Roman authorities, who appointed them, rather than to the people) collaborated with the colonizers in an inhuman system of taxation that reduced the colonized people's currency to sheer dirt. It was this symbol of Roman despotism that Jesus ridiculed when he looked at a coin bearing Caesar's image — with the inscription *Supreme Pontiff* to indicate the emperor's connection with the divinity — and tossed it back to where it belonged: the dustbin of Caesar's treasury. And he fearlessly explained his action at the risk of being crucified for treason: that human beings, by virtue of the image of God they bear, are totally God's; and Caesar has no power over them (Matt. 22:15–21). Jesus thus reminded them of the old credal formula: "we have no king but Yahweh"; it was this proclamation of freedom that God's people, now Rome's slaves, countered by shouting: "we have no king but Caesar" (John 19:15).

In fact, many times before his death Jesus warned his little flock that they should never be slaves of the Roman model; they should not copy that system of government; "it shall not be so among you," he pleaded with his finger obviously pointing to the Roman representative in Palestine (Matt. 20:23–28). This warning does not seem to have had any effect except on the first few generations of Christians!

It was certainly in reaction to the Roman captivity of the church that some of the early monastic forms of religious life evolved. It was a movement of men and women who abandoned Rome and fled to the desert "to seek a society where all are equal, where the only authority comes from God through wisdom, experience, and love" as Merton is said to have explained.[6] Religious life, according to the seed-idea we have discovered in revelation, is not a churchy form of existence with vows serving only as a means of personal holiness. It is also a protest against any social order, civil or ecclesiastical, that serves other gods. It is a contrast society which, through opted poverty and evangelical obedience, partakes in Yahweh's vow to struggle with the oppressed against the principalities and powers that oppress them. In short, the obedience religious men and women vow is obedience to a God who calls them in the poor and calls them to be poor; a God who calls them to speak for the poor and struggle with the poor. Religious congregations that fail to respond to this call must suffer the fate of salt that has lost its flavor (Matt. 5:13) and of being replaced by other contrast societies.

WHEN CELIBACY IS NOT PROPHETIC

Obedience and poverty as practiced by religious orders were, as we have indicated, originally two indispensable means, the one positive and the other negative, of proclaiming the supremacy of God and the inviolable dignity of every man and woman. By the first we confess our faith in the only God who can make us human; by the second we openly renounce every form of slavery to all other gods and idols. Obedience and poverty, in other words, are kerygmatic vows to be practiced by the whole church and in an eminent manner by religious men and women.

But celibacy, the vow that is specific to communities of religious persons, is a different matter; its history, both in Christian and other monastic traditions, demonstrates that this vow is endowed with an innate potentiality to make itself a god, an idol, a cult of a kind. It can neutralize the prophetic thrust of the two kerygmatic vows and, consequently, turn the religious into counterwitnesses to Yahweh's Reign. There is therefore a great need to be vigilant.

This is why I warned at the beginning of this discussion that the circles of virgins and ascetics of the early church should not be taken as the origin of religious life. Rather, it is in the seed-idea of religious life that we find the origins of the institution of virginity. The inspiration for it could not have come directly from the gospels, which make no issue of virginity, even of Jesus' virginity; for the leitmotif of the gospel narratives is Jesus' obedience to God and his continuous confrontation with Mammon.[7]

Even Paul's teaching and personal example do not appear to have converted celibacy into a specifically Christian institution in the apostolic church. For the Jewish scriptures held virginity sacred only in terms of mar-

---

6. Bonnie Thurston, "Thomas Merton on the Contemplative Life: An Analysis," *Contemplative Review,* 17, 1984, 2.

7. See Aloysius Pieris, "To Be Poor as Jesus Was Poor?" *The Way,* 24, 1984, 186–97. Also in *ATL,* 15–23.

riage and not for its own sake (Deut. 22:13–18). Notwithstanding exceptions like Jeremiah, John the Baptizer and perhaps a few others, the general trend was to celebrate sexuality and its enjoyment as a gift of God. The New Testament does not go out of its way to annul this teaching, but it certainly repudiates the cult of sex that prevailed at that time.

This brings us to the conclusion that the idea of ascetical virgins, or at least the occasion for that idea, could have emanated from the Greco-Roman culture in which the church had to live its core message of obedience and poverty. In that non-Christian milieu not only a practice but a veritable cult of virginity seemed to have served as a sociological antidote against the contagion of sexual licentiousness which heralded the imminent downfall of that civilization. Employing the gnostic idiom of Hellenism in a creative manner, the church announced the Good News by presenting a Christian version of virginity not only as a protest against the promiscuity of that society, but also as an anticipation of the end-time of God's Reign when marriage will not be necessary (Mark 12:25). By imitating Jesus also in his virginity, they expressed their hope in God's new order of love, by means of a christic appropriation of an evangelical value which had been practiced by non-Christians for less praiseworthy motives. It was an excellent example of inculturation in that the church discovered a way of being prophetically present in and through a "kingdom value" of another culture.

Let me sum up. The protest against the order of sin (here, the sexual exploitation of the weak) and the immediate realization of the ultimate future are the context which made virginity and celibacy prophetic. In other words, the ascesis of virginity was the historical form by which the seed-idea of religious life, namely, a contrast society contesting the present by anticipating the future, came to be sociologically registered in the church. It is when this seed-idea is eclipsed by its own historical manifestations that religious life and, in this case, virginity and celibacy, cease to be prophetic by becoming values in themselves, a god of a sort. Let me indicate four examples of such deviations.

Spiritual Pride

The clearest instance is the elevation of virgins to a privileged class in the Hellenistic churches. Virginity had soon become a spiritual form of riches capable of generating power. Once dead, the virgins were mentioned immediately after the martyrs; while yet alive, they occupied places of honor in the Sunday liturgy. It is hardly surprising that the spiritual pride of some virgins in this period drew many letters of warning from their pastors. About seventeen centuries later we meet their successors in the Jansenists who, according to the verdict of their contemporaries, were "pure as angels and proud as devils."

The link between virginity and aristocracy in the Roman Catholic tradition must never be overlooked. Many famous virgins who begin the tradition were noble ladies bored with Rome and seeking the company of saints and scholars — as Paula and Melania did with St. Jerome.[8] We are informed that a very high infant mortality rate and the consequent need to produce many children to ensure continuity in the family lineage, coupled with the absence of a reliable birth-control method, had often created a surplus of female children. Given the expenses involved in the initiation of girls into adulthood, by way of dowries, etc., consecrated virginity often became a money-saving device. Later, as in St. Ambrose's order of virgins, infants began to be consecrated almost at birth, took their vow of chastity at puberty, and continued to live in the parental home.[9]

Though one cannot generalize, one must reckon with the fact that the aristocratic origins of the Roman tradition of the order of virgins could have turned this institution into a means of social mobility for the commoners. This danger certainly exists in the Third World even today. Virginity and celibacy can serve as a status symbol for the poor who are not attracted to poverty and obedience, which are harsh realities in the world they abandon when they join religious communities. The vocation boom in the Third World must, therefore, be critically assessed in order to make sure that the two kerygmatic vows continue to serve as the prophetic basis of celibacy. One must also note with regret that the church's overemphasis on clerical celibacy, with scant reference to the obedience and poverty of the gospels, is the root cause of ecclesiastical careerism, the most vulgar manifestation of Mammon in the ministerial church.

Misogyny

We must, however, concede that in a church dominated by a male clergy, virginity could have been the only way open for talented women to rise to public recognition. Thus Paula, who studied the Hebrew scriptures, and her sister Melania, who was involved in getting Origenism condemned, could rub shoulders with church leaders. But this tendency, far from challenging the androcratic church order, helped only to reinforce its misogynic foundations. For the Eve-Mary polarity, which has infected the Christian view of woman, was given a further boost by this form of virginal asceticism: woman by nature is Eve, the temptress; she is safe only as Mary, the virgin! This view of women as intrinsically prone to sexual sin and meriting compassion has deep roots in the canonical tradition of the Roman church.[10]

Unfortunately, the comparison between Mary and Eve was made to revolve around sexual purity, with no biblical foundation for it, rather than in terms of obedience and disobedience, poverty and ambition. I suspect that the artists and poets of the modern period of European history who took up

---

8. Yarbrough, "Christianization in the Fourth Century," 159–60.
9. Ibid., 160–61.
10. Brundage, "Prostitution in the Medieval Canon Law," *Signs: Journal of Women in Culture and Society,* 1 (4) Summer 1976, 835.

the theme of Mary Magdalene (prostitute turned mystic) were perhaps groping for an alternative model of womanhood, a blend of Mary and Eve, eros
and agape, a symbol of saintly sensuality and affective maturity — chastity
glowing with the ardor of charity.

Two-Tiered Spirituality

Celibacy uprooted from the basic vows normally tends to create a two-
tiered spirituality; an elite class of "asexual" beings imitating the angels
are at the top, and married commoners or sexual beings are at the bottom.
When this happens, a need is felt to maintain a social balance by imposing
a puritanical discipline at the higher level of celibate life and an ethos of
permissiveness at the lower. The reciprocity between the cult of virginity and
the cult of sex in the gnostic milieu in which the church lived her early centuries reflects this social balance. It is observed even today in some gnostic
cultures in Asia.[11]

This tradition still continues in the church, despite the Second Vatican
Council. Religious tend to turn their specific vow into a symbol of a spiritual
aristocracy, relegating the laity to a lower rung in the ladder of perfection.
We have not yet fully realized the implications of the conciliar teachings on
the universal call to holiness, namely, that the commandments of God, far
from being a minimalist spirituality for "ordinary" Christians, are the very
foundation of Yahweh's community of love, freedom, and justice; celibacy,
an evangelical counsel, not a status symbol, is prophetic only in the context
of such a society, not outside it and not above it.

Eschatological Illusion

Finally, we must record here the most ridiculous outcome of not allowing
celibacy to grow in a community founded on obedience and poverty. For
want of a better term, I call it "the eschatological illusion." Many monks and
nuns began to interpret the end-time purely in terms of an asexual existence
similar to that of angels. Instead of anticipating Yahweh's Kingdom through
the basic vows, they tested their eschatological freedom by trying to live
as if they were discarnate spirits. Monks and virgins lived together, bathed
together, as Evagrius boasted, and even slept together.[12]

Misreading 1 Cor. 7:36–38, where only those who "burn" are advised to
marry, these men and women tried to live as if they did not burn! They did
not honestly come to terms with their own sexuality. St. Jerome is indignant
about the *virgines subintroductae* (loosely translated, "virgins slipped in the
back door") whom he refers to as the "darlings" or *agapetae* (Ep. 22:14), for
they have betrayed virginity "by swelling wombs" (Ep. 22:13–14)! Referring

---

11. See, e.g., "Buddhism in a Permissive Society," *Ching Feng* IV (4), 153ff.
12. See Clark, "John Chrysostom and the Subintroductor," *Church History* 46, June 1977,
171–85.

to the scandal of the Valentinians, Irenaeus (Ad. H., 1.6.3) speaks of religious brothers and sisters living together until the sisters become mothers![13]

If, indeed, the Kingdom of God is interpreted only in terms of sexuality and its absence, and not in terms of radical obedience which involves Yahweh's Reign of love, and radical poverty which incarnates that love as human solidarity, then celibacy becomes the object of a cult. This species of idolatry is known in history as encretism, an obsession with chastity, which in reality is only a disguised form of an obsession with sex. Thus celibacy and sex enthrone each other as gods in the lives of those who fail to base their spirituality on allegiance to God alone and on the renunciation of Mammon.

Let me conclude by insisting that allegiance to God alone (obedience) is not primarily a renunciation of marriage or sex (celibacy) but a renunciation of power and riches (poverty). Hence, with no intention to make direct allusions to recent happenings in the church, I wish to recall that the great scandal among the disciples of Jesus was not failure in celibacy, as most of them were married, but that the man who controlled the finances of the Apostolic College found it so easy to exchange Christ for money.

---

13. Ibid., 172–73.

17

Ignatian Exercises against a Buddhist Background

PRESUPPOSITIONS

"The ocean can be compared only to the ocean, the sky only to the sky." So runs an old Sanskrit proverb. Buddhism and Christianity are so unique, each stamped by its own irrepeatable identity, that they truly defy comparison. Nevertheless, like the ocean and the sky, they are not only compatible in their incomparable distinctiveness, but are even complementary. I have explored this complementary at length elsewhere.[1] In this chapter, I want to take up a few of the highlights in the Buddhist-Christian dialogue and apply them to the Ignatian Exercises.

The two religions are complementary in that they respond to two different but mutually corrective instincts of the human spirit. Buddhism satisfies our innate thirst to *know* the liberating truth in its metapersonal ultimacy. Christianity fulfills our need to *love* the redemptive source of all beings in interpersonal intimacy. Buddhism is predominantly gnostic but not unilaterally so. For it has evolved from its inception an "affective" spirituality which moves in contrapuntal harmony with its "sapiential" soteriology. Conversely, Christianity is not exclusively agapeic. There has been a gnostic current of mysticism that received a strong impetus from Hellenism and stayed within the confines of orthodoxy; without it Christianity would be greatly diminished.

This general observation hides two crucial axioms. The first is that *gnosis* and *agape* are two languages of liberation which the spirit speaks within each one of us and therefore no religion can spur us to the fullness of the humanum without educating us to be fluent in both of them. The implication

---

First published in *The Way: Supplement* 68, Summer 1990, 98–111.

1. See my *Love Meets Wisdom,* 9–12, 111–19.

is that what the Buddhist speaks in each of us, in the sapiential idiom, the Christian in each of us must understand and respond to in the language of love. And vice versa. The second axiom is that only a person accustomed to monitor this interior dialogue introspectively is qualified to participate in the rewarding encounter between the two irreducibly distinct cultural moods which these religions have created in the societies they animate.

The twofold principle is eminently valid also where a particular stream of Christianity — in this case, Ignatian spirituality — seeks to be at home in a culture shaped by one particular branch of Buddhism, say the *Theravada* tradition, such as we encounter in Sri Lanka. A Jesuit working in such a context is called to be an "integrated person," familiar with both spiritualities, rooted in two soils, so to speak. This, obviously, is far from easy. An unguided zeal for personal integration, however, might expose him to two temptations. One would be to mix up the two idioms to form a kind of hybrid spirituality, a sort of cocktail in which we taste both components though not in the purity of their individual flavors. We call this "syncretism." The other is more sophisticated; the creation of a tertium quid (a third reality) in which neither one nor the other retains its identity even in a mixed form. This is known as "synthesis." Neither of these methods is ecumenically helpful or spiritually fruitful.

Our option is for "symbiosis," a cultivated form of reciprocal proexistence whereby each idiom sharpens its identity in conversation with the other. For their mutual exposure reveals the authentic character of each in such a way that it is possible to recognize that which is not genuine in either of them. Hence the most significant outcome of the symbiotic approach is the discovery and the consequent elimination of that which is spurious in each tradition.

In the course of retreats and recollections which I have been conducting for mixed groups of Buddhists and Christians, I have been able to collect many such unauthentic elements from both traditions. As for Ignatian spirituality — the main focus of this chapter — I have a rather long list from which I have selected only the following three items for this present discussion: (1) the theological framework of the Ignatian Exercises; (2) the concept of "contemplation"; and (3) the notion of "self" in Ignatian anthropology.

A THEOLOGY OF IGNATIAN EXERCISES

Praxis is the first formulation of its own theory. Regrettably, the theory implicit in the Ignatian theopraxis has not evolved into a theology commensurate with the transforming power of the Exercises. One reason, I suspect, is that Ignatius himself was a victim of decadent scholasticism taught in his day in Paris. The study of this theology left his spiritual health so weakened that he needed much time and prayer to have it restored. It was this experience that he institutionalized into what is called "tertianship," also known as the *scola affectus*. It is a period of rehabilitation offered to the Jesuits, an opportunity for recuperating from the ravages of scholastic studies.

The Exercises themselves contain the suffocating effects of this theological method. The Principle and Foundation (*Exercises*, 23), the quintessence of the affective spirituality fostered during the four weeks of exercises, is distorted by the scholastic formula it is crammed into. The pernicious doctrine of using creatures to go to God (the instrumental theory of creation) advocated here — the polar opposite of the ecological approach of the Buddhists — also comes from decadent scholasticism and contrasts with the sacramental theory of creation that emerges clearly in the climactic exercise, the Contemplation to Obtain Love (*Exercises,* 230–37) — notwithstanding the use of a few terms borrowed from the schoolmen. Even in the key exercises of the First Week, the exercitant with a Buddhist sensitivity tends to be confused by the forensic theology of the Latins, which places the accent on guilt and justification.

The early Jesuits allowed the Exercises to stagnate as a mere manual of spirituality, while they overdeveloped scholastic theology to its abstract extremes. Even such eminent men as Bellarmine contributed to this dichotomy. Hence any incompatibility with Buddhist spirituality springs, in most instances, from an incongruous theology surrounding the Exercises rather than from the essence of the Ignatian praxis. The theological idiom of the Exercises does not always resonate with their affective content.

Its interaction with Buddhist spirituality may suggest one possible direction along which to look for an appropriate Ignatian theology. Though not entirely uncontaminated by scholasticism, *Theravada* spirituality has retained its original *therapeutic* framework. The Buddha is the physician who diagnoses the human predicament (what Christians call "fallenness") as a chronically fatal "dis-ease": *dukkha* (pain), and its cause as *tanhā* (greed). These are the first two noble truths. The third declares that the disease cannot be cured without removing its cause; for it is in greedlessness that health and wholeness are to be found! The fourth is the remedy; the prescription is known as the eightfold noble path; it is the sum and substance of Buddhist spirituality. It is the way to eradicate greed or self-centeredness.

It is wrong to perceive this therapeutic framework as supportive of an individualistic spirituality. Lay Buddhists as well as monks involved in liberation struggles today exploit to the maximum the explosive social doctrine concealed in the Buddha's prescription. Greed they rightly diagnose as the cause of social illness, in the sense that this perverse psychological urge is ideologically organized into a dehumanizing socioeconomic system; this means, also, that the removal of greed cannot be left to individual initiatives alone. A "correct analysis and understanding of things as they are" (*yathābhūtaññāna,* to use the Buddha's favorite phrase), demands collective and organized effort to remove this institutionalized greed.

The ideology behind this interpretation is that greedlessness or *alpecchatā* (literally, "seeking the bare necessities of life without any surplus") should serve as the ethical principle governing every form of social organization if we wish to eradicate the misery of the "oppressed masses," or *dalidda* (a word and a concept which the Buddhist scriptures seem to have introduced into the Indic languages[2] presumably because the Buddhists were among the first in India to recognize mass poverty as a social evil).

This principle is also the basis of emergent liberation theologies in Asia: the practice of evangelical poverty (*alpecchata*) and the removal of forced poverty (*daridrata*) are inseparably linked,[3] as eradication of the cause of illness is to the healing of that illness. After all, was not the coming of the Kingdom, too, presented by the first evangelizers as God's healing mission in Jesus? Is not the entire gospel permeated with the message of human wholeness guaranteed in the resurrection and anticipated here and now through the *via crucis* of selfless love and greedless sharing?

In fact Ignatius appropriates this language in the very idea of "Exercises" in that they are intended as a means for keeping our spiritual muscles fit for action (*Exercises,* 1). Iparraguirre observes that, among the binomials Ignatius resorts to when expressing the key ideas of the Exercises, the word *salvation* (Exod. 1) is coupled with *salud,* "health."[4] One is, therefore, curious to know whether a nonscholastic theology using the therapeutic idiom was ever available to Ignatius. History seems to have an answer.

Though by no means a professional theologian, Ignatius was practical enough to have recognized, both in the Exercises (*Exercises,* 363) and in the Constitutions,[5] the need for a "positive theology" complementing "scholastic theology." The former is a kind of theology tending to excite "affections," claims Ignatius, while the latter is for defining, explaining, and defending the truths against heterodoxy (*Exercises,* 363). His followers, however, showed excessive zeal for this rational, apologetical type of theology and neglected the former.

It is true that Jesuits like Petau, the "father of positive theology," and the even more creative Montoya, tried to restore the positive method, but by that time "positive theology" had degenerated into a mere function of the scholastic method. Congar says that Ignatius (together with Juan Mair, who is said to have made the first-ever reference to this twofold method in his commentary on the *Sentences* [Paris 1509]) offers us the earlier notion of "positive theology."[6] It is a theology or a method of doing theology which reflects a spiritual praxis rather than a concern for a rational justification of dogmas. Or should

2. Chakravarty, "The Social Philosophy of Buddhism and the Problem of Inequality," *Social Compass,* 33, 1986: 205.

3. See my *ATL,* 20–23, 38–50, 75f., 121ff.

4. I. Iparraguirre, *A Key to the Study of the Spiritual Exercises,* Allahabad, St. Paul, 2nd ed., 1960, 35.

5. See *The Constitution of the Jesuits,* trans. George E. Ganss, Institute of Jesuit Sources, St. Louis, 1970, numbers 351, 446, 464.

6. Yves Congar, *A History of Theology,* Doubleday, New York, 1968, 171–74.

we say, it is a theology in the practice of human liberation? Could theology ever be anything else? At the Council of Trent there were two voices crying in the wilderness, pleading for a return to a kind of theology which we, following Ignatius, would like to recognize as "positive" and nonscholastic. These voices, unfortunately, were not those of the two Jesuits who served the council as papal theologians, and who were hailed as champions of the status quo. Rather, they were those of the Italian Benedictines, Chiari and Ottoni, who wished that the Roman Church obviate the imminent Western schism by abandoning its forensic paradigm of guilt, punishment, and justification and adopting a biblico-patristic approach, such as, for instance, the Antiochean model developed by Chrysostom, which employed the therapeutic idiom. They charged that the whole controversy on faith and good works originated from the Latin forensic theology in which not only the Roman theologians but even the Reformers were imprisoned.

These two men were virtually shouted down by the scholastics! Were the two Jesuits among those who accused them of "Protestantism"? The followers of Ignatius would do well to ponder over this episode as narrated by Barry Collett.[7] The Antiochean theology preserved by the Benedictines of the *Congregazione Casinese* which extended from Messina to Provence, taught that what we inherited was not the guilt of Adam, but mortality, and therefore it was eternal death that Christ's grace delivered us from. But the healing process by which our fatally wounded nature is restored to wholeness is left to our faith and good works.

Had Ignatius been there and understood Latin well enough, he would have recognized a type of positive theology that his Exercises needed. If this theology disappeared after the Council,[8] was it because there was no Ignatius to appropriate it? After all, both the *devotio moderna* (which he absorbed from the *Imitation of Christ*) and the structure of the *Ejercitatorio* of Cisneros (which he seems to have picked up at Montserrat) were radically transformed, in the laboratory of his own personal experience, into a new medium of spiritual renewal in the church. His Benedictine connection, which lasted only a few days at Montserrat, may not have put him in contact with the "positive theology" of the *Congregazione Casinese*, which certainly extended its influence over that little monastery. Had he chanced upon such a theology, he could have been the initiator of a theological renewal as he certainly was of a spiritual movement.

Though this critical observation was inspired by my Buddhist experience, it deserves to be treated as an Ignatian critique of the Jesuit theological tradition. It is not too late to allow the Exercises to evolve into a positive theology, at least where it has to meet the challenge of Buddhist soteriology.

---

7. Barry Collett, *Italian Benedictine Scholars and the Reformation,* Oxford, 1985, see chapters 4–8.

8. See Barry Collett, "The Benedictine Origins of a Mid-Sixteenth Century Heresy," *The Journal of Religious History,* June 1986, 17f.

CONTEMPLATION OR AWARENESS?

A certain unchecked tendency, as I shall explain a little later, has allowed the word *contemplation* to function as a blanket term for the spiritual. Contemplation, accordingly, is identified as that which gives spiritual value to everything else: action without it is activism; liturgy without it is ritualism. In fact a theory is gaining ground among certain ashramite theologians in South Asia that "the universal call to holiness" is in fact a universal call to "contemplation." Evidently, the word has become a synonym for God-experience.

Now, the occurrence of the term in Christian literature reveals at least three semantic variants. The Exercises often employ the term *contemplation* to indicate a manner of using the imagination to evoke *affective* sentiments, which by the very fact of their being affective, do not remain in the speculative regions of the mind but sink gradually into the very depths of the *heart,* the locus where the person is touched fundamentally and totally. The contemplations on the life, events, and the person of Jesus in the Second, Third, and the Fourth Weeks of the Exercises *(Exercises,* 101ff.) come under this category. The visual image dominates in these exercises, but other interior senses are also employed. In fact, using the gustatory idiom, Ignatius alludes to this affective experience as "interior relishing" to be preferred to mere accumulation of (intellectual) knowledge *(Exercises,* 1).

This species of contemplation corresponds to what Buddhists call *anussati,* profound awareness, or *anupassanā,* interiorized vision of various objects of meditation such as the person of the Buddha or even a decomposing body.

Secondly, *contemplation* is also a technical term for the most elevated and the climactic mystical state of infused prayer. But a theology that has grown around this meaning of contemplation regards mysticism (or "immediate experience of God") as something that really happens only in contemplative prayer. Action is spiritual only when it leads to or overflows from contemplation. This meaning determines our definition of spirituality today.

The Buddhist equivalent of this ultimate state of mysticism is *paññā,* the highest form of gnosis leading to nirvanic freedom. It is often referred to with expressions that use the visual idiom: e.g., *vipassanā, vidassanā,* which can be paraphrased as the liberative "insight" into the ultimate truth.

What concerns us here is yet another, a typically Ignatian, understanding of contemplation, not dissociated completely from the previous two variants, and indicated by the phrase *"seeking* God in all things and all things in God," or as *"finding* God in all things." The Buddhist terms given above do not correspond to this notion at all. Nor is it quite the same as the "infused prayer" of the traditional mystics. Rather it denotes an abidingly affective *awareness* of God — preferably accompanied by consolation — in the midst of and through the mediation of apostolic labors undertaken in charity and obedience. The phrase "contemplative in action," I believe, was coined by one of the early Jesuits to describe a person endowed with this habitual state of heart and mind.

Unfortunately the word *contemplative* in that phrase cannot prevent the intrusion of the second meaning given above; hence it runs the risk of misrepresenting the Ignatian mind. Any implication that apostolic action or works of charity and justice would receive the character of a God-experience secondarily and indirectly from the experience of God given in contemplative prayer must be removed from that phrase. From a valuable clue found in the *Memoirs* (n. 129) of Blessed Pierre Favre, a reliable interpreter of the Ignatian mind, we can infer that the *actual* encounter with God ("possessing Christ" as he calls it) is in doing God's will, in obedience, in getting involved in the mission of Jesus on earth, in apostolic activity, in works of love and justice; whereas, contemplation, if that word has to be used, must mean the *affective* encounter with God in prayer. To sum up, *contemplation* is the affective awareness of the actual God-experience mediated by works of charity and justice. This is the spirituality that social activists all over the world are hungering for.

It is clear that the visual idiom employed in the words *contemplation* or *anupassanā, vipassanā,* etc., does not adequately express the notion of God-consciousness implied in the Ignatian mysticism of service. *Seeking* God in all things is more than just *seeing* God. Perhaps we should look in the direction of the Buddhist practice of *sati,* an uninterrupted "awareness" or "mindfulness" accompanying day-to-day activity. The most pervasive spiritual exercise in *Theravada* Buddhism is known as *sati-paṭṭhāna,* "establishment of mindfulness, training in constant attentiveness."

The cardinal concepts of Buddhist spirituality — *appamāda, amoha, bodhi* — all refer to this habitual state of alertness and wakefulness, or full awareness. It is the Buddhist counterpart of *nepsis* (vigilance) and *diakrisis* (discernment) of Hellenistic Christians. The pilgrim on the eightfold path discovered by the Buddha, too, adopts a permanent posture of attention to what is conducive to liberation (wholeness) and what is not.

May I suggest, here, that the auditory idiom might succeed in bringing out this dimension of vigilance more than the visual does? *Theravada* Buddhism is essentially a religion of the word and not of sacraments. The technical term for the disciple is *sāvaka,* "the hearer" (of the salvific word, *dhamma*), also a synonym for the "saint." In fact in the Indian tradition, revelation is primarily *shruti,* an act of hearing rather than of seeing.

Now the Ignatian concept of Jesuit ministry, too, was essentially one of prophetic service to the Word more than a cultic one revolving around the administration of sacraments,[9] and the axis of Ignatian spirituality is "obedi-

---

9. See Michael J. Buckley, "Jesuit Priesthood: Its Meaning and Commitments," *Studies in the Spirituality of Jesuits,* December 1976, 18 and *passim.*

ence" or "listening" (*obaudire*), being ever open to God revealing the divine plan for us. This posture of alertness to the Word coincides with that much misunderstood term *indifference* which really connotes a trained proneness to hear and execute God's word, a positive attitude of love which regards everything else secondary to what "the divine Majesty" commands for our salvation and for the salvation of our people (*Exercises,* 23). It is the habitual *awareness* of the goal — the wholeness and the wholesomeness to be attained (for oneself and for all creation) by *doing* what one hears God say (*Exercises,* 1). This is the dynamic sense of "discernment" or "discerning love" — which is summed up as a "mysticism of service." This is why the daily examination of consciousness plays such a central role in Ignatian spirituality.

The word and the concept of contemplation not only fail to bring out this rich meaning common to both traditions, but can also be misleading even within the Ignatian spirituality. Let me insist that the reason is not to be located merely in the visual idiom it employs, but in the fact that in its early history, the occurrence of this word reveals two dangerous shifts in emphasis. The first is the Hellenistic manner of "seeing" God as supreme beauty to be contemplated, and of relegating all action as secondary and preparatory to that beatific vision. This is unbiblical. By contrast, the prayerful activist Ignatius wanted his sons to regard (apostolic) action as the context and the purpose of prayer.[10]

The second is the cultural shift from *orality* to *literacy;* from the Word proclaimed and heard in the present historical moment in the midst of a people, to the written word of the scriptures read in private and reflected upon. In the *lectio divina,* the Word could cease to speak through history and community, and thus distance itself away as an ahistorical object of contemplation! The dynamism and the immediacy of the Word demanding response through action could be compromised; the alertness, the awareness, the vigilance and all the urgency of attention to the *hic et nunc* which both *Theravada* and the Ignatian spirituality inculcate tend to be replaced by a self-hypnotic trance.

We should be wary, therefore, about the dominant role that the word *contemplation* has traditionally played in determining the very definition of spirituality. A change of paradigm, I submit, will ensure a rediscovery of the authentic meaning of spirituality. This is true at least where Ignatian and *Theravada* spiritualities have to meet and interact. For, in both these traditions, the focal point of spirituality is self-denial, not contemplation as such, though the latter is an "exercise" that is useful and even necessary.

---

10. See J. de Guibert, *The Jesuits: Their Spiritual Doctrine and Practice, a Historical Study,* St. Louis, Institute of Jesuit Sources, 1972, 585.

A SELF WITHOUT SELF

The most challenging experience in a Buddhist-Christian encounter is the discovery of the pivotal role that "self-denial" plays in the *Theravada* as well as Ignatian spirituality. For self-love is as much a hindrance to Buddhist gnosis as it is a rejection of Christian agape.

The contemporary emphasis on self-assertion and self-fulfillment — an understandable reaction against certain masochistic spiritualities of the past — does not create a comfortable climate to discuss this question. Yet the spiritual journeys of the founder of Buddhism and the founder of the Jesuits bear a striking similarity in the way they came to the discovery of this basic truth. Each of them was a warrior hailing from a noble family; each became intensely aware of an impulse to change his course of life radically and embarked on a path of excessive asceticism that bordered on self-torture (*atta-kilamatha*). Only then did each of them discover that true freedom lay in the middle path of "self-realization through self-negation."

I am aware that this perspective has to vindicate its validity against criticism coming from three different directions: from liberal theologians, from liberation theologians, and from feminist theologians.

In western liberal theology, there is an emphasis on the "dignity of the human person" together with a theological discourse on human rights — at least in many contemporary writers. This makes the sovereignty of the individual self the basis, center, and apex of a just society. Hence self-realization receives more than due emphasis in this scheme. It is not surprising that an unqualified demand for self-abnegation is viewed with suspicion.

Here two remarks are in order. First, the liberal theologian's perception of the self does not seem to withstand the devastating critique of Latin American liberation theologians.[11] Second, we pose the whole question here from the perspective of the *other* rather than of the self, of duties rather than rights. The Jewish scriptures, for instance, situate the problem in the covenantal scheme of "obligations" to others, especially to the weak.[12] In the Indic cultural paradigm implicitly accepted by Buddhists, self-abnegation is a corollary to the thesis that self's innate orientation toward *others* in terms of a prior existence of obligations (*dharmāh*), makes it impossible to realize one's own self except with self-restraint. Also in the Ignatian scheme, the "otherward" orientation enters the very definition of self so that its "realization" cannot take place except as an "eccentric" movement toward the self's innermost center, which is, in fact, situated outside the self, i.e., in the Totally Other.

As for the liberation theologians, I endorse their suspicion that this doc-

---

11. See chapter 10 in the present work, "Human Rights Language and Liberation Theology."

12. See Sieghart, "Christianity and Human Rights," *The Month,* February 1949, 49.

trine of "self-abnegation for the sake of self-realization" could lead to a self-centered, antisocial manner of defining spirituality. Note, however, that in the vast project of human liberation, person, and society are interlaced. Our study here is only a "close-up" of one aspect and in no way implies a denial of the other. Furthermore, the debate among the tricontinental third-world theologians has confirmed that social analysis is not by itself adequate in the context of liberative struggles. Introspective analysis of the self is the other face of class analysis, as I have argued in the course of that debate.[13]

I, too, join the feminists in declaring that the way this doctrine has been misused in the past to build an aggressive male-dominated church and society on the graves of female egos is to be condemned as deplorable and intolerable. However, instead of questioning the validity of the doctrine of self-abnegation, as some feminists do, I would rather demand that the males begin to practice it with the same zeal with which they had earlier imposed it on the other half of humanity. The abuse of a good thing is no reason to abandon it.

Whoever, guided by Ignatius, has made the First Week's "journey to the hell of self-knowledge," to borrow Balthasar's powerful expression,[14] does not hesitate to confess that self is self's only enemy. Hence the rather common teaching that other creatures could be a hindrance to our encounter with God is a misreading of what goes on in the hidden corners of the human psyche. (Such a negative view of creatures was insinuated in the scholastics' "instrumental theory of creation," which crept into the Principle and Foundation [*Exercises*, 23].) The only agent that keeps God away from us is our own self. It is the self as self's own creature that resists the Creator and uses other creatures as tools for self-gratification or greed. In fact to use creatures *tantum quantum* (simply as a means) to arrive at God is a sinful exercise that can never be a God-experience. Self-centeredness in whatever form is a sin against others, besides being self-destructive.

However, the Ignatian Exercises, where they are less tied to scholastic theology, persuade us that love shows itself in deeds of self-giving (*Exercises*, 231). Love compels the isolated self to die that it may rise as a related self. This growth of the individual to the fullness of personhood through communion involves the most central message of Christ: that the freedom of my own *self* essentially revolves around that of *others* who, as the proxy of the Supreme Other, are both the recipients and the agents of that freedom (Matt. 25:34–46).

This is why Ignatius was mulishly stubborn in maintaining, against all currents to the contrary both within and outside the order, that the real index of spiritual maturity is not formal prayer, not even contemplative prayer, but self-abnegation (see *Exercises*, 189). By self-abnegation he especially meant

---

13. See my *ATL*, 80f., 15–20, and *passim*.
14. Hans Urs von Balthasar, *Church and World*, Herder, New York, 1967, 104.

the hardships and trials that our apostolic action undertaken in obedience and charity necessarily brings with it, and which we embrace cheerfully for love of God and neighbor. Hence Ignatius defines the goal of the Exercises not as perfection in prayer but as freeing the self of selfish tendencies *and* seeking/finding God's will (*Exercises,* 1); while elsewhere he simply says that the purpose of the Exercises is self-conquest (*Exercises,* 21). There is no contradiction here. Called by God to assume any role God would assign to us in Jesus' mission on earth (apostolic spirituality as radical obedience), we are also summoned to sacrifice all, even our own self, for the apostolic end (spirituality as radical poverty). The essence of the Ignatian doctrine is that "continuous self-abnegation" accompanying our apostolic involvement is precisely what facilitates prayer and makes our action mystical.

The Buddha's concept of self-abnegation, however, is more than ascetical, it is ontological, as the Theravadins interpret it, and therefore more radical than the Ignatian version of it. So it appears at first sight. That the human person is soulless (*anatta*), that is to say, a series of fluctuating psychophysical moments with no permanent immortal substratum, is the liberating truth realized through gnosis. There is no *I* or *me* or *mine* in the Buddhist claim, in contrast with the Vedantin's "You are That."

The Buddha's denial of the self, accompanied by his insistence that self is one's only refuge (*atta-sarana*) and the only island (*atta-dīpa*) in this ocean of existence, has led to much speculation among contemporary scholars, some postulating the existence of two selves, one to be noughted and the other to be cultivated. I would refrain from reducing the mystery of the self to numerical terms. The paradox must remain: There is one self in me, and "in reality" (*paramatthato*) it does not exist.

If this doctrine sounds nihilistic, could it be because, like Ignatius, we have subscribed to the Hellenistic belief in the existence of an immortal and incorruptible soul, instead of working within the biblical anthropology, which, to put it mildly, does not cling to such a belief? Ignatius's image of our fallen nature, as a "soul imprisoned in this corruptible body" (*Exercises,* 47) projects a theory that is not essential to Christian spirituality. The Buddhists' absolute denial of an unchanging, undying spiritual substance in humans is the most articulate extrabiblical approximation to the biblical teaching about our creatureliness, our dustness, i.e., our absolutely indebted existence. Who are we but breakable pots made of clay? Are we not mere mud sustained as living beings by the gratuitous infusion of divine breath but for which we would crumble back to the dust whence we came?[15]

This anthropology, totally absent in the Ignatian Exercises, does, nevertheless, emerge faintly from the "christology" of the Second and Third Weeks. One, of course, needs a bit of imagination and creativity to educe the true na-

---

15. See L. de Silva, *The Problem of the Self in Buddhism and Christianity,* Study Center for Religion and Society, Colombo, 1975, 72–81.

ture of the human person from what is revealed there of the person of Jesus. Here, Ignatius shows he had truly *known* Jesus, by *following* him. (Has anyone found another way to know him?) It is the Jesus of positive theology, not of the scholastics.

This Ignatian image of Jesus can be brought into sharper focus with the aid of a "Spirit christology" that would tilt more toward the Fathers than the scholastics. Such a christology sees Jesus to be empty of all self. In taking our human form, he became, like us, a brittle earthen pot kept in one piece by our maternal Father's life-giving breath of love, the Spirit. He is the fragile container of this Spirit, *pneumatophor* — what by sin we refuse to be. Like us he too had no self, an *attā* of his own, so to say, save that of God.

According to an accepted version of "Spirit christology," Jesus is "sheer obedience" and "perfect availability," a perpetual "yes to existence pure and simple" (Kasper), so that, as the Spirit-bearing pot of clay, he was destined to crash on the cross of failure and break to bits, spilling out the healing waters of the Spirit on all the world. Jesus is God's "eccentric" act of seeking God's center outside the divine circle, in the human other: *propter nos homines et propter nostram salutem descendit de caelis.*

This Jesus who reveals himself to anyone who is prepared to follow him in the "third degree of humility" (*Exercises,* 167) on the *suññatā* (*kenosis*) of the cross, is the giver of the Spirit, the true Self who holds us from succumbing irreversibly to the dustward pull of our mortal nature; who breathes upon us the name by which each of us is gratuitously suspended in his or her fragile identity. To know one's true self as utterly nonexistent except in relation to the Other is the wisdom that comes from the cross; gnosis born of agape.

18

The Vows as Ingredients of Authentic Humanism

An Autobiographical Essay on the Religious Vows

Two considerations have guided me in choosing and developing the theme of this essay. The first is the man in whose honor I write it: Samuel Rayan, a great humanist living his Christian faith within the Ignatian spiritual tradition. The other is the time and the location in which I am writing: Sri Lanka, 1990. I gather my thoughts and feelings in the midst of a chaos that this country has to live through, with nothing to hold on to, except whatever is left of the human within a suffering people. At no time in the history of our people has the humanum been so tantalizingly present by its apparent absence — and, therefore, desperately desired and sanguineously sought. Yet my indomitable faith and hope in the love that we humans are still capable of imbue my thoughts and feelings with a stubborn optimism. What I write is my own testimony to the humanum I have encountered in those who continue to speak and work for peace.

A CHRISTIAN READING OF THE HUMANUM

Christ and the Human: A Theological Mood

When caught up in a chaotic whirlpool of political and ideological confusion, such as the one I have just referred to, the safest strategy is to plunge into the ever-available currents of humanism, whatever be their immediate source; they are sure to direct us into the right stream. One learns this strategy from *Gaudium et Spes;* in this document, the Second Vatican Council did not content itself with the earlier ecclesiastical habit of resorting to "natural

First published in *Vidyajyoti Journal of Theological Reflection* 56, January 1992, 3–22.

law" and "reason" as the only means to save social ethics from the deluge of ideological misinterpretation; the council (GS, Pt. I, chaps. 1–3) seems to have tempered this stoic maneuver of the past by consciously turning to contemporary humanism for possible avenues on which the church can engage God's redeeming (i.e., humanizing) presence in the world of structural sin.

We would do well to follow this lead of the council in our efforts to fathom not only the mystery of God but also the mystery of man and woman! What if we would abandon our addiction to philosophical definitions of the divine and resort, instead, to the saner praxis of fathoming the human in order to encounter the divine. This would keep in check our compulsion to possess divine knowledge — the ever-recurrent cause of our Fall (Gen. 3:5–6). Such a compulsion, as we see in the aftermath of Chalcedon, all too easily leads to the political elimination of persons, to ecclesiastical intrigues, the deposition of pastors from their seats, and other inhuman deeds in the name of a rationally defined truth about God's inner nature.

If a definition is what matters, why not begin our search with Yahweh's own humanistic self-definition as the Liberator who dares to stand in open conflict with the slave masters of this world, compelling them to release their slaves to serve Yahweh alone and thus become a family of free humans (Exod. 20:2; Lev. 26:12–13; etc.)?

Adam, the dust-man who lives in us, crawls up heavenly heights to steal the form of God in knowledge and power, only to be hurled down to the depths of nakedness and cunning, taking on the form of the serpent (Gen. 3). But the Christ into whom we are baptized, as the early Christians sang (Phil. 2:6–11), did not have to steal the form of God, since he possessed it, but plunged down, truly *falling* in love with our humanity, becoming like us both "in appearance" (*homoiomati*) and in (psychophysical) "structure" (*schemati*), accepting the lowest social condition, namely, that of a slave, both in life (v.7) and in death (v.8); and so he could be raised in his humanity as Master and Lord in solidarity with all who have been made slaves by the inhumanity of ambitious, serpent-inspired, and power-hungry Adams.

It is not merely in our definition of God that we slip into the antihumanist groove; we do so even in the way we have been trying to define the human as *animal rationale*. The underlying equation, "beast+reason=human person," tells us only of the hominized beast (i.e., Adam as the unredeemed cosmos) who still continues to live by the law of the jungle, the law of "survival of the fittest"; furthermore, reason, left to itself, is often the most deceptive part of our being, justifying what the beast in us desires; it is the creator of dehumanizing ideologies.

But the evolution of the hominized beast into a humanized angel — "angel" in the literal sense of a "messenger" of flesh and blood who announces the imminent liberation — is the transformation that heralds the new earth and the new heavens. The *hominization* of the cosmos is a process that has littered the earth with "rational animals," i.e., hominized beasts [Adams];

being an unfinished series of events, it ceases to be redemptive if it does not continue as a process of *humanization,* that is to say, as a progressive movement toward the humanum.

Humanism is the rubric under which we understand our own consciously organized and willful "taking over" of this process. Obviously, a movement or an organization does not become humanist simply because its advocates name it such. Hence we need to begin our inquiry with a tentative declaration about (not a definition of) humanism. My suggestion is that humanism can be understood as an indefinable psychosocial ethos charged with a personal and communitarian agitation for and an incessant reaffirmation of the humanum; and we can understand the humanum as the interior abyss to be fathomed both in the depths of our personal being as well as on the ultimate horizon of our societal strivings. In this framework, humanism directs us to our Absolute Future (Total Liberation) which is drawing us from a purely "hominal" seed-stage to the full flowering of a "humanized" cosmos, that is to say, to the birth of the Cosmic Wo/Man.

Since the "human" is our immanent center that lies transcendentally *outside* our "hominal" circumference, our growth toward it is an "eccentric" movement. But God-in-Jesus, who loves us with a human heart and constitutes our Center, is equally eccentric in that this God, too, gravitates toward the humanum as God's own Center lying outside the divine circle (Phil. 2:6–11). One embraces Christianity officially when one believes that Jesus is God's eccentricity and that in Jesus we all become human by being eccentric ourselves, i.e., by striving to make God our human center.

A Christian, in other words, is one who believes that Jesus is the focus of God's human concern, a concern that coincides with our Godward ascent. Jesus is the nucleus of the humanum, the nucleus which — not without our efforts at continuing his struggle for fullness and freedom — is ever growing toward the "pleroma of the humanum" — or, in technical terms, *the fullness of Christ.* Since, however, all of Jesus is Christ but not all of Christ is Jesus, it follows that to proclaim "Jesus is Christ" is to demonstrate by word and deed that by following Jesus the Man in his eccentricity, we, together with all creation, are becoming in him and with him the epiphany of full humanity. Therefore, to strive toward the humanum — as the great Jesuit humanist, Teilhard de Chardin, taught us — is to exercise our obligatory role in christogenesis.

The Three Vows of the Humanist: A Personal Discovery

Once I develop a taste for the humanist flavor of Christian discipleship and the christological savor of humanism, I start to wonder why some men and women who have vowed to follow Jesus by evangelical poverty, obedience, and chastity are sometimes avowed enemies of the humanum.

Very early in my Jesuit life, I found myself fearing the vows of religious life as agents of dehumanization; I feared that those first years of formation were deceiving me. The vows, I said to myself, were not worth living if they could not evoke the human in me. And apparently they failed the humanist test: the capacity to transform the hominized beast in me into a human announcer of freedom.

After a long period of doubt and search, after seeking advice from a few Jesuit counselors (who were more Jansenists than Jesuits), I fell back on Fr. Luigi de Mattia's suggestion that I should suspend for a while my preoccupation with the vows and focus my attention, instead, on events or tendencies in my life which stood the litmus test, that is to say, which brought out the human not only in me but in all who were associated with me.

This was a great experiment and a successful one. I realized to my pleasant surprise that there were in me — and therefore, presumably in most others — three impulses which could easily be designated as the three vows of the humanist: an intense search for beauty, frequent explosions of humor, and an insatiable thirst for intimacy. Though each of these was an Immanent Force recreating my spirit from within me, I discovered that each was also a response to the seductive power of a Transcendent Source that was totally other than my own being.

This discovery made me even more inquisitive about the role of the three religious vows I was made to pronounce as a condition for being accepted into religious life. For it seemed that my bridled passion for aesthetic pleasure was in direct conflict with the vow of poverty; my humor tended to ridicule the possibility of other humans demanding of me an obedience due only to God; and my success at "particular friendship" right from the first flowering of youth seemed to flout the basic requirements of vowed chastity.

At the end of a dark corridor of conflicts and constraints lived through with stubborn determination and rash adventurism — which at that time did not seem to merit the title *faith* or *hope,* though it certainly does now — I came out with a clearer vision of what I had always sensed in the subliminal zones of my being as the most profound implication of the three religious vows:

- that it was the spirit of evangelical poverty that made me seek nothing less than what is most desirable for the whole of my being: "beauty ever ancient and ever new."

- that it was my sense of humor that made obedience (contrary to my Novice Master's pessimistic predictions) a celebration of God's word personally addressed to me.

- and that human intimacy which was warned against as a direct violation of chastity, was in fact the guarantor of the affective maturity which that vow was meant to produce in me.

Thus the three vows — not in the way they were explained to me in the fifties, but in their merger with the three humanizing experiences of my life — became for me (I repeat, *for me*), the three pillars of authentic humanism, or at least of *my* humanism. Could this be true of others, too? I wonder.

Beauty First

Our sense of beauty is our capacity to see the invisible wholeness asserting itself beneath our fragmented existence; to taste the bliss of final emancipation already in the passing joys that linger in our memory; and to touch the intangible glory of the end-time in every step taken toward its light; to discover and venerate every one of God's countless icons (Gen. 2:27) made of earth's dust and divine breath (Gen. 2:7) and zealously guard even the least of them from every kind of desecration; and above all, to delight in the glory of our Maker's image which we humans, each and all, "bare" in the very process of cocreating with her, the final artifact: our truly human future, indeed a New Creation.

"To seek Beauty in all things and all things in Beauty" — if I may reformulate the classical Ignatian ideal in the light of the climactic contemplation in the *Spiritual Exercises* — is one of the three foundational experiences of humanism. Therefore, the humanist's starting point is Beauty, not the Beast. Mary of Magdala was able to recognize what was ugly in her and wash it off with a warm gush of tears only when she had her first irresistible glimpse into the exquisite beauty of the Man Jesus. She has, since then, become an object lesson for educating people in the aesthetics of the Kingdom. "She has done a beautiful thing to me," says Jesus (Mark 14:6). The gospel, which is the wonder of God's human fellowship, can never be told anywhere in the world without mentioning this event, as Jesus himself forecast (Mark 14:9) — so normative is her experience for all generations.

By contrast, those who are prone to begin their spiritual journey with the elimination of the ugly, rather than discerning it in the light of the beautiful, generally fall into one or the other of two antihumanist grooves: stoic indifferentism or pathological messianism. Neither is capable of the revolutionary change that humanism promises.

Let me first deal with stoicism, a poison that has infected many streams of spirituality. The stoics begin their spiritual journey with an encounter with the ugly; hence they search for the realm of Beauty in the solitudinal bliss of their individual selves, seeking support from "reason" (or "natural law"?), to justify their passive self-complacency. Theirs is a degenerate form of gnosticism. They escape from the present reality, the very shrine in which Beauty resides, for they claim to contemplate it in what they consider to be its "pure" form, which obviously is an abstraction.

Such words as *indifference* or *apatheia,* which denote interior freedom and equanimity are interpreted negatively and, of course, falsely, as a refusal to be sullied by the squalor of contemporary social reality, whereas in a humanist context they connote our aesthetic predisposition to desire first and thus to discover the beautiful in the midst of the ugly. When God, the supremely delectable one, is recognized as the source of our enjoyment of the world, then everything takes its place in relation to that source (*Exercises,* 23). Such is not what stoics mean by indifference. Their preoccupation is to immunize themselves from all contact with the ugly.

"Why waste time weaving a gigantic piece of leather to cover the thorny path that leads to freedom?" they seem to argue. "Let each one cover one's feet with a pair of leather shoes and walk on the thorns!" They do not remove evil; they simply insulate themselves from it, each one individually. By contrast, humanists who have a foretaste of freedom, and for whom beauty is the *forma a priori* even in their perception of the ugly, would rather clear the ground before them as they walk, knowing that the weaker brothers and sisters will follow them sooner or later.

The stoic, to change the metaphor, acts like the Tropical Monitor, that massive amphibian reptile which inflates itself with its own breath to make itself insensitive to the pain inflicted by stones and sticks of "human" enemies. I presume that one can discipline oneself to acquire this kind of "stoic indifference" in the face of the ugly only in so far as one has not risked tasting the bitterness of the ugly; but to avoid the risk of the ugly, one has to avoid savoring the beauty that hides in everyday life. Indeed, how can one fight the foul without first feasting on the fair?

The principle we are educing by means of these reflections is a simple one: aesthetic pleasure does not intoxicate our inner senses but sharpens them to perceive the ugly that lurks even in beauteous things. The horrid reality of sin, oppression, and injustice is monitored only by those whose minds and hearts have, in some ways, savored the exquisite taste of Beauty. In fact, beauty recognized and relished tends to make us not merely sensitive but even *oversensitive* to the unsightly. And this is the danger which stoics strive to avoid by numbing their senses to the foul and the fair alike, misnaming it *indifference.*

Humor as Celebration of Beauty

The most repulsive sight that has ever met my eyes, so far, was the crimson waters of our rivers with the bloated bodies of once beautiful boys and girls floating supine, crying to heaven for vengeance. Uglier still was the stoic withdrawal of religious men and women from this arena of sin under the pretext of not being called (by God, allegedly) to dabble in politics. Ugly too was the pathological messianism of the so-called Sinhala freedom fighters who, in their zeal to eliminate the hideous monster of state terrorism and in their justifiable determination to restore human wholeness to our chronically diseased society, resorted to the ugliest possible means that hominized beasts are capable of: liquidation of the noblest of humans and the destruction of life-sustaining structures of our society.

I would not belittle the bravery with which they battled with the Beast to bring Beauty back from its grip. But their assault on the Beast was so beastly that it succumbed to the very beastliness it was meant to remove. They turned reckless, ruthless, and remorseless to the point of insanity. They only helped the demon of state terrorism to go from strength to strength. The Tamil militants in the North, at the time of writing, have not succeeded totally in avoiding a similar rut of isolation.

We need to recognize, first, that sensitivity to what is lovely is simultaneously a sensitivity to what is not lovely. Hence our aesthetic urge runs the risk of reinforcing our natural revulsion toward the unpleasant and of generating rancor and bitterness, unless a sense of humor is allowed to temper our sense of beauty.

A true revolutionary's first qualification is to have acquired the humanist's art of smiling at the ugly in one's own self. Hitler and Stalin were not capable of laughing at themselves. They took their egos so seriously that, gradually, their own selves replaced the cause they idolized: the Super Man or the Communist Society. And at what devastation to humanity! The collapse of the Soviet experiment in Eastern Europe is history's monumental verdict on pathological messianism; it is the tragedy of a revolutionary program that had no place for comedy. True freedom fighters are not megalomaniacs who sacrifice the basic right of the masses on the altar of an alleged revolution.

Every organized society, civil or ecclesiastical, that does away with the court jester and the cartoonist has eliminated an effective means of prophetic humanism: humor which exposes the nudity of the hominized Beast that sits on the throne, robed in Beauty invisible.

Humor is Beauty in possession of itself, and, therefore, brings out the ridiculous or the laughable elements in the ugly. There are many instances in which the ugly can be laughed out of existence. For, when the light of the end-time is allowed to expose the ridiculous in the follies and foibles of humankind, we can share God's laughter at the wickedness of our nation (Ps. 59:8). God is, as the psalmist says (Ps. 2:4), "enthroned in heaven" and laughs before she rebukes the oppressive nations. One sure sign of the coming of the kingdom, as Jesus clearly tells us in the third beatitude (Luke 6:21), is the laughter that dries up our tears. From Psalm 126 we learn how even a small experience of God's liberative intervention on behalf of those who dare to dream can bring laughter to their mouths and songs to their tongues (verses 1–2).

True humor, therefore, is a celebration of Beauty; a foretaste of the resurrection of Jesus which, after all, is God's last laugh at death and its ugly agents! The true activists, the genuine zealots of ultimate beauty, the authentic humanists, are recognized by their readiness to celebrate in the midst of the struggle. What made the Nicaraguan Revolution so unique is that the people were able to feast together and laugh their way through the postrevolutionary reconstruction of their nation in the face of diabolical constraints. This was totally unheard of in previous "revolutions."

This is why liturgy is so essential a feature of Christian activism. It is the pathological messiahs who cannot distinguish an empty rite which is not born of liberative struggles, from an authentic liturgy which is an ecclesial celebration of the paschal mystery into which we are thrown by our passion for the humanum. It is their inability to celebrate that make their messianism pathological. The *Minjung* theology of Korea, the first articulation of a truly Asian liberation theology, teaches us how crucially important humor and celebration are in life struggles of the *Minjung* (the masses). In practically all cosmic religions the role of prophecy is exercised through mask dances.

On the other hand, cynicism and sarcasm which pass for humor, are actually caricatures, that is to say, unaesthetic deviations of it. They are humor without beauty. When Abraham and Sarah laughed (Gen. 17:17; 18:12), it was not humor: it was cynicism, for they did not see their prospective parenthood in God's light, in the perspective of the future. For, authentic humor is rooted in the (theological) virtue of hope. Hence all laughter that is not of the Kingdom turns into mourning (Luke 6:25) and must be avoided (Jas. 4:9).

Thus I am persuaded that the twofold act of desiring the comely and discerning the comic in all things around us is, so to say, an eschatologically inseparable experience. When, therefore, I hear someone cite Dostoievsky's saying that Beauty alone is indispensable for humanity's survival, I always hasten to add "but not without humor."

Friendship: The Sacrament of the Human

Our sense of beauty is an act of faith in our glorious future anticipated here and now in our struggle against the ugly. Our sense of humor is an act of hope which makes us celebrate the certitude of our victory in the midst of false starts, setbacks, and failures. But love is the greatest of the three, St. Paul insists (1 Cor. 13:13). Without love there is no music, but only noise (1 Cor. 13:1). It is love that beautifies us with truly human qualities (1 Cor. 13:4–7).

Can faith last and hope endure without love as their basis? That Beauty "ever ancient and ever new" which exposes the ugly and makes us smile in hope, is also the very Love by which we love one another; that is to say, God who can be known only by way of human love (1 John 4:7–8). This love, therefore, cannot be reduced to philanthropy or allowed to evaporate into a platonic sublimation; it must sink its roots in the particular and the concrete; it must be contextualized in interpersonal intimacy. It necessarily begins with one before it spreads to many, like God's friendship with Abraham. Love knows a way of multiplying without dividing.

Friendship, which cannot but be particular, is the most tangible proof of humanism, the most glowingly visible presence of the humanum, since it is by far the most cathartic encounter with the transcendent in that it threatens one's ego by destroying its insulations and making it fall from the secure heights of ignorance and innocence to the risk-ridden terrain of affective growth.

Friendship, if I may dare to use terms borrowed from mystical theology, is an "infused love," so to say, which gives me courage to welcome the dissolution of my ego through the invasion of another into the frantically fortified armory of my interior castle. Once my defenses are broken, once I am totally disarmed by love received and love given, then I emerge crucified and risen, in a spirit of self-transcending openness toward that Other who it is that meets me in all others.

For what friendship does to me is to expose everything ugly in me to the purifying love flames of someone already recognized as beautiful. The agony of this catharsis turns into an ecstasy of intimacy only to the degree humor enters the process. Weakness artfully hidden from my childhood, the ugly stains and scars of my subconscious skirmishes with reality, and stacks of uncleared garbage, now seen for the first time with the eyes of another, could indeed be a shattering blow to my self-image and absolutely humiliating; hence it would hardly be a healing and wholesome experience if laughter and celebration are not there to prevent that humiliation from degenerating into an aggressive self-pity.

Our search for intimacy is, incontestably, a perilous voyage of discovery; but there is a pearl of great price which makes it worth the risk: chaste beauty and pure humor.

No wonder, some spiritual masters in the Middle Ages stressed the indispensable role that friendship plays in spiritual life. Abelard and Heloise, Francis and Clara, Beatrice and Dante, the two monks Bernard and Malachi, and many others since then have witnessed to this healthy tradition. The Buddha too believed in the need of a "beautiful friend" (*kalyana mitra*) for anyone keen on spiritual progress.

All these men and women were great humanists. Jesus went furthest of all in practically identifying the whole process of redemption as friendship, God's friendship with us in Jesus, to be spread contagiously through our friendship with one another (John 15:9–17); and by friendship, he obviously meant *intimacy,* that is, self-disclosure (John 15:15). And self-disclosure is self-exposure, which is another name for disarmament, an absolute condition for total peace.

A HUMANIST READING OF THE RELIGIOUS VOWS

Some Theological Presuppositions

My next step is to develop further the coincidence between the three ingredients of humanism explained so far and the three religious vows. The observations I offer in this chapter presuppose the theology of religious life, which I have already outlined in chapter 16. To make my reflections more intelligible, I wish to sum up the major ingredients of that argument.

In that chapter, I proposed that obedience and poverty could not have originally been two "counsels of perfection" but merely two aspects of one basic baptismal commitment. By the evangelical obedience we proclaim in word and deed that Yahweh (God of Moses, the God of Jesus, God universally known through creation and conscience) is the only Sovereign Ruler of our life; and by evangelical poverty, we declare in word and deed that no other god (be it Capital/Mammon, the civil state, or the church; the individual self or the collective ego; dogma, rite or law, language or race; color, creed, or class, in short, any human-made or God-made creature) shall be allowed to replace Yahweh as the supreme Law of our life. The first is a positive declaration, while the second is the negative formulation of one and the same faith proclaimed in both liturgy and life: "We have no Sovereign other than Yahweh."

Poverty and obedience, as we had demonstrated in that chapter, are more than just vows to be taken by a few seekers of perfection; rather, they are the kerygmatic and prophetic commitment of the whole body of Christ, which is the church. Through them we proclaim and anticipate Yahweh's Reign as a reign of love and freedom based on justice and equality, believing as we do that all gods other than Yahweh are manufactured and manipulated by the rich and the powerful who thrive on slave labor, whereas the *humanum* reappears in the center of our world only when Yahweh Who is Love and Justice is installed as the sole Ruler. This is the Good News of the Reign of God for which Jesus died and for which the church lives.

I also pointed out that the word of God in the Bible unfolds against the background of slave empires such as Egypt, Babylonia, Assyria, and later Greece and Rome. Their ignorance of Yahweh and their consequent idolatry accounted for their oppression of the weak. Despite such examples of dehumanization, the chosen people, too, renounced their exclusive allegiance to Yahweh when they adopted the socioeconomic model of those same "developed" nations and grew, like them, into a pyramidally structured society, drawing the wrath of the prophets and the curse of God's poor.

Regretfully, the church too has absorbed from an idolatrous secular society a feudal and imperial model of "hierarchology" (Congar's term) and the mentality that goes with it. Although Vatican II moved church law to recognize an ecclesiology based on communion, still the canonical understanding of episcopal authority including that of the Pope is hardly free of the feudal framework. No renewal is possible till "poverty" and "obedience" which characterize the follower of Jesus leave the dead letter of church documents and become the pulsating core of its organizational existence. Until then, the church remains a countersign of its own baptismal proclamation: "We have no Ruler other than Yahweh."

Moreover, the traditional attitude of expecting a few men and women (so-called "Religious") to practice vicariously the twofold baptismal vow that the whole church is called to pronounce prevents the church from becoming what it is called to be: a "contrast society" by means of which the God of Jesus could challenge the Babylons and Egypts of our time and reveal to all nations God's project of a truly human community of peoples. What must we do with salt that is no more salty?

The sociopolitical implications of the two proclamational vows (obedience and poverty) that I described in chapter 16 are not set aside but presupposed in the following reflections, which focus more on the personal dimension of the Christian vocation. In this chapter I am also presupposing the other suggestion I made in chapter 16, which I also substantiated with examples from the history of religious life — namely, that celibacy ceases to be prophetic and becomes a countersign of the kingdom whenever it is not practiced in the context of the two kerygmatic vows.

Against the background of these presuppositions, I will try to reflect on the humanist contents of the three religious vows.

Small Is Beautiful: Evangelical Poverty as an Aesthetic Experience

The Ignatian exercises encourage me to become an activist ever engaged in the service of the least of Jesus' sisters and brothers but not without an aesthetic enjoyment of God in all things and of all things in God. This ideal of a perpetual feasting on God's creation in the midst of work had been described as "contemplation in the action." The key word that suggests this ideal in the Ignatian vocabulary is *consolation* rather than contemplation; the true meaning of this word was revealed to me only when I began to satisfy my God-given right to relish God's creation, in the midst of my activity. But soon, experience showed me that such "consolation" does not come automatically. Rather, it is a spiritual mood that coincides with the attitude that Ignatius describes as *indifference,* i.e., "that interior freedom which comes from evangelical poverty." Let me try to describe it in the light of my own experience.

There are two prerequisites for an aesthetic experience of God in all things and all things in God. Nonaddiction to anything whatsoever is the first. The other is critical distance from everything on earth. Both prerequisites are a mental mood that one is not born with; they have to be acquired and fostered until they become a permanent posture of the heart. This arduous process is what evangelical poverty is all about: a growth in aesthetic sensibility.

By vowing religious poverty, I have taken upon myself the responsibility to free myself from addiction to or obsessive dependence on any creature. For such dependence would dull my aesthetic sensibility; I would become an "alcoholic" of a sort, incapable of relishing my potion because I intoxicate myself with it. Addiction prevents me from distinguishing ecstasy from inebriation. Surfeit kills the taste and the person. A bee that gets glued to honey through gluttony turns its source of nourishment into a lethal drug. To enjoy its food without dying in it, the bee must suck no surplus, but take just what is necessary, *tantum quantum* (in proportion) (*Exercises,* 23).

Evangelical poverty is a name for nonaddictive gratification of all my senses, interior and exterior, with the wonder that all of God's creation is.

The aesthetic intensity guaranteed by religious poverty, then, is in inverse proportion to the exertion of my acquisitive powers of the goods of this earth. Little is beautiful; surfeit is hideous. This is even more true of spiritual goods which I crave to store up, ostensibly for eventual disposal in the field of the apostolate, but subconsciously for enriching myself with knowledge that generates power. Ignatius sounds a timely warning: Not a surfeit knowledge, but only an interior relishing of things satiates our spiritual senses (*non abundantia scientiae satiat animam sed res interne gustare*) (*Exercises,* 1). Beginning with this warning, Ignatius leads me step by step to the climactic exercise in which he persuades me to live in a permanent mood of relishing God in all things and all things in God (*Exercises,* 230ff.).

In this graduated process of spiritual training, Ignatius has intertwined two themes to form one unifying thread weaving all the various exercises into a meaningful whole. The first theme revolves around evangelical poverty (both actual and spiritual, i.e., external and internal) as the constitutive core of Christian discipleship; and the other is the perpetual enjoyment of God as an inexhaustible source of delight (i.e., source of "consolation") — indeed, a desirable sign and permanent fruit of that discipleship. For the aesthetics of the Reign of God and the vow of poverty are inseparable if not indistinguishable. They are the foundation of a "Kingdom praxis," or to use the more traditional term, an "apostolic spirituality."

If that is what the principle of nonaddiction implies for someone yearning for a gratifying experience of God in creatures, then the second principle, that of critical distance, ensures the converse, namely, that all creatures are delectable only in God.

By critical distance, I mean the optimum range of perception that permits the "in-God" perspective to be ever present in our day-to-day encounter with creation. Drawn too near or driven too far, a creature fails in its mission to mediate "tears and consolation" that mark out an authentically human life from a merely hominal existence. A theology that coherently reflects such humanism is not conspicuously present in the main stream of Roman Catholic "orthodoxy."

Our Catholic theological tradition is too often circumscribed by our adulation of that which is said to be *wissenschaftlich* (scientific). This is why we have turned works of art into objects of science. Through the microscope of rational precision, we "close in" on the canvas, our eyes roving over the blotches of paints in search of what is allegedly true and genuine. The beautiful escapes us. The followers of Jesus, by contrast, keep a creative

distance because their concern is not power that accrues from "an accumulation of knowledge," but the willingness to "relish things interiorly"; for,
these things are all a summons from the Creator to receive her outpourings
of self-communication (*Exercises*, 1). Not greed for knowledge, but love of
beauty makes us truly human.

The type of "cerebral theology" we have inherited from a long tradition
of scholastic speculation (now respectably called *wissenschaftlich*), with its
obsessive concern for close-range observation and dissection of things, has
developed a cult of disproportion (i.e., a cult of the Ugly) in the very understanding of creation which is God's body. We are made to project before us
that of which we are an inseparable part. This distancing is responsible for
stoicism, which is the other side of rationalism.

This paradox represents a very valuable theological principle. Stoic indifferentism or distancing is a spirituality that accompanies a rationally "closing
up" of things. This is the cult of disproportion we just referred to. A good
analogy would be the present generation's insane compromise with noise.
The strategy is to cut the distance between our ear and the source of sound,
to the point of reducing our auditory sensitivity to zero. Our high-tech culture
entices us to drown ourselves in the din of superamplified sonic waves that
eventually make us deaf to all music! Distancing by closing in, alienation
through excessive familiarity.

The figure of the Buddha reclining restfully says it all: a taste of paradise
in this vale of tears. Totally at ease with himself and with everything around,
he greets us with a compassionate smile that is eloquently instructive: "I am
distant enough to enjoy the world in which you drown yourself to death."
That sums up the aesthetics of the Kingdom.

There is, of course, a more creative dimension to our sense of Beauty;
through our partnership with God we are creating an ultimate artifact: God's
Reign, or the new continuum called Christ. The inner dynamic of this creation is evangelical obedience to God's saving will. The creative movement
of the aesthetics of the Reign of God is what obedience is about, while
the passive and appreciative aspect of experiencing the final fruit of God's
Reign, already now, is ensured by evangelical poverty. For obedience (our
"ascetical" act of collaborating with God in creation and redemption) and
poverty (our "mystical" absorption into the ecstasies of God's creative and
redemptive presence around us) are but two aspects of the same aesthetic
experience.

Since our excursus on poverty dwelt long enough on the aesthetic dimension, it would be redundant to go over the same terrain with regard to
obedience. Hence I shall focus my attention now on the sense of hope that
the eschaton — the final outcome of our obedience — brings for us in this
vale of tears. In humanistic terms, I'm talking about that sense of humor,
which obedience implies as a celebration of beauty — a beauty guaranteed
by poverty.

Anticipating the Last Laugh:
Evangelical Obedience as a Celebration of Hope

"We must obey God rather than human beings" (Acts 5:29). These defiant words epitomize all that I promised on the day I vowed obedience as a religious, thus confirming my baptismal consecration. They are the words that the followers of Jesus hurled at the religious hierarchy of their day. It is none other than Israel's ancient profession of faith which Jesus confirmed on the cross: we have no sovereign other than Yahweh.

To submit to the will of a man or a woman is the fate of unredeemed beasts. No human being can cringe before another human being without both of them becoming subhuman. There was once a man who for our sake was made "worm and no man" because some persons degraded themselves by usurping God's place in human affairs. Yet he was not the slave of such men; he was the Suffering Servant of Yahweh. It was in obedience to God that he let humans make asses of themselves by riding on his shoulders. God it is whom he obeyed even under the yoke of such asinine people.

Asses do have a role to play in God's world. It was, after all, thanks to his own ass that Balaam learned of Yahweh's will and obeyed it (Num. 22:21–32). The ass, nevertheless, remained an ass, and not God's substitute. And so I have found it difficult to accept any human being as someone "taking the place of Divine Law-giver," which is why I have always felt rather uncomfortable with the phrase *locum Christi tenens* (taking the place of Christ) used exclusively as an epithet for a superior. In the mouth of Jesus, it is the poor and the powerless who were declared to be his proxy, and the first apostles eminently qualified themselves for this by renouncing power and possessions. Those who listened to ("obeyed") them, listened to (obeyed) Christ.

Christopher (Christ-bearer) is a better term and reminds all superiors of the donkey that carried the Messiah on the streets of Jerusalem. In Chesterton's poem, this donkey boasts of the cheers it received from the crowds and the palms they laid before its feet. The donkey would not be a donkey if it knew it was one! It identified itself with Christ who rode on it and appropriated for itself what was due to Christ. As a superior, I can cease to be a donkey the moment I know I am one, and if — unlike Chesterton's donkey — I let Christ receive the deference of the obedient. If, as a superior, I do not have the sense of humor to take myself to be the ass that I am, soon the community will have to exercise its sense of humor lest this comedy take on a tragic finale.

Ecclesiastical superiors, in particular, must take pride in their humble vocation. Let them know that the Messiah has no taste for horses and that his preferential option is for donkeys (see Zech. 9:9–10). The verdict of sacred history falls heavy on King Solomon who had to build stables in the process of erecting his slave empire (1 Kings 4:26–28). Whoever could own horses could also own slaves! His idolatry (1 Kings 11:4–8) may explain the emergence of the pyramidal structure among God's People, though he had the wisdom to know that serving (not enslaving) one's brothers and sisters as God's revered icons was true worship rendered to the one and only God.

To restore this ideal of service, the Messiah came as Servant-King, a fool in the world of power, choosing in his wisdom, to ride on a donkey (Matt. 21:2–6) to symbolize the arrival of God's Reign in his person and in his message. But a donkey that thinks itself to be a stallion might strut about in style and toss the rider down. In the perspective of God's kingdom, it is a privilege and a grace to be an ass.

Though not officially appointed a superior, I have, since the mid-seventies, assumed leadership in a community made of men and women, young and old, lay and religious, Christian and non-Christian. It took some time before I acknowledged that this community is, if at all, the one that takes the place of Christ (*locum Christi tenens*) and I am the ass privileged to carry the One whose burden is light, whose yoke is sweet; nevertheless a burden and a yoke.

I am sure many of my superiors would have brayed to God in the words of Moses, "Is it because you do not love me that you *burdened* me with these people?" (Num. 11:11). On my part, however, I have always tried to sit lightly on the backs of my superiors. I have learned that they should not be overburdened with weights their conscience cannot carry. Hence in a few crucial matters I took upon my own conscience the responsibility for certain decisions which certain superiors, if approached, would have been too weak to make their own.

Such exercise of charity toward one's superior involves proper discernment, and comes under the category of "prudential judgments"; *prudence* (from Latin *prudentia,* a contraction of the word *providentia* [providence]) implies our judicious entry into God's providential scheme of things by taking courageous steps in the direction of the end toward which all things are ordained. *Prudence* was presumably the nearest equivalent in the vocabulary of Aquinas to what other mystics understood by "discernment."

Besides, Ignatius taught me to practice obedience of judgment rather than obedience of execution. This means, in my understanding of this scholastic term, that I am not expected to immolate my will under the ax of my superior's will. We are informed that the authority to rule (*imperium*), according to the then accepted (Thomistic) theology, belongs to the realm of the intellect and not of the will. Would I be temerarious if I extend this interpretation also to the Ignatian idea of "judgment" — the scholastics' *judicium?* Superior and the subject must arrive at a common "judgment" (i.e., an understanding) about God's will, so that both may opt for it in unison.

In practice, this ideal is not believed in. To follow the superior's will seems easier than struggling together with the superior to understand God's will. Is not blind obedience a regression to the subhuman? Was it not a disobedient and stiff-necked people that found it more convenient to "slave" (*abad*) under a human ruler than to "serve" (*abad*), i.e., worship Yahweh in the freedom of the desert (Exod. 14:12)?

Obedience to Yahweh as the only Sovereign coincides with service to one another; God's Reign is a cosmic community of free humans, characterized by the elimination of all despots (Isa. 14:1–27). For what Yahweh demands is not sacrifice of victims, but obedience to this law of love (1 Sam. 15:22). Those who obey Yahweh alone, would not sell their freedom for religion. They worship unhampered by rites; they live uncrushed by laws; they believe unobsessed by dogmas. They strive to anticipate, as far as possible, the freedom of the end-time. Their obedience is "prudential" in the sense explained above; a joyful celebration of hope.

Yet such people reveal their authenticity only when a nondiscerning ecclesiastical superior dares to "take the place of Christ" and commands without striving to accept his or her role as the Christ-bearing donkey. Faith is not enough in this case; one requires the virtue of hope. One must ever look toward the ultimate end, which is a God who provides. It is a situation in which the riders are at the mercy of the donkey.

In such circumstances, a humorous episode in the life of Ignatius can be illuminating. Ignatius mounted on a donkey pursued a Muslim blasphemer in order to kill him, but lost sight of him at a place where the road bifurcated. So Ignatius allowed his donkey to choose the "correct" road. The animal, however, took the "wrong road" and the Muslim's life was saved.

Once, as the leader of my community I advised a confused companion: "Since you sense that very serious issues are at stake and you lack clarity of vision, I suggest that, as Ignatius did when a Muslim blasphemer's life was in his hands, you should let the ass decide!" And so I decided for him!

The Book of Revelation, which is a reading of the signs of the time, educates us to look up to God as the God of hosts, the *Pantocrator.* (In the times of the Book of Revelation, human rulers had made themselves divinely appointed and infallible decision-makers of the Roman Empire — a discomforting Roman feature that dies slowly). I did not understand the full import of the title *Pantocrator* until I saw an artist's interpretation of it in a church in Rome: Christ with hands raised as those of a maestro! He is in charge of the cosmic orchestra. He conducts. The flutes may blow flat; the sopranos may sound hoarse; the drummers may break the beat and ruin the rhythm. But the *Pantocrator* knows how to handle it all. And in the end there is harmony, followed by rounds of cheers.

The end-time is a time for laughter, when great errors of judgment will be seen as minor "diversions"; humor which is an anticipation of this laughter makes obedience a celebration of hope. The cynics are too proud to laugh at themselves; they laugh at others. But the humble can obey because they are the target of their own humor. It is only when I learned not to take myself too seriously that I began to celebrate God's providence in what prima facie appeared to be myopic decisions of some of my superiors.

Chastity and Friendship:
Interpersonal Communion of the Obedient Poor

That Christmas night in 1955 when I was pronouncing my vow of chastity in the Society of Jesus, I was not aware that my parents had done just that on the solemn occasion of their marriage, over four decades before me. They had vowed to be chaste in their marital intimacy; my vows, too, would lead me to a nonmarital intimacy within my celibate chastity.

This conviction dawned on me after I had cleared four misconceptions with regard to the vows. Let me expose these rather widespread errors, listing them in the ascending order of their gravity.

The tendency to equate celibacy with chastity is the first source of confusion. In fact, they are two different species, altogether! Celibacy is a voluntary renunciation of conjugal and family life, made for the sake of the gospel; chastity is an obligatory attitude of mind and heart. Celibacy is an "evangelical counsel" which practically defines and distinguishes the canonically recognized status of religious life; it is for the few. Chastity, on the contrary, is the "universal" quality of nonidolatrous communion with creatures — something that necessarily accompanies our common baptismal commitment to obedience and poverty. It is for all.

The second misconception accounts for the common belief that chastity and intimacy are incompatible outside wedlock. This erroneous judgment results from not posing this question within the perspective of biblical humanism (cf. Jer. 8 onward). There, it is idolatry (Jer. 8:1–5; 10:1–16) that disrupts anthropocosmic euphony (Jer. 8:13–22) and disintegrates interhuman communion (Jer. 9:4–8). The implication is that it is our single-heartedness (Jer. 17:5–8) — by which we covenant ourselves with Yahweh and Yahweh alone (obedience), without any other god to usurp Yahweh's place (poverty) — that guarantees our intimacy with nature and with one another. This single-heartedness is chastity; and as such it is none other than the nonidolatrous character of obedience and poverty; intimacy both cosmic and interpersonal, therefore, is the glowing visibility of chastity. In other words, chastity (celibate or marital) and intimacy are not only compatible, but are as inseparable as fire and its glow.

The third in the series of misapprehensions needs a lengthy analysis before it can be gotten rid of. It consists of a very unwholesome assumption about marital intimacy, against which celibate chastity is contrasted and its meaning distorted.

Some homilists at nuptial masses tend to present marriage as a contract in which partners vow to take each other as the mutual center of their lives. This is a pseudotheological concession to an infantile perception of the nuptial alliance, often expressed by affectively immature lovers with such words of endearment as "You are my only love, my only light"; "You and you alone are the ultimate purpose of my life, the sole source of my happiness, the absolute center of my existence"; "Minus you, I am zero"; "The day I lose you, I lose everything"; and so on.

Fortunately, many young people do not take these expressions literally. If they do, they flout their baptismal vows. It is a pity, therefore, if they hear from the pulpit that marital chastity is a way of avoiding adultery by conceding to idolatry.

Yahweh found her people adulterous precisely because they were idolatrous. The first lesson that our vows of obedience and poverty teach us is that no human being — let alone other creatures — can ever be the absolute center, the ultimate source of happiness, or the exclusive focus of attention of another human being; not even in the holy sacrament of matrimony. No creature can quench another's thirst for love. Only God can.

It is not seldom the case that people who enter marriage worshiping each other as gods end up hating each other as demons. No man or woman can play God to another man or woman. In marital and nonmarital intimacy, one relates to the other merely as a sacrament of God, never as a substitute for God. In fact, lovers who face each other too long will be bored with each other. All true intimacy is between two people arm in arm and facing God together. In scripture, idolatry and interpersonal communion cancel each other. They cannot coexist.

This means unchastity is the manifestation of idolatry. The most common forms in which it occurs among the married are possessiveness, jealousy, and suspicion, to list them in the order of their genesis.

Possessiveness is as much an attack on evangelical obedience (I am your God; I own you) as it is a sin against evangelical poverty (you are my God; I cannot do without you). Jealousy which issues from it, is a species of hatred that masquerades as love. Suspicion, the third step, is a mental hang-up and almost a psychotic disorder. In the Buddha's analysis, *lobha,* or greed (possessiveness); *dosa,* or hatred (of which jealousy is a species); and *moha,* or mental disorientation (such as suspicion is) are the three roots of spiritual slavery. Their absence is declared to be true freedom (*nirvana*). Chastity is the transparency of that freedom; intimacy is sheer reveling in it.

This is why I maintain that nonidolatrous communication between persons is what chastity is, and that intimacy is included in its definition. It is that quality of friendship which prevents partners from gazing at each other in an exclusive "short-circuit relationship." In other words, chastity is the very transparency of obedience and poverty, the baptismal vows which alone generate all forms of communion and all degrees of intimacy.

This premised, could we now turn to the question of chastity and intimacy among celibates?

The vow of celibacy is not an option for a solitary life. Even the celibate's life is governed by the Creator's ordinance: "It is not good for man or woman to be alone" (Gen. 2:18). The individual self that is unrelated ceases to be a human person. But human relatedness can never be nonsocial, nonmaterial, or disincarnate. The humanum which constitutes God's Center — Christians call it Christ — is made of us, of cosmic stuff, of matter and energy, tested and refined in the crucible of Jesus' passion and death in which the whole creation is made resurgent. Thus intimacy which is the very essence of God is shaped by this cosmic/human center. Intimacy, therefore, is coterminous with our very existence. Celibate or married, we are all called to intimacy of various kinds and degrees.

We learn our first lessons in intimacy in our mother's womb, which enfleshes the warmth of the "Father's bosom" (John 1:18), where the eternal Word was conceived and nurtured in the Love that was the Spirit. This Word, by the overshadowing of the same Spirit of Love, was made flesh (John 1:14), so that all flesh is now endowed with the communicative force of the Word. Intimacy is discourse, or more precisely, intercourse, that is, a psychophysical exchange of selves through the Word in the Spirit.

This last thought leads us to the fourth and final misconception in our list, the most consequential of them, namely, the tendency to define chastity as sexual purity. Here all the other three misapprehensions are compounded into one, in particular that which equates chastity with celibacy. The result is that intimacy is judged chaste or unchaste in terms of sex. We do not deny that sexuality and even genitality can enter the picture at any time, but chastity and intimacy which are inseparable because they together constitute the non-idolatrous communion of the obedient poor, cannot be related essentially to sex. It is celibacy that takes the genital/sexual factor into its definition.

Unchastity is idolatry, basically, not necessarily sexual impurity. Thus encretism (the cult of carnal continence) is as unchaste as pornography (cult of sex).

Since our discourse is about enfleshed intimacy (creation as intended by God does not know any other, as demonstrated above), we can gain much clarity by resorting to the distinction made today between the sexual and the genital. All intimacies are said to be sexual, that is to say, determined by the dominance of the male or female element in our psychophysical makeup. Jesus' friendship with John was sexual. His intimacy with Mary Magdalene was sexual. Joseph's close relationship with Mary was sexual. Mary's maternal love for her divine Son was sexual.

Now, celibate intimacies differ from the marital in that the former are not per se genital, while the latter are. However, the nongenital is not equivalent to the platonic. For the sexual and the genital are two aspects of our makeup, which, like two circles that intersect, leave a common area which is at once sexual and genital. In some people, the circle S and circle G touch each other only at the circumference. Such persons know exactly when they cross from one circle to the other.

But most people have an area in which the two circles overlap, and where the sexual is not clearly separable from the genital, as far as human feelings are concerned. Here one is one's own educator and guide. It is through trial and error that one learns to cope with twilight zones in a spirit of inner tranquility. Chastity is not an anesthesia that benumbs the genital component of our essentially sexual being, but a way of being honest toward the One who is the real Center of our interpersonal communion. Only a conscience thoroughly formed by the practice of evangelical obedience and poverty is honest enough to learn the exquisite art of friendship.

Or should I put it more bluntly in terms of the humanistic idiom I have employed in analyzing the two kerygmatic vows?

The restlessness that accompanies the almost irresistible desire to express intimacy genitally is handled with consummate dexterity by a celibate who has acquired a taste for that which is truly beautiful and is endowed with just enough humor to celebrate little certitudes amid unsettling anxiety. If I educate myself in the aesthetics of the Kingdom by adopting the principles of nonaddiction and critical distance and grow in my ability to smile at the ugly in me in the light of that last great laugh of the resurgent cosmos, then I am equipping myself to advance in celibate chastity.

Neither chastity nor intimacy, which is the glow of chastity, is a static virtue; it is a long journey, a lifelong process of growth. The vows are a program of struggle for full humanity, not an automatic *saltus* to a supercosmic state. Thus it is good to take our bearing and check our direction by keeping our communication apparatus (i.e., our conscience) always tuned to the final destiny: the humanum. If, on the other hand, we glue our selfish eyes on ourselves, or idolatrously on a copilgrim, instead of keeping them fixed on the One who stands on the horizon summoning us and guiding our journey, we can well miss our orientation altogether.

And yet however much we fix our gaze on the goal before us, our motion toward it will not and cannot be a straight line. Neither an arrow shot by the most skilled archer nor a technologically accurate launching of a rocket, escapes this law of zigzag motion. So also in the journey of our vows, we too may now swerve to the right and now to the left, but such deviations are not dangerous as long as we can continuously correct and recorrect our path with the aid of the information ever communicated to us from the One who is the sole source of our life, the Fount of our freedom, the Goal of our Long March: Yahweh, who gathers all of us within herself as a resurgent cosmos, as a human bundle of ecstatic intimacy for which we already have a name: *Christ.*

Index

Other Titles in the Faith Meets Faith Series